PARADING PATRIOTISM

PARADING PATRIOTISM

Independence Day Celebrations in the
Urban Midwest, 1826–1876

ADAM CRIBLEZ

NIU Press
DEKALB

Published by the Northern Illinois University Press
DeKalb, Illinois 60115

Library of Congress Cataloging-in-Publication-Data

Criblez, Adam.
    Parading patriotism : Independence Day celebrations in the urban midwest,
1826–1876 / Adam Criblez.
        pages cm
    Includes bibliographical references and index.
    ISBN 978-0-87580-692-1 (pbk : alk. paper)
    ISBN 978-1-60909-088-3 (e-book)
    1. Fourth of July celebrations—Middle West—History—19th century.
I. Title.
E286.A12624 2013
977'.02—dc23

                                                        2013012979

Contents

Acknowledgements

In 2005, when I began conducting research for this project, my wife was pregnant with our first child and I intended to study the culture of public drinking in the urban Midwest. Today, nearly eight years later, I have three wonderful daughters and many people to thank for the transformations this project has undergone.

I would like first to thank John Larson, my advisor and mentor at Purdue University. His advice was always timely and pointed. He pushed me to revise and revisit chapters constantly as the project took shape. Thanks also to the other three members of my dissertation committee. Douglas Hurt, Caroline Janney, and Jon Teaford provided thoughtful analyses of my work and helped me to take the all-important step of thinking about this work as a book project rather than as a dissertation.

While in West Lafayette, I also had the good fortune to interact with an amazing cohort of graduate student colleagues. Whether playing "Peep Ball" in Recitation Hall or taking part in deeply philosophical conversations at Chumley's over schooners of Rolling Rock, I was influenced by the ways that they thought about history, and I appreciate the support they provided me throughout my graduate studies. Special mention must go to the homebrewers—Darrin, Doug, Mauricio, Patrick, Scott, and Tim—for the wonderful conversations and the tasty pints.

Long before I intended to revise the manuscript, Gretchen Adams convinced me to submit it for publication. Her enthusiasm for this project kept me going even when I doubted myself. Thanks, Gretchen.

Of my colleagues and students at Purdue, Ohio State-Mansfield, and Southeast Missouri State, three merit special praise. Kathy Friedley conducted some vital last-minute research, helping me focus the introduction. Dan Amsterdam took the time to thoughtfully read and provide suggestions on various chapters. His insight was invaluable. Patrick Pospisek likewise read parts of the manuscript and provided feedback that helped me situate the celebrations in better historical context. Without these three individuals, this work would have certainly suffered.

Most importantly, I would like to thank my family. My parents cheered at every stage (although I am still waiting for my postdoctorate steak dinner . . .). My daughters, Avery, Eliza, and Charlotte, have been sources of inspiration and welcome comic relief from the isolation inherent in writing. And my wife, Jennie, has been by my side at every step. Her love and understanding has allowed me to work on this book at odd hours and in odd places. Thanks, Jen!

Finally, I would like to thank Mark Heineke, my editor at Northern Illinois; Tim Roberts, the Managing Editor of the Early American Places Initiative; and the two anonymous readers, who all provided tremendous insight and pushed me to examine my writing more critically. Their tireless effort has made this work immeasurably better. Any mistakes that remain are, of course, my own.

America is a Tune. It must be sung together.[1]
—GERALD STANLEY LEE

The Fourth of July, 1845, arrived in Cleveland as "the sun rose in an unclouded sky, [and] the air from the lake was free and breezy." Shortly after dawn, artillerists stationed in the city square boomed an Independence Day greeting, breaking the serenity of the otherwise early morning calm. By late morning, Clevelanders poured from their homes and into the city streets to welcome the anniversary of the nation's birth. Boys shot firecrackers while men and women gathered to watch the much-anticipated firemen's parade. After this procession, the populace split; some Clevelanders congregated at the Second Presbyterian Church to sing patriotic hymns, listen to an Independence Day message delivered by George Willey, and marvel at the proficiency of Professor Long on "the finest tuned organ in the city," while others retired to a nearby grove for a hearty meal. The presence of a Revolutionary War survivor, Mr. Warren of Warrensville, enlivened dinner, while the guests reportedly "did justice to the edibles with a gusto quite equal to their patriotism." In the evening, Clevelanders reconvened in the public square "to gaze upon the splendid pyrotechnic exhibition." After the fireworks, most residents returned home, abandoning the city streets as young boys fired incendiaries until late in the night.[2]

The seeming orderliness and ordinariness of this Independence Day celebration masked undercurrents of discord prevalent in Cleveland, and elsewhere, in mid-nineteenth-century commemorations of the Fourth of July. One editorial published after this particular celebration remarked that the day was "cheering to every patriotic heart" despite the efforts of

"Native Americanism" to shout down Willey's oration. The same commentator praised the nonpartisan nature of the day's festivities, contrasting it with Independence Day the previous year, when a "political party attempted . . . to turn the patriotism and hallowed associations of this great day to party aggrandizement." Four years later in Cleveland, a German immigrant named Jakob Mueller would remark that, "the procession on the Fourth of July, which was observed annually by the Americans in a mechanical and spiritless manner, was so unworthy of the historic nature of the event that we [Cleveland Germans] parted ways with the Americans, holding our own celebrations in nearby groves in keeping with the esthetic style of the free men, abandoning ourselves to the happiest of patriotic moods."[3]

Between 1826 and 1876, the semicentennial and centennial anniversaries of the signing of the Declaration of Independence, urban midwesterners, spurred by conflict over the proper mode of commemorating the Fourth of July, developed distinct notions about how their Independence Day celebrations reflected patriotic loyalty and American nationalism. In 1826, Fourth of July festivities revolved around community-sponsored parades, long-winded patriotic oratory, and rounds of toasts to the leaders of the American Revolution. Both Thomas Jefferson and John Adams passed away that day, symbolically bringing closure to the generation of the founders and transferring power to a new cohort just as the nation passed a momentous milestone. Fifty years later, following a bloody civil war and in the midst of tenuous reconstruction efforts, midwesterners spent the Fourth of July picnicking, watching baseball games, and buying red, white, and blue merchandise while deciding how to best commemorate the American centennial, revealing important tensions between lauding the past and promoting an even brighter future. Between these semicentennial and centennial celebrations, regionalism, ethnic identification, and cultural imperatives transformed midwestern Independence Day commemorations into segregated affairs split by ethnicity, social class, race, political party identification, religious affiliation, and gender. Because of these cultural schisms dividing urban midwesterners, the proper veneration of the Fourth of July became a hotly contested topic not only in defining regional conceptions of American nationalism, but also in staking claim to the nation's past through controlling historical memory.

The Urban Midwest

This study focuses on the experiences of residents in five midwestern metropolises—Chicago, Cincinnati, Cleveland, Columbus, and Indianapolis. The development of these cities in the mid-nineteenth century reflects a diversity in the maturation of the region: Chicago began as a small military outpost but expanded rapidly with the advent of rail travel, Cincinnati was the first western boomtown but lost its inherent geographical advantages when rail lines outpaced river travel, Cleveland's fortuitous position on Lake Erie at the terminus of the Ohio and Erie Canal provided the basis for a meteoric rise late in the century, and legislators created the cities of Columbus and Indianapolis as centrally located state capitals. In addition to urbanization, these cities witnessed tremendous demographic change as immigration and industrialization swelled city populations. While other midwestern cities (particularly Detroit, Kansas City, Milwaukee, Minneapolis, and St. Louis) certainly played important roles in the development of the Midwest, the experiences of residents in Chicago, Cincinnati, Cleveland, Columbus, and Indianapolis exemplify the relationship between urban midwesterners and American nationalism and patriotism.

Defining the geographic boundaries of the Midwest is a daunting task. Today the United States Census Bureau includes twelve states in its official definition—stretching from Ohio in the east to the Dakotas, Nebraska, and Kansas in the west. In fact, the three states included in this study form just the southeastern-most portion of the modern region. Yet for much of the nineteenth century, Americans knew the modern Midwest by a different term—"the West." And even that characterization became troublesome as, by mid-century, Ohio, Illinois, and Indiana no longer seemed sufficiently isolated or pastoral to satisfy the mysterious allure afforded "the West." For a time, this area floundered in namelessness as epithets like the Great Lakes region, the Old Northwest, and the interior never really caught on. By the 1880s, when contemporaries popularized the term "Middle West," it no longer strictly applied to the now-urbanized areas bordering the Ohio River and instead better described the rural plains region of Kansas and Nebraska. A more accurate name, then, for the three states included in this work would probably be the Census Bureau's linguistically cumbersome "East North Central" terminology as the name "Midwest" is somewhat of a misnomer. Yet Americans—both modern and historical—have well-developed understandings of what constitutes the Midwest, or midwesterners, even if they lack the ability to precisely mark the geographic boundaries of the region. So while I acknowledge the limitations of using "Midwest" as a geographical place and "midwesterners" as a way to name the region's inhabitants, they are the most useful terms we have to easily describe such a geographically, economically, and culturally diverse area at the crossroads of the nineteenth-century United States.[4]

Between 1826 and 1876, the midwestern states of Ohio, Indiana, and Illinois grew rapidly, transforming villages from isolated frontier outposts into thriving commercial, industrial, and political centers. The accompanying population explosion included both newly arrived European immigrants and American citizens migrating westward from New York, New England, Virginia, and the Upper South. In this cultural climate, residents of these states developed a sense of regional distinctiveness, mixing emergent American traditions from the East with customs brought by the Germans and Irish. As historian Jon Teaford explains, the people of the urban Midwest "possessed certain social, political, economic, cultural, and ethnic characteristics that distinguished them as a class apart from the other metropolises in the nation." Another commentator describes the Midwest as representing "common sense and decency and normal Americanness incarnate," considered by contemporaries "as the most moderate, the most average, the most normal part of the country, whatever these terms might mean." Perhaps most importantly, these states were neither former British colonies, which allowed residents to dissociate themselves from ties to European colonialism and dependence on a mother country, nor slaveholding regions, permitting midwesterners to distance themselves from the racial turmoil plaguing the South. This created not only regional distinctiveness, but also inherent regionalism as the states carved from the Northwest Territory seemed compelled at times to justify their very existence as latecomers to the creation of the American nation. Just as many German and Irish immigrants exuberantly celebrated Independence Day to outwardly demonstrate their love of adopted country, so too did residents of Ohio, Indiana, and Illinois strive to define for themselves the meaning of being an American through enthusiastically commemorating the birth of their adopted nation.[5]

Transformations in Celebrating the Fourth of July

The method of celebrating the Fourth of July in these emerging cities changed drastically over the course of the nineteenth century. Settlers in fledgling midwestern pioneer towns commemorated Independence Day in the early republic in a very formulaic, premeditated manner. Cannon and pistol fire welcomed the dawn while, in late morning, citizens gathered for a military parade through the city streets, stopping at a courthouse or church. At this prearranged gathering point, an orator (usually a lawyer or preacher) provided a long, drawn-out speech laced with allusions to the greatness of the Founding Fathers. Then another prominent citizen read the Declaration of Independence aloud before men congregated at local drinking establishments, offering rounds of toasts and drinking until late in the night. By the centennial year, this behavior had long since disappeared as recreation and leisure dominated postbellum Fourth of July celebrations. Baseball, horse racing, and picnicking took the place of civic parades, long-winded orations, and universal toasting, while residents focused increased attention on the progress and potential of the nation rather than universally lauding the glorious heroes of their colonial past. Understanding this fundamental shift requires tracing how ethnocultural imperatives, the American Civil War, historical memory, and changing patterns of consumption and commercialism altered midwestern perceptions of patriotic American nationalism which, in turn, transformed holiday practices.

While the methods of celebrating Independence Day changed drastically over this 50-year period, debates over nationalism and definitions of patriotic loyalty remained central to commemorations of the nation's birth throughout this era. More specifically, midwesterners disputed the constituent elements of American national identity. Regional distinctiveness, ethnocentrism, and political culture formed the basis of these debates. Midwesterners contended that they were, somewhat paradoxically, not only archetypal Americans but that their particular geography and history uniquely positioned them to represent the best aspects of the American nation and, as such, provided added impetus to properly celebrating the Fourth of July holiday. Issues of ethnicity played into this developing sense of region as immigrants settling in these midwestern cities latched onto Independence Day as an opportunity to both defend their ethnic heritage and exhibit patriotic loyalty to their adopted nation. Despite tension between new states and old, and immigrants and native-born Americans, this was not so much a political debate as a cultural one. Midwesterners seemed to care little for Congressional dictums regarding naturalization and political citizenship. Instead, citizens heatedly argued the merits of regionalism, ethnicity, and political culture in defining cultural citizenship. The Fourth of July provided an apt occasion for these discussions about patriotic plurality, which, in turn, were manifested in debates about the proper mode of commemorating Independence Day. Even as parading and bombastic oratory gave way to picnic excursions and extravagant fireworks displays, midwesterners of all creeds defended their actions on the Fourth of July as acts of transformative patriotism representing the best of the American nation.

What Is This American?

In 1782, Michel-Guillaume Jean de Crèvecoeur famously asked, "What then is this American, this new man?" in his *Letters from an American Farmer*. Historians still wrestle with Crèvecoeur's question when trying to define American cultural identity in the eighteenth and nineteenth centuries. In the United States, unlike most European nations, there was no long-standing historical tradition or cultural homogeneity from which to construct a unified national identity. Nationalism in the United States, therefore, necessarily relied on weaving together an assortment of ethnic characteristics to create a uniquely American tapestry. Generations of historians have examined this process and the inevitable clashes between immigrants and native-born Americans accompanying cross-cultural interaction. Oscar Handlin and John Higham were two of the earliest historians to specifically address this issue in a scholarly manner, arguing that immigrants relinquished their ethnicity through Americanization and that nineteenth-century American identity did not allow for ethnic pluralism. Assimilationist arguments like those presented by Handlin and Higham dominated discourse of American national identity for decades, positing that European immigrants quickly and willingly exchanged their Old World heritage for the benefits of American cultural citizenship.[6]

Rather than focus on immigrants surrendering their cultural identity to the hegemonic majority, a new generation of historians debate the merits of culturally constructed national identity. This approach introduces greater cultural give-and-take, exploring how immigrants introduced Old World traditions into Anglo-American society while adopting certain New World customs. Likewise, native-born Americans added ethnic customs to their own traditions even while pressing immigrants to conform to mainstream conceptions of American national identity. This invention of ethnicity complicates not only our understanding of immigration and assimilation, but also conceptions of Americanization and patriotic nationalism, as contemporaries closely linked national identity to ethnicity. Thus cross-cultural interaction both helped define American nationalism and allowed immigrants to assert their patriotic loyalty without entirely surrendering their ethnic heritage.[7]

Cross-cultural interaction and a developing collective sense of belonging coalesced in the evolving concept of cultural citizenship. Unlike political citizenship, which confers voting rights and requires paying taxes, cultural citizenship, in the words of one scholar, "defends that peoples may continue to be different yet contribute to a participatory democracy." In the nineteenth century, cultural citizenship allowed for multiculturalism and ethnic plurality but also required unwavering loyalty to the ideals and symbols of the United States of America. In the mid-nineteenth century, urban midwesterners sometimes welcomed immigrants and ethnic Americans migrating from the east with open arms and readily included them in the growing cultural polity, while on other occasions local native-born majorities acted to exclude immigrants and minorities from being considered truly American. Cultural citizenship, then, is central to understanding how urban midwesterners interpreted the meaning of the Fourth of July and shaped commemorations of the holiday to define patriotism, ethnic and national identity, and the sense of cultural belonging uniquely interacting in the mid-nineteenth century.[8]

Conceptions of patriotism likewise evolved over the course of the nineteenth century. Was listening to a droning July Fourth orator in 1826 inherently more patriotic than spending time with family and friends at a picnic 50 years later? Did Fourth of July revelers marching in antebellum parades necessarily love their country more than their postbellum equivalents enjoying a game of baseball? Instead of declaring certain actions to be explicitly patriotic or unpatriotic, this study focuses on how midwesterners defined the propriety of Independence Day activities in their particular context of time and place. In the postbellum Midwest, citizens insisted that recreation and leisure signified patriotic loyalty as surely as their antebellum counterparts relied on rousing public oratory and readings of the Declaration of Independence. Throughout the period, civic leaders certainly believed—or at least publicly proclaimed—that "old-fashioned" celebrations revolving around military parades and long-winded orations epitomized patriotic loyalty. But many midwesterners disagreed, arguing that non-civic-directed commemorations equally revealed patriotism and perhaps more accurately reflected contemporary American culture. Midwesterners, then, dynamically defined how Independence Day influenced cultural citizenship and patriotism in the nineteenth century, changing their parameters over time to fit particular political, social, and cultural circumstances.[9]

Studies of Independence Day

The developing understandings of American national identity, cultural citizenship, and patriotic loyalty intersected on the Fourth of July in the mid-nineteenth century urban Midwest in the guise of celebratory actions. Historians have long recognized the role of celebrations in defining cultural characteristics and the means by which these festivities diffused or instigated partisan, class, racial, and ethnic tension. Most studies, however, overlook both the mid-nineteenth-century urban Midwest and Fourth of July commemorations in that era. Instead, monographs about Independence Day often focus on either the late eighteenth century (highlighting the tension between Federalists and Anti-Federalists in remembering the nation's birth) or on the Progressive Era (examining shifts in twentieth-century celebrations toward a Safe and Sane holiday free from alcohol and dangerous fireworks). But between these eras, the Fourth of July moved beyond partisan clashes to address issues of ethnicity, class, race, and gender while remaining an important part of the nation's social, cultural, and political calendar. Historians of Americans holidays, noting some of these shifts, can be divided into two broad categories: scholars like Robert Pettus Hay, Len Travers, and Diana Karter Appelbaum who argue that Independence Day could bring together, even if just briefly, disparate elements of American society, and historians including Ellen Litwicki, Scott Martin, Roy Rosenzweig, and Richard Gowers, who contend that celebrating the holiday was a divisive, and potentially explosive, occasion.[10]

Historians arguing for the unifying potential of the Fourth of July generally interpret the rhetoric of inclusive holidays espoused by civic leaders as clear evidence that Americans banded together to celebrate the holiday, ignoring ingrained ethnic, racial, sectional, or social animosities for a day of blissful togetherness. These studies occasionally over-romanticize Independence Day celebrations, arguing that they briefly brought together a diverse socioeconomic, ethnic, and racial population in a shared moment of nationalistic revelry that helped hide the disturbing political and social ills of the early republic amidst the sights, sounds, and overflowing patriotism of the day's festivities.[11]

Unlike historians focusing on the inclusive potential of nationalistic holidays, a second group of scholars minimizes the cooperation facilitated by the Fourth of July and instead examines the tension created by intensely nationalistic commemorations. Three authors in particular, Ellen Litwicki, Scott Martin, and Richard Gowers, have greatly added to understandings of nationalistic holidays in the nineteenth century. Ellen Litwicki considers the confluence of ethnicity and assimilation on public holidays, including the Fourth of July, throughout much of the nineteenth and early twentieth centuries, focusing specifically on the cities of Tucson, Chicago, and Richmond. Her analysis taps into a sociological vein drawing liberally from the works of Benedict Anderson and Eric Hobsbawm in suggesting that immigrants navigated bounds of Americanization through a shared "imagined community" tying recognition of ethnicity by both native- and foreign-born Americans to understandings of political nationalism. Operating on a much smaller geographic scale, focusing exclusively on southwestern Pennsylvania, Scott Martin promotes the potential divisiveness of Independence Day, noting that "the Fourth was contested cultural space from which a variety of ideas, values, and models of behavior emerged in response to new social, economic, and political circumstances." Between 1800 and 1850, the growing partisanship of Independence Day celebrations fragmented, rather than unified, the Pittsburgh-area populace, driving them toward either commercialized recreation or overtly moral and religious remembrances of the Fourth, typified by Sunday School picnics, temperance rallies, and abolitionist lectures. Richard Gowers examines postbellum Independence Day celebrations, revealing deep schisms on the basis of class, ethnicity, gender, and race. Gowers demonstrates that American nationalism could tear apart communities in New York City, Chicago, San Francisco, and Atlanta, especially as ethnic and racial heterogeneity increased in the latter part of the nineteenth century. With the possible exception of Chicago, however, the urban centers in Gowers's study faced atypical, rather than representative, racial and ethnic circumstances that make his work unique; residents of Atlanta vividly recalled the strict antebellum racial hierarchy, the New York Irish were renowned for their boss system of corrupt politics, and in San Francisco, droves of Asian immigrants provided a visible reminder of ethnic boundaries and racialized definitions of Americanness.[12]

Rather than focus on this traditional subset of locations (New York City, Boston, and Philadelphia are popular choices) and eras (typically colonial or Progressive), *Parading Patriotism* analyzes an underrepresented region receiving both new European immigrants and internal migrants from the "old states" like New York, Massachusetts,

Pennsylvania, and Virginia in the midst of a period witnessing budding nationalism. During the middle of the nineteenth century, Americans wrestled with issues of national growth and historical memory as the nation expanded geographically beyond the eastern seaboard and citizens attempted to construct a coherent sense of national character without an extensive shared history. The Midwest held matchless transformative potential for this young, developing nation, offering a region without long-standing ties to England or the troubling social ills accompanying race-based slavery. *Parading Patriotism* explores this unique intersection of time and place, explaining how regionalism, ethnic identity, and celebratory culture in the mid-nineteenth-century urban Midwest broadly defined nascent national character. Between 1826 and 1876, urban midwesterners consciously constructed their own distinct interpretations of this American nation through components of cultural citizenship and used Independence Day as a vehicle to define patriotic nationalism—occasionally with community-wide support but more often with a split populace.

Chapter Summaries

This study is divided into an introduction and five chronological chapters. The introduction focuses on a single year, 1826, the semicentennial anniversary of the signing of the Declaration of Independence, and serves as a baseline for discussing change over time in the balance of the work. Here I argue that the manner in which midwesterners celebrated the Fourth of July was typical of the era—parades, orations, and toasts dominated the day's fare—but that the year also portended important turning points in both commemorations of the holiday and the direction of American nationalism. In particular, I focus on the ongoing debates among midwesterners over memorializing the past and celebrating the present and future. At the heart of this issue was the role of historical memory for the so-called "first generation of Americans" in the Midwest, questioning their ability to assume the mantle of American liberty and patriotism from the founding generation. The introduction also examines the origins of midwestern regional distinctiveness, and how residents came to the realization that the near-simultaneous deaths of John Adams and Thomas Jefferson on July 4, 1826, indicated the end of an era in American history.

Chapter One spans the years 1827 to 1849: a period in which a cadre of citizens came of age in the early republic and struggled with their revolutionary legacy. In these two decades civic boosters unsuccessfully tried to maintain control of the holiday, insisting that the day be celebrated as they thought it had been in the past—with all the pomp and circumstance of colonial fetes and without partisan, ethnic, or racial dissent. But instead, political parties, antislavery and temperance advocates, and revelers bent on improving the religiosity of the day by unequivocally linking American Protestantism with American patriotism gained control of the holiday. This chapter continues the theme of past versus present by looking at how reformers transformed the meaning of the holiday to represent their particular visions of constructing an American national identity predicated on links between the nation's Puritanical heritage and their own reform agendas.

Chapter Two examines the late antebellum period, 1850 to 1856, in which ethnic animosity dominated Independence Day rhetoric and activities. Rising numbers of immigrants (and the accompanying increase in nativist fervor) triggered ethnocentric arguments about who belonged in the American cultural polity, which, in turn, caused particularly vicious debates over the meaning of being an American. I spotlight three events in this chapter, all occurring in 1855, highlighting this ethnic animosity: the Chicago Lager Beer Riots, a split in Cincinnati's Independence Day festivities pitting an explicitly nativist celebration against an ethnically inclusive commemoration, and the Bloody Fourth riot in Columbus. In this era, native-born Americans sought to define their national identity more stringently, while their foreign-born counterparts demanded the rights of citizenship promised by the founding generation.

Chapter Three moves chronologically forward to commemorations of Independence Day in the era of the American Civil War. In the urban Midwest, there was a definite ebb and flow in enthusiasm for patriotic celebrations and support for the war effort; early optimism gave way to harsh reality as the brutal and bloody conflict continued unabated. Fourth of July celebrations reflected this growing unease. Ultimately, the brutality of the Civil War forced midwesterners to reassess the meanings of liberty, nationalism, patriotism, and freedom associated with Independence Day and to reconsider its place on America's social calendar.

Chapter Four examines the postwar years, 1866 to 1875, focusing on three distinct trends in commemorations of the Fourth of July. First, the holiday developed a commercialized aura as recreational and leisure pursuits replaced somber remembrances for the majority of celebrants. At the same time, Independence Day became a marketable commodity as businessmen utilized the holiday to explicitly link product advertisement to patriotic loyalty. And finally, sectional reconciliation and issues of race and memory forced postbellum midwesterners to wrestle with their nation's contentious past.

The final chapter brings the study full circle, again focusing on a single year—1876, the one hundredth year of American independence. Centennial commemorations exacerbated disagreements over the proper way to celebrate the past and present. In the urban Midwest, commentators attempted to reconcile progress and prosperity with the history and traditions linked invariably to the one hundredth Fourth of July. Just as celebrants 50 years earlier struggled with assuming the mantle of patriotism from the founding generation, midwesterners in 1876 felt a conflicted sense of remembering the past while lauding America's seemingly unlimited potential.

In 1913, Gerald Stanley Lee penned the phrase that opens this work: "America is a Tune. It must be sung together." Between 1826 and 1876, urban midwesterners of all ethnicities, socioeconomic classes, and races composed this Tune, using the Fourth of July as an opportunity to orchestrate the complexities of American nationalism. The problem was that they could not sing in harmony.

Introduction. "Freedom's Jubilee": Commemorations of the 1826 Semicentennial

"If great blessings, gained by the wisdom and blood of our forefathers, have descended upon us, it becomes a solemn duty, not only to hand down to posterity unimpaired the bright inheritance, but also to make our contributions to the great cause of human prosperity"[1]

—BENJAMIN DRAKE

In 1826 Benjamin Drake, a Cincinnati lawyer, delivered a Fourth of July address to a local chapter of the Phi Alpha Theta Society. Drake's lecture focused on the American Revolution and the long shadow cast by those "illustrious patriots." He argued that "the sun of that glorious event . . . brought the blessings of freedom to our country," but insisted that contemporaries also celebrate that the United States was now "in the meridian of her prosperity, full of years, great in population, in physical resources, and in high renown." Drake's oration mirrored a larger disconnect taking place in the United States as Americans balanced paying tribute to the successes of the founding generation with expectations of an even brighter future. Several momentous events taking place in 1826 forced revelers to reconcile historical memory of the nation's past with its present state and future promise. Most coincidentally, the deaths of Thomas Jefferson and John Adams on the Fourth—50 years to the day after the first Independence Day—brought symbolic closure to the founding era. For midwesterners after 1826, balancing allusions to the nation's past with predictions of its bright future would become increasingly arduous as they wrestled with the weighty mantle of the founding generation while seeking to define how memory and interpretations of the past should influence developing notions of patriotic loyalty and American nationalism.[2]

In 1826, American citizens recognized that the United States stood at a crossroads. Fifty years had passed since the signing of the immortal Declaration of Independence and, in the intervening decades, America had grown from a tenuous federation of 13 British colonies to an independent nation of 24 states stretching past the Mississippi River. Most of the leading political figures of the colonial era no longer held office, replaced by a new generation of citizens unfamiliar with life as a British subject or the social upheaval of the Revolutionary War. Additionally, thousands of immigrants arrived on the shores of the new nation and thousands more poured across the Appalachian Mountains into the rugged western lands constituting the modern Midwest. This Midwest was not yet a politically or culturally coherent region, and most settlements remained small and scattered across the vast interior wilderness.

The Growth of the Urban Midwest

Europeans, primarily French voyageurs, first arrived in the early seventeenth century to explore the upper Mississippi River valley and the region that would become the American Midwest, but the population remained sparse until late in the eighteenth century as militant Native American confederations and poor transportation conditions slowed colonial westward expansion. After winning their independence from Britain, various eastern states claimed the prized territory, arguing that colonial charters entitled them to these western lands. To minimize internal squabbles and to settle land disputes, the Confederation Congress reached a compromise. The states—primarily Virginia, New York, Connecticut, and Pennsylvania—rescinded their land claims in return for the right to use the territory to settle accounts with Revolutionary War veterans. To formalize this decision, Congress passed the Northwest Ordinance in 1787. The Northwest Ordinance accomplished several very important tasks: creating a territory free from slavery, establishing precedents for the geographic expansion of the nation, and laying out the process by which a territory could become a state on equal standing with the original 13. After 1787 settlers poured into the Northwest Territory, especially along navigable rivers, giving birth to the five cities considered in this study.[3]

CINCINNATI

Due in large part to transportation innovation and industrialization, Cincinnati emerged as the first western boomtown, gaining renown as one of the nation's undisputed population and economic leaders. In 1788, John Cleves Symmes, a member of the Continental Congress and appointed governor of the Northwest Territory, formed the Miami

Company to buy, subdivide, and sell tracts of land on the northern bank of the Ohio River. The original three settlements proposed by Symmes merged as the newly christened Cincinnati in 1803. At the center of a fertile valley encompassing portions of Ohio, Kentucky, and Indiana, Cincinnati quickly became an important regional marketplace, providing nearby farmers with an outlet for surplus agricultural goods. The introduction of steam travel to and from the Queen City in 1817 marked the inauguration of Cincinnati's ascent from frontier trading center to thriving commercial metropolis. Population increases quantitatively demonstrate this change. In 1800, just 750 residents called Cincinnati home. By 1810 that number was nearly 2,500 and a decade later, Cincinnati was the seventh most populous city in the entire nation, numbering 10,000. Early residents of Cincinnati exhibited remarkable homogeneity, as white, native-born Protestants dominated the population. Even as late as 1825, white native-born residents constituted over 95 percent of the city's 16,230 residents. Nearly a quarter of Cincinnati's residents were involved in manufacture and trade, allowing the city to import $2.5 million worth of goods in 1826, a fivefold increase over its total less than a decade earlier, marking an impressive recovery from the economic depression accompanying the end of the War of 1812 and the financial panic of 1819. Cincinnati also grew culturally during the early nineteenth century: residents established a college, local magnate Daniel Drake founded a medical school in 1819, and the Western Museum—essentially a glorified cabinet of curiosities—housed thousands of exhibits in natural history, painting, and sculpture.[4]

CLEVELAND

Englishmen founded Cleveland shortly after their counterparts settled in Cincinnati, although they met with much less immediate success. Established at the confluence of the Cuyahoga River and Lake Erie, Cleveland's geographic potential drew the attention of investors in the Connecticut Land Company who, in 1796, sent a surveying expedition to determine the future prospects of this lakeshore wilderness. Their investment paid little immediate dividends: by 1800 census takers counted only 1,500 people in the entire Western Reserve, an area encompassing nearly three million acres of land. By 1810, the fledgling hamlet of Cleveland remained small and insignificant, including only 57 residents and outnumbered by several other villages within its own county. Cleveland remained an agricultural backwater well into the nineteenth century: it took an act of Cleveland magistrates in 1820 to keep swine and cattle from grazing in

FIGURE 1. "Alfred Kelley." Courtesy of the Ohio Historical Society.

the village streets. But the 1820s marked the beginning of a turning point for Cleveland's fortunes due, in large part, to the efforts of Alfred Kelley, the district's state representative. Kelley focused on improving transportation routes—both overland and by water—to Cleveland, recognizing that accessibility would be essential for the future prospects of the lakeside village. In 1825, the state of Ohio, due in large measure to Kelley's tireless campaigning, fixed the terminus of the planned Ohio & Erie Canal at the mouth of the Cuyahoga River, encouraging investment in Cleveland from both local residents and eastern financiers. Clevelanders enthusiastically celebrated the canal groundbreaking at Newark, Ohio, which took place on the Fourth of July, 1825. Kelley also coaxed the federal government into awarding Cleveland a $5,000 grant to improve its harbor, another boon in this era of rapid transportation development and canal mania and, by 1826, Cleveland began emerging as a Great Lakes commercial hub, linking western hinterlands to the newly completed Erie Canal in upstate New York. Cleveland, bolstered by the prospect of its impending growth and a burgeoning commercial sector, despite a meager population of only one thousand, held a great deal of potential.[5]

COLUMBUS

Despite the early growth of Cincinnati and the fortuitous location of Cleveland, state lawmakers met in 1803 and determined that neither would be granted status as the state capital. Neither would Chillicothe, a town in southeastern Ohio functioning as the temporary capital, be awarded that honor. Instead, lawmakers proposed locating the capital in the underdeveloped center of Ohio, on a navigable body of water equally accessible to residents throughout the state. In 1812, shortly before the United States entered a war with Great Britain, land sales began in the newly formed central city of Columbus. The War of 1812 stimulated economic and population growth in the town (which housed both British prisoners and American soldiers—sometimes as many as three thousand at a time), providing substantial profits to local merchants. But, as in many American cities, recession followed victory in the war and land prices plummeted. Many of the almost two thousand residents that called Columbus home in 1826 came because of the city's status as the political hub of the state. To maintain this political stature (there were numerous attempts to remove the capital to a more industrializing or populated area of the state until nearly mid-century) local residents concentrated on transportation innovation, building several roads to and from Columbus to accentuate the benefits afforded by a centrally located capital. In 1826, for instance, planners for the National Road projected running the thoroughfare through Columbus, and began surveying in earnest that year. Columbus, though growing much more slowly than Cincinnati and with less commercial potential than Cleveland, also looked to the future with optimism, encouraged by its central location in the state, its future transportation prospects, and its solidifying status as Ohio's political capital.[6]

INDIANAPOLIS

The state legislature of Indiana mimicked their counterparts in Ohio, establishing Indianapolis as a centrally located capital city even though there was no established settlement in the area. Town lots went on sale in October 1821 but the public responded lukewarmly. By 1831, the state still owned three-fourths of the properties in the mile-square location set aside for downtown, as malarial, disease-riddled swampland surrounding the city and poor relations with local Native Americans hindered the development of the fledgling capital. Additionally, territorial governor William Henry Harrison's ruthless dealings with Native American tribes and forced land cessions caused tension in the early nineteenth century, as did Tecumseh's pan-Indian movement, centered just 50 miles from Indianapolis. Yet Indianapolis residents could soon point to several signs of progress. In 1822, the *Indianapolis Gazette* newspaper published its first issue, postal service began, and the first session of the circuit court returned 22 indictments, mostly for illegal sales of homemade alcohol. Additionally, in 1826, a treaty with local Potawatomi removed most vestiges of indigenous peoples from central Indiana, freeing land near the new state capital for settlers and economic expansion, while farmers slowly reclaimed and drained swampland around Indianapolis, thus promoting both agriculture and better health. Also, fortuitously for early settlers, in 1826, the city's first stagecoach lines began regular traffic between Indianapolis and other towns throughout the state. Despite poor health conditions, a fledgling and untested transportation system, and less than promising commercial conditions, Indianapolis officially became the state capital in 1825. In that year, Indianapolis residents cheered as the state government relocated, giving the city's 762 citizens hope for future success.[7]

CHICAGO

Residents incorporated Chicago as a town in 1833 and as a city four years later. But as early as 1803, it was the site of Fort Dearborn, an American military outpost. In August 1812, Native Americans attacked the sparsely populated and lightly defended fort. Potawatomi warriors ambushed a column of soldiers, women, and children fleeing the attack, killing 86 of the 148 evacuees and enslaving the survivors. The victorious Potawatomies burned Fort Dearborn to the ground, forcing the Americans to rebuild the structure after regaining control of the region in 1816. European settlement remained minimal in the area around Fort Dearborn for over a decade. By 1823, American leaders facing more pressing concerns deemed the military protection provided by Fort Dearborn unnecessary and emptied the barracks, causing a void in Chicago's already tenuous society. Weakened by the departure of American troops, residents of the area did not formally organize Chicago as a town until a decade later, in 1833, when the population remained a paltry 350.[8]

In each of these growing midwestern cities, debates concerning historical memory and regional uniqueness resonated in celebrations of the national semicentennial in 1826, mirroring discussions among midwesterners about how they measured up against their counterparts from eastern states that had declared independence from Britain 50 years earlier. As the oration given by Drake suggests, midwesterners sought to properly honor the sacrifices made by Revolutionary War veterans prior to the establishment of midwestern states while still lauding the progress made in the intervening years, in which they had taken part. Thus the fiftieth anniversary of the nation's independence, known alternatively as the year of Jubilee, marked an important milestone in midwestern conceptualizations of American nationalism and patriotic pride and, as such, provides an excellent starting point for exploring the evolution of nineteenth-century Independence Day celebrations and associated conceptions of American patriotism. To midwestern men and women, the semicentennial marked not only a chronological landmark, but an ideological and cultural one as well. Midwesterners used the occasion to publicly proclaim their opinions on American independence and nationalistic loyalty. They employed patriotic oratory, parading, and toasting (all deemed proper modes of celebrating the nation's birth in the antebellum era) to discuss what it meant to be an American citizen. And they used their actions and rhetoric to explain the importance of the semicentennial in developing understandings of regionalism, ethnic identity, and culture citizenship.

The Rising Middle Class

During the first half of the nineteenth century, these growing midwestern cities nurtured the rise of an economic and ideological middle class, emerging as a dominant political, cultural, and social force. The twin impulses of industrialization (minimizing skilled manual labor) and consumerism (making middle-class as much a lifestyle as an economic category) collaborated to form a distinct middling class in the urban Midwest, as it did elsewhere in the United States. Middle-class American citizens, guided by an ethos of moderation and self-control, molded conceptions of American cultural identity, and by extension July Fourth celebrations, to fit their own evolving notions of a virtuous citizenry. Middle-class commentators described "good" Americans as non-slaveholding, native-born, white Protestants. Good Americans consumed alcohol only in moderation or abstained entirely and refrained from physical violence. As these middle-class urban midwesterners came to define themselves (and, at least in their eyes, the culture of the entire nation), they became increasingly exclusive, withholding the rights of cultural citizenship and control of public commemorations of the Fourth of July from outsiders claiming an entitlement in natural law. Urban centers proved especially problematic for idealistic middle-class reformers attempting to regulate American morality because, as notorious hotbeds of pauperism, crime, corruption, and vice,they were the very antitheses of the traits of good Americans. Some celebrations of the Fourth of July in these urban centers also proved antithetical to middle-class notions of good Americanism, as violence, excessive drinking, and historical irreverence plagued Independence Day commemorations.[9]

This rising middle class included a group of men historians dubbed civic boosters. Civic boosters promoted their cities to both outside investors (usually from the east coast) and local citizens in efforts to improve the economic and ethical stature of their particular communities, simultaneously encouraging good business and the development of a moral citizenry. Civic boosters in the mid-nineteenth century can be divided into four categories, each with their own unique agendas and methods for defining what it meant to be a good American. Elected municipal officials were important, and usually highly visible, civic boosters. Their motivation seems clear: the creation of a more moral and prosperous city reflected positively on their leadership abilities and probably meant a longer tenure in office. Newspaper editors constituted a second cadre of boosters, acting in concert with elected officials by publishing partisan political organs capable of bestowing or withdrawing patronage to favored politicians and legislative action. Businessmen, including wholesalers, merchants, and manufacturers, comprised a third group of civic boosters, each with a well-defined economic reason to support an exuberant midsummer celebration. The final group of civic boosters consisted of various professionals, including clergy, physicians, and attorneys, who relied on maintaining social standing to remain in positions of community leadership. Civic boosters' practices differed: Cleveland's Alfred Kelley pursued public funds for internal improvements while Cincinnati's Daniel Drake sought eastern investment and inexpensive immigrant labor to bolster the local economy. But whatever their method, civic boosters constantly extolled the virtues of their particular cities and urged local residents to act more patriotically.[10]

Boosters' support of civic-sponsored, community-wide commemorations constituted a vitally important aspect of antebellum Independence Day festivities. Formal celebrations of the Fourth of July typically included parading, an oration, and the reading of the Declaration of Independence in either the principal city streets or near civic buildings like the statehouse or county courthouse. The ideal celebration, at least for these boosters, followed a well-defined and tightly controlled pattern in which each group played a prescribed role: city councilmen led the Fourth of July parade, a local clergyman or attorney delivered the oration, businessmen organized trade associations to march in orderly procession, and newspapermen diligently reported on the conviviality of the day, praising fellow boosters for their benign, nonpartisan patriotism.[11]

Pre-1826 National Celebrations of Independence Day

Understanding the national history of the Fourth of July is vital to appreciating the changes that took place in nineteenth-century urban midwestern commemorations of the holiday. Americans first celebrated Independence Day during the American Revolution, binding former British subjects together through the shared experience of liberty and wartime sacrifice, helping to unite a fragile nation. In the years following the war, the Fourth of July remained a unifying event, giving Americans the opportunity to solemnly remember their fallen comrades who had suffered and died so that they might live as free men and women. But this necessity for togetherness slowly faded after the Redcoats were defeated, replaced by arguments over the political future of the young nation epitomized in the framing of the United States Constitution. The Constitutional Convention entrusted with writing a unifying document instead produced political factionalism—Federalists supporting the proposed Constitution and Anti-Federalists opposing its immediate adoption. These politicians latched on to the Fourth of July as a symbolic opportunity to claim the mantle of the revolution as their own, and thus validate their stance on the Constitutional ratification.[12]

Between 1787 and 1826, political division pitting Federalists and Anti-Federalists—and later Federalists and Democratic-Republicans— in ongoing contests of one-upmanship dominated eastern Independence Day celebrations. Federalists held stoic dinners on the Fourth of July, toasting only their own leaders like George Washington, John Adams, and Alexander Hamilton, and somberly, if not always soberly, extolling the virtues of a strong national government and sound fiscal policy. The opposing Anti-Federalists vied for political preeminence in their commemorations, replacing honorifics to Adams and Hamilton with toasts to Thomas Jefferson and the Bill of Rights on July Fourth as 13-gun salutes, political toasts, military parades and orations became sites of contestation, with both political camps vying for the all-important title of most patriotic.[13]

Celebrants occasionally came to blows defending their particular visions of how properly commemorating Independence Day reflected American nationalism. In Albany, New York, on the Fourth of July in 1788, 50 Anti-Federalists marched through the city streets, loudly proclaiming their political loyalties. At the conclusion of their trek through Albany's thoroughfares, celebrants burnt a likeness of the Constitution, both demonstrating their firm opposition to the document and infuriating the city's pro-Constitution forces. Incensed Federalists, themselves celebrating Virginia's recent ratification of the Constitution, responded to this challenge by attacking the Anti-Federalists, resulting in the two sides battling through the city streets armed with swords, clubs, stones, and bayonets. Although few celebrations in the late eighteenth and early nineteenth centuries resulted in bloodshed, political divisiveness became a hallmark of the holiday during the post-revolutionary period as both political parties sought to position themselves as the true heirs to the revolutionary legacy by symbolically controlling patriotic commemorations of Independence Day.[14]

Democratic-Republicans, emerging at the turn of the nineteenth century from a coalition of former Anti-Federalists and others opposed to Alexander Hamilton's fiscal policies, sought their own control of the patriotic holiday. In particular, Democratic-Republicans, upset at the continued Federalist use of what historian Simon Newman terms "patriotism for partisan purposes" on the Fourth of July, converted the day into a festive occasion promoting white, male egalitarianism. Unwilling to allow Democratic-Republican domination of the anniversary of the nation's birth, Federalists fought back, reforming their own festivities in an attempt to showcase the diversity of the American populace led by a duly elected (and more importantly, Federalist) government, including women, African-Americans, and ethnic minorities in their fetes. In eastern urban centers by 1826, then, partisanship threatened the intended conviviality of the Fourth and created discord over the meaning and proper commemoration of the nationalist holiday.[15]

Pre-1826 Midwestern Commemorations

Many emerging midwestern villages also celebrated the Fourth of July before the semicentennial, albeit with far less political conflict and far more unanimity. Cincinnati first commemorated Independence Day in 1799, when the small populace turned out en masse for the village's first community-wide festival. The revelry began with a salute at dawn from cannons housed at nearby Fort Washington, followed by a militia parade in the late morning. The festivities stretched into the evening with a community-wide dinner and hours of dancing at Mr. Yeatman's tavern. Charles Cist, a Cincinnati resident writing about this memorable celebration nearly 50 years later, reported that the toasts given that evening were "in good spirit and taste" and that a crowd of gentlemen and "a brilliant assembly of ladies" attended the gala event. Celebrating the Fourth of July in early Cincinnati, with a small homogeneous population, apparently united the citizenry for a day in which, according to historian Steven Ross, even "masters and journeymen marched together not as employer and employee, but as fellow citizens."[16]

Moses Cleaveland's band of Connecticut Land Company surveyors celebrated the first Fourth of July in Ohio's Western Reserve shortly after landing on the banks of Lake Erie on Independence Day, 1796. Cleaveland and his followers commemorated their landing, and the holiday, by firing a musket salute and drinking rounds of toasts, including one to their benefactors, the Connecticut Land Company. During the evening, the company drank "several pails of grog" before retiring "in remarkable good order." Following the lead of this first celebration, pioneer Clevelanders remembered the Fourth of July with unusual exuberance as a day marking both the anniversary of American Independence and the arrival of Cleaveland's band of intrepid surveyors. For instance, in 1821, Cleveland held three separate events, all including (relatively) large numbers of celebrants. Despite the multiple celebrations, local newspapers reported no violence between participants or division among revelers.

Instead, the three groups spent the day peacefully and, by all accounts, cheerfully. Emily Nash, a teenage girl and budding socialite, attended one of the commemorations that year. In her journal, Nash detailed her recollections growing up in the region and eagerly related her Fourth of July experiences. She went to a dance with a young man, whose feelings she had hurt after giving him "the mitten" (turning down his advances). Two years later she accompanied other "young folks" to a dance, remarking that, "it rained some but we don't mind the rain when independance [*sic*] day comes." She apparently enjoyed the festivities, joined by a young man named Peter Beals, and left in high spirits, remarking that "we had a fine dance."[17]

Residents of the planned capital city at Columbus commemorated early Independence Days in similar fashion, with toasting and parading at the forefront of their revelry. The Fourth of July festivities of 1818 typified those marking Columbus's early history, as local residents gathered in a tavern and marched in procession through the city streets before returning to the drinking establishment for dinner. After feasting, residents honored George Washington, Revolutionary War heroes, the president and vice president, other leading political figures, and the State of Ohio in successive toasts before retiring in high spirits.[18]

Indianapolis's Fourth of July celebrations mirrored those of its Ohio counterparts, beginning with its inaugural fete in 1822. The village's first Independence Day program took place on the militia muster grounds and included readings from the Declaration of Independence and George Washington's Inaugural Address as well as a sermon given by Rev. John McClung. McClung's oration included an invocation that nothing "take place . . . to injure the . . . morals of a place whose character is now forming," clearly fearful of the tenuous state of Indianapolis's developing society. The revelry continued with a feast of barbecued deer—shot while wandering on one of the city's largest roads—and, "enlivened with whisky," included fourteen toasts, after which revelers enjoyed a huge bonfire and a dance at a local tavern spent "in hilarity and mirth."[19]

Independence Day festivities in early Chicago necessarily revolved around life at nearby Fort Dearborn. In 1816, a company of troops spent the holiday rebuilding the burned fort and burying the skeletons of those who died in the massacre four years earlier. In 1819, American soldiers at the newly rebuilt fort celebrated by firing cannons, shotguns, and pistols into the air, commemorating both the Fourth of July and the end of hostilities with the British in the region. When American forces withdrew from Fort Dearborn in 1823, Independence Day celebrations went as well, disappearing until after Chicago's incorporation a decade later.[20]

Celebrating the Semicentennial

As July 4, 1826, approached, citizens throughout the nation began making extensive preparations for the national Jubilee. Among the more notable national events was the arrival of the Marquis de Lafayette from France and his journey through the United States in 1824 and 1825. The famed Revolutionary War hero traveled extensively throughout the country and encountered warm receptions at each stop. On May 19, 1825, Lafayette visited Cincinnati, the only midwestern urban center he encountered on his travels. Cincinnatians greeted the Marquis with a 13-gun salute and shouts of praise, even though he stayed just briefly in the Queen City. Other cities heralded his arrival just as affectionately, as Lafayette visited the Hermitage, the White House, New York City, and various other points across the young nation, bringing with him good cheer and, most importantly, a visible reminder of the sacrifices made by the patriots of 1776. This tour marked the last journey of the Marquis de Lafayette through the United States and, coupled with other historic events, added to a sense of closure found in commemorating the nation's semicentennial.[21]

Indeed, spurred by the return of Lafayette, many eastern cities heartily celebrated the Jubilee Fourth of July, embracing the duality of a day set aside to both pay tribute to the past and laud the present and future. In New York, the Common Council created four golden medals signifying American ingenuity. Tellingly, three went to surviving signers of the Declaration of Independence while Council presented the fourth to the son of Robert Fulton, promoter of the technology of steamboat travel. With a similar nod to the past and present, Worcester, Massachusetts native Isaiah Thomas read the Declaration of Independence in the same spot where he originally read the document in 1776 after its adoption by the Continental Congress. In Boston, the chosen orator "illustrated, that our fathers had honoured their fathers and themselves, and had done justice to us their posterity," noting that, "it was our duty to follow their high example." Even Thomas Jefferson, in a letter written on June 24 declining an invitation to celebrate the holiday in Washington, D.C., shed light on the relationship between historical memory and the present. He would have been delighted, he wrote, "to have enjoyed with them the consolatory fact, that our fellow citizens, after half a century of experience and prosperity, continue to approve the choice we made," adding his hope that "the annual return of this day forever refresh our recollections of these rights, and an undiminished devotion to them." Clearly commemorating the Jubilee throughout the nation necessarily involved reconciling the past and present.[22]

On the semicentennial Independence Day in the urban Midwest, revelers focused their celebratory energy on three main patriotic pursuits—parades, orations, and toasts. The nature of these activities provides insight into trends that defined the holiday in succeeding decades. The actions of midwestern Fourth of July celebrants in 1826 demonstrate developing ethnocultural schisms, indications of partisan squabbles, and a growing regionality emphasizing moral reform. Differences existed in the content of the respective festivities in midwestern cities, but the results remained consistent—midwesterners began to construct distinct interpretations of American nationalism and to utilize the Fourth of July, and control of the memory of the holiday, to shape these interpretations.

PARADING

Independence Day celebrations in 1826 typically began at sunrise, marked by a salute of rifles or cannon shot by a local militia or military company. Shortly after this gunpowder revelry, celebrants gathered and marched in a civic-sponsored procession through the village streets, led by local political leaders and firing pistols or fireworks while loudly proclaiming the coming of the anniversary of the nation's birth. In Columbus, 300 residents, constituting nearly one-sixth of the village's entire population, joined 24 war veterans in marching to a nearby grove. In Cincinnati, Revolutionary War survivors joined militiamen, mechanical societies, and agriculturists in their annual parade. In Medina, near Cleveland, 24 "Female Youth," dressed all in white and representing the number of states in the Union in 1826, promenaded along the city's concourse accompanied by numerous war veterans. As several historians have capably demonstrated, this type of parading could function as a form of popular politics during the early republic by providing men, women, and even children an acceptable forum to air grievances or public concerns. As the population of these midwestern urban centers grew during the nineteenth century, parades did become sites of symbolic contestation. But in 1826, the small size of these towns and their relatively homogeneous populations afforded revelers the opportunity to use parading as a means to publicly proclaim patriotic loyalty.[23]

ORATORY

Parades usually terminated at a church or nearby grove, typical sites designated for the day's oration. Newspaper editorials often primed these orations (traditionally delivered by a local lawyer, pastor, or Revolutionary War veteran) with articles emphasizing similar themes. Speeches and editorials recalled the glories of 1776, lauded the efforts of America's republican government, and promoted the continued progress and prosperity of the growing nation. In these patriotic overtures, orators and editors cast the past and the present in perfect harmony: the present represented the logical extension of the revolutionary era. Columbus's *Ohio State Journal* included a typical Fourth of July editorial in 1826, praising the progress of the Midwest in the years between the signing of the Declaration and the semicentennial by proclaiming that, "the coming fourth of July will complete fifty years of liberty, prosperity, and happiness." Clearly, the editor, Philo Olmsted, believed that the Jubilee celebration ended an important era in American history. But Olmsted also remarked that Ohio, in particular, responded favorably to this great transformation. In that 50-year span, he wrote, Ohio grew from a wilderness "almost unknown to civilized man" into a place populated by "eight hundred thousand souls." Tellingly, Olmsted did not attribute this growth and unparalleled success to fertile soil or navigable waterways, but instead to "the intelligence of the people, and the freedom of their government." New York governor DeWitt Clinton made similar remarks when breaking ground for the Ohio and Erie Canal in 1825. Clinton lauded the progress of Ohio as being "without a parallel in the history of mankind," and the state as being populated by a "moral, patriotic, and intelligent" people. That a republican government brought out the best in its citizens served as a recurring theme in editorials printed in midwestern newspapers on the Fourth of July during the early nineteenth century, allowing midwesterners to spread unimpeded across the continent and dominate the supposedly virginal landscape through technological and intellectual superiority. For their part, midwesterners viewed themselves as uniquely patriotic, representing the strongest points of a republican nation and fulfilling DeWitt Clinton's promise as moral, patriotic, intelligent—and perhaps most importantly, discerning and responsible—American citizens. The emergence of the Midwest as a coherent region, and more importantly, one capable of fulfilling the promise of the revolutionary generation, began to materialize during the Jubilee celebrations, often in the guise of such laudatory oratory.[24]

Just as printed editorials applauded the accomplishments of the American people (and midwesterners in particular), Fourth of July orators heaped optimistic praise upon the region in their speeches, using their addresses as forums to define evolving midwestern regional identity. Cincinnatians initially quarreled over the civic-sponsored speaker for the 1826 holiday. Some wanted Benjamin Drake while others preferred William Henry Harrison Jr., the son of the former Indiana governor and future president of the United States. Unable to choose, Cincinnatians welcomed both orators in 1826: some citizens assembled at the First Presbyterian Church to listen to Harrison, who "reflected much credit upon his taste and judgment," while others chose the celebration of the Phi Alpha Theta Society, held in the town's Baptist Church, for Drake's speech. Drake spoke at length about the preeminence of the young republic, lauding the fertility of its land, the virtue of representative republican government—especially should Jackson ascend to his rightful post in 1828—and the prosperity of its merchants. Newspaper accounts indicated that revelers celebrated the day "with much spirit, according to the different arrangements," before uniting for a general celebration to close the day's festivities. Despite a split populace, Queen City orators clearly recognized the path speechmakers should take in the year of Jubilee, lauding American progress while recognizing the nation's historical legacy.[25]

In Indianapolis, nearly all of the city's 762 citizens turned out for an oration given by Calvin Fletcher, a well-known and highly respected local attorney. Fletcher began, as did most orators of his day, with an appropriate ode to the heroes of 1776 and the signers of the Declaration of Independence. Fletcher then recounted the ability of the Fourth of July to tie together Americans "in whatever country, and in whatever clime their destinies may have called them," before imploring listeners to "unite in solemn reading" of the Declaration, extolling the timelessness of the document. After this lofty remembrance and laudatory speech reconciling past and present, Fletcher took a unique turn, commenting on the institution of slavery, a topic often deemed off-limits at early Fourth of July speeches. "On this day of national congratulation, let us not pass unnoticed one sin, one national evil," Fletcher began, railing against "the involuntary slavery of a part of the human family." He concluded his oratory conservatively, with an obligatory nod to American progress and ingenuity, praising the "rich rewards of virtue and religion" uniquely exhibited in the growing Midwest.[26]

Although atypical among midwestern Independence Day orations, Fletcher's connection between slavery and the Fourth of July reflected a time-honored practice in eastern commemorations of Independence Day. Clearly orators understood that their words, often immortalized in newspaper columns published after the holiday, held the power to shape and define public opinion, which, in turn, could shape and define emerging definitions of American nationalism. George Buchanan gave the first abolitionist Fourth of July oration before the Maryland Society for Promoting the Abolition of Slavery in 1791. A little over a decade later, Lemuel Haynes became the first African-American to give a public Independence Day speech. In Salem, New York in 1826, Nathaniel Prime delivered a discourse entitled "The Year of Jubilee, but not of Africans," intended to combat the budding anti-colonization movement. In his oration, Prime lamented the fact that, although the year of Jubilee celebrated freedom, "a million and a half of our fellow men . . . are at this moment groaning under the chains of bondage." Clearly, orators in the year of Jubilee recognized the paradox of celebrating independence while slavery bound African-Americans in chains. But despite the efforts of Buchanan, Haynes, Prime, Fletcher, and others, the Fourth of July often marked just another opportunity to turn a blind eye to the suffering of enslaved African-Americans while celebrating the supposed freedom of the young country. Not until the 1830s would the debate over slavery gain notice as an accepted, if controversial, subject for Fourth of July oratory.[27]

In Cleveland, the city's one thousand citizens celebrated the Fourth of July in 1826 with "the usual demonstrations of joy." Residents made minimal preparations for the event; a committee appointed to make arrangements for the celebration extended a "general invitation" to Clevelanders and citizens of the nearby towns to attend the day's festivities. Reports of the resulting celebration were favorable, if not especially noteworthy. The day began with a salute at sunrise, formally commencing the Jubilee in Cleveland, as it did in many other cities and villages across the United States that morning. The *Cleveland Herald* deemed the salute part of the "recollection of the prosperity and happiness enjoyed during the first half century of our existence as a Nation," and reported that the time-honored ceremony undoubtedly touched every patriotic heart. Several hours later, at eleven o'clock, Reverend Bradstreet delivered a public oration, constructed as a traditional ode to the heroes of the Revolution and the progress made by the young nation in the 50 intervening years, before the celebrants retired to a local tavern, where the keeper provided a hearty meal and the men drank extensive toasts.[28]

TOASTING

Bouts of collective drinking served as an accepted forum for airing politically contentious viewpoints and demonstrating unabashed partisanship and discord even during the American Revolution. As Americans battled the British, drinking toasts in colonial taverns constituted an important, if sometimes controversial, aspect of Independence Day celebrations. Patriotic citizens drank heartily to military victories and republican institutions while damning the English crown and parliament. By 1826, in the now-independent nation, toasts lauding both the virtuousness of the Founding Fathers and the various symbols associated with American patriotism replaced rounds berating the English monarchy. Yet toasts retained their earlier ability to incite division and discord. An 1823 celebration in Washington, D.C. exemplifies this potential; organizers made a special point of encouraging the mixed crowd of Federalists and Democrats to "drink *all* the toasts that they might alternatively offer" rather than just ones reflecting pro-Federalist or pro-Democratic sentiment. Clearly, the toastmaster intended that the holiday unite Americans of all political persuasions rather than promote discord. Toasting, although usually done with wine, whisky, or other available liquor, was not simply an antebellum drinking game (revelers drank to excess after toasting concluded). Instead, toasting various political, economic, social, and cultural ideals on the Fourth of July provided nineteenth-century patriots with an accepted, time-honored opportunity to voice their particular conceptions of nationalism and patriotic loyalty.[29]

Celebrants divided toasts into two groups—planned "regulars" and spontaneous "voluntaries." As their names suggest, revelers generally toasted regulars universally and, as planned toasts, fashioned them well in advance, paying tribute to war heroes (especially politically innocuous ones), republican institutions, and vague patriotic ideologies like liberty and freedom. Although partisan squabbles sometimes found their way into regular toasts, celebrants usually saved such divisiveness (already enlivened by previous rounds of regular toasting) for voluntaries. Thirteen regulars, in honor of the number of original colonies, was an accepted number passed down from the revolutionary era and rarely varied. Revelers usually drank the first regular toast to Independence Day and traditionally followed it with one honoring George Washington. After they toasted Washington, the order varied, although celebrants regularly included rounds of drinks honoring heroes of the Revolution,

FIGURE 2. "The Apotheosis of Washington," artist and date unknown. Morristown National Historical Park.

symbols of the nation—such as the eagle or American flag—local leaders, and both current and former presidents. Celebrants often offered the thirteenth, and final, regular toast to women, reserved as a position of honor before the unruliness of voluntary toasts. For example, with their final regular, the men of Columbus in 1826 honored "The Fair of America," and promised lightheartedly that "yours are the only arms to which freemen delight to yield." Overall, this general pattern for regular toasting continued into the early nineteenth century, tied by the common thread of historical memory, as most regulars honored the nation's revolutionary legacy and symbols passed down from the founders.[30]

Unlike regular toasts, celebrants spontaneously conceived voluntaries, often after the effects of alcohol lowered inhibitions and loosened tongues. Voluntaries could be both inflammatory and divisive because, instead of lauding politically innocuous symbols like the American eagle, the flag, or figures culled from the nation's collective memory, voluntary toasts spoke to local concerns, regionality, and contentious national issues. Voluntaries provided a valuable opportunity for inebriated citizens to air grievances or loudly proclaim political loyalties in a safe, time-honored, exclusively male environment. Voluntary toasts, therefore, tend to reveal much more about the cultural and political climate of midwestern urban centers on the Fourth of July (and the evolving self-conceptions of what it meant to be a patriotic American) than the carefully planned, and usually unobjectionable, regular toasts.

Contentious voluntary toasts often revolved around timely national political issues. In Columbus in 1826, one voluntary celebrated the army and navy as fine "instruments for the protection of our rights," recalling their glorious roles in American victories in the War of 1812 and the American Revolution. A second voluntary in Columbus in 1826 recognized American manufacturers, adding the caveat that "sound policy and genuine patriotism will always give them the preference." Like their neighbors in the state capital, Clevelanders drank to important economic and political symbols, including "The American Yeomanry—Good at the plough, true with the rifle, and our guardians at the ballot-boxes." The iconography of this toast is unmistakable; Clevelanders drinking to yeoman farmers clearly utilized images from the nation's past to construct an idealized vision of what America should be. Promoting the yeoman farmer, particularly at the ballot box, meant not only romanticizing the hardscrabble pioneer lifestyle, but also the notion that this hardworking citizen best represented what it meant to be a patriotic and loyal American.[31]

Another popular topic covered by voluntary toasts involved internal improvements, an issue of great interest in the Midwest following the successful opening of New York's Erie Canal in 1825, and the groundbreaking of the Ohio and Erie that same year. Residents of Cleveland drank semicentennial toasts to Henry Clay and, sarcastically, "enemies of Internal Improvement—May they live upon cat-fish and hominy, and drink tobacco juice," conflating opposition to roads, harbors, and canals with ignorant, uneducated backwardness. With transportation fever striking otherwise isolated regions of the growing Midwest, its residents maintained strong opinions on funding, building, and maintaining internal improvements. Citizens of Columbus, clearly interested in the possibility of connecting the city to the surrounding hinterland, toasted the coming of the Ohio and Erie and the hopes that "this Gigantic under-taking of an infant state" be "crowned with complete success." These toasts had clear political implications, and residents of Cleveland and Columbus voted accordingly, supporting internal improvements and championing the cause of Henry Clay's American System in most 1820s elections. Tellingly, the final voluntary toast in Cleveland in 1826 was for "the present toasts" and the hope that they grow "better and better for years to come."[32]

The Deaths of Adams and Jefferson

Revelers usually included the first three presidents (Washington, Adams, and Jefferson) in their rounds of Independence Day toasts. While all political parties could hail Washington's accomplishments, John Adams, a leading Federalist, and Thomas Jefferson, the founder of the Democratic-Republican faction, often drew especially partisan con-sideration for their roles in establishing political freedom and republi-can government as well as their associations with the nation's leading political parties. By 1826, Adams and Jefferson constituted two of a small number of important surviving revolutionary figures, symbolic as for-mer presidents, leading patriots, and political factionalists.

On the Fourth of July, 1826, both John Adams and Thomas Jefferson drew near the ends of their illustrious lives. Jefferson remained bedridden in Monticello, drifting in and out of consciousness and attended almost constantly by doting physicians. On the evening of July 3, he reportedly revived sufficiently to ask one doctor, "Is it the Fourth?" Jefferson barely survived the night, waking only briefly on Independence Day morning before taking his last breath, shortly after noon. Similarly, John Adams remained confined to his Boston home in early July, suffering from a debilitating cough. On the morning of the Fourth, ringing bells and can-non fire awoke Adams, indicative that the holiday had arrived. Adams reportedly told a servant that "It is the glorious Fourth of July—God bless it," and sat down in an armchair to await his coming death, which greeted him in the early afternoon. Thus on the Fourth of July, 1826, two great statesmen breathed their last, 50 years to the day after the first Independence Day—a coincidence with symbolism lost on no one.[33]

In Cleveland, the *Herald* discussed the coincidental losses of Adams and Jefferson, and their payments of "the debt of nature," shortly after receiving word of their deaths. The *Herald* delved deeply into the symbolic potential of the coincidence and the implications of their passing, spending a great deal of space detailing the fact that these great patriots "lived to witness the great . . . Jubilee—the exact completion of 50 years." The occasion, the editor remarked, was "the most extraordinary on record; and will perpetuate it, as not the least event in the annals of our Republic."[34]

Within a week, Cincinnatians first heard the news of Jefferson's and Adams's deaths. One newspaper remembered Jefferson as "one of the most illustrious benefactors of his species that ever lived in any age." More tellingly, however, the newspaper discussed the remarkable timing of their unlikely departures at length. It was "as if Providence had spared" the ex-presidents, proclaimed one editorial, attributing divine intervention to their longevity. Speaking of Jefferson, the paper surmised that, "while the anniversary was celebrating, as a jubilee on earth, the illustrious writer . . . departed to join his comrades in Heaven."[35]

Perhaps less religiously, but no less zealously, Columbus newspapers relayed details of their deaths to local citizens on the twentieth of July. Besides reciting many of the accomplishments of the ex-presidents, city newspapers also addressed the coincidence of their nearly simultaneous deaths. Even in this era of staunch partisanship, Phil Olmsted's Democratic *Ohio State Journal* willingly laid aside its political animosity in addressing their remarkable lives. "Whatever may have been our feelings" of John Adams, the paper began, the nation's second president provided "many and valuable services to his country." Commenting on the coincidence of their deaths, the *Journal* admitted that it "excited our surprise," but also that "they should die on the anniversary day of our Independence, and that anniversary should be the commencement of a new half century, must mingle our surprise with superstitious astonishment."[36]

Surprise and astonishment are possibly expected responses to the deaths of two of the nation's most prominent founders. However, the commencement of a new half-century described by Olmsted meant more than just the beginning of the 50-year march toward the Centennial. Instead, this new half-century also symbolically brought forth a new generation of leaders, struggling with the mantle of their forefathers.

Midwestern celebrations of the semicentennial Fourth of July varied little from those of previous Independence Day holidays. Parades, patriotic orations, and rounds of regular and voluntary toasts remained standard in every city, as they had been for decades. But the manner in which midwesterners celebrated the semicentennial revealed important differences and foreshadowed coming debates over the meaning of the holiday. Regional uniqueness, cultural imperatives, and ethnic identification emerged in this era as portents of future divisiveness. But perhaps most important in 1826, the seemingly symbolic deaths of Adams and Jefferson appeared to confirm the sense that the American nation was on the threshold of a new era in its history and that the Fourth of July not only played an important role in its past, but would also serve as a prominent part of its future.

1 / "The Sabbath of Liberty": Morally Reforming the Fourth of July, 1827–1849

"Although the merchants had with one consent agreed to observe the day as a sort of republican Sabbath, and give their boys a holy-day, it soon became apparent that must change their purpose, and open their customers a place of rest and shelter; for the streets were literally thronged."[1]
—Columbus Ohio State Journal, 1848

Midwestern celebrations of the Fourth of July began to change in 1826 as celebrants argued about the importance of the nation's past in commemorating the nation's birth. Over the next two decades, Independence Day celebrations became increasingly disjointed as urban midwesterners split over the proper way to honor the occasion. Civic boosters remained insistent that old-fashioned, civic-sponsored festivities could unite the populace in solemn patriotic remembrance of a shared past. Yet instead of adhering to this prescription, most midwesterners used the holiday as an opportunity to reflect on how cultural issues revolving around alcohol consumption, violence, race, gender, and religion defined American nationalism and patriotic loyalty. Middle-class midwesterners then used these categories and celebratory experiences to construct restrictive cultural guidelines about what constituted a "good" American citizen. As the definition of "good" evolved, the Fourth of July slowly transformed into a holiday pulling citizens apart, rather than drawing them together, in commemorating the nation's birth.

The years between 1827 and 1849 marked a tumultuous time in American history. In 1830, South Carolina nullified a federal tariff, forcing Americans throughout the nation to reconsider and defend their own understandings of the meaning of the Union. Later in the decade, a financial panic brought about primarily by Andrew Jackson's personal crusade against Nicholas Biddle and the national bank threatened the administration of Jackson's successor, Martin Van Buren, as well as the economic well-being of thousands of Americans, including many midwesterners. Farmers lost their life savings and eastern financiers beat a hasty retreat from midwestern investments to protect their assets. In the 1840s, the nation stood on more solid economic footing, but faced disagreements about territorial expansion, the future of slavery, reform ideologies, and the place of women in legal and political arenas.

The Growing Midwest

During this era, the Midwest rapidly urbanized, stimulated by industrialization and westward expansion. As it expanded demographically, the Midwest also began to develop a stronger sense of regional identity. It was no longer a stepchild of the republic, a remote backwater populated by inconsequential villages and isolated pioneers. Instead, the Midwest became increasingly geographically distinct, blending European immigrants and eastern migrants to create a regional culture that managed to be both unique and representative of the expanding United States. Celebrations of the Fourth of July reflected this transformation as, rather than uniting to prove their collective patriotism, urban midwesterners divided on how best to individually proclaim political and cultural loyalty to the growing nation.

Cincinnati, the largest of these cities, led this tremendous regional expansion, its population swelling from 16,000 in 1826 to nearly 115,000 by mid-century. During the 1840s, the Queen City's rapid population boom was rivaled only by its industrial output—both nearly tripled in the decade—justifying one traveler's observation that Cincinnati was "one of the most industrious places in the world." Much of this demographic and economic growth resulted from the construction of the Miami and Erie Canal, completed in 1845, and the continued importance of river transportation bringing both native- and foreign-born migrants to the growing city on the banks of the Ohio River and allowing Cincinnati to become one of the nation's leading economic centers.[2]

Cleveland's growth and prosperity during this era also relied upon transportation innovation and its fortuitous location. On July 4, 1827, workers completed the final stages of the Ohio and Erie Canal (ten years to the day after the groundbreaking of New York's Erie Canal), connecting inland areas of northeastern Ohio to Lake Erie at Cleveland. This ambitious building project solidified Cleveland as an important regional marketplace, connecting Ohio's rich agricultural hinterlands to valuable eastern markets through the Great Lakes and canal systems. Population grew apace: between 1825 and 1845, Cleveland expanded from fewer than 500 residents to more than 12,000 and, by mid-century, Clevelanders confidently expected continued economic growth and prosperity.[3]

Although it lacked the water connections of Cincinnati and Cleveland, Columbus also grew substantially between 1827 and 1849, in large part due to its status as Ohio's political capital. During that time, the population increased from 2,000 isolated souls to a more robust 15,000, many of them part of the city's political institutions. Both Whigs and Democrats exploited Columbus's advantageous central location and increasing political importance, holding nominating conventions on numerous occasions in the state capital. In 1840, a political rally promoting William Henry Harrison's "Log Cabin and Hard Cider" campaign drew nearly 20,000 supporters to Columbus while Democrats regularly met in the statehouse square to promote their candidates. In spite of its promise as a government center, Columbus faced numerous setbacks. In 1849, a cholera outbreak forced a quarter of Columbus citizens to evacuate. Of those who remained, over three hundred perished while hundreds more battled the debilitating illness. Also, despite its growth, Columbus remained a relatively unimportant commercial and industrial center—its central location ensured political importance but stymied economic growth, with limited access to canals, rivers, and lakes.[4]

Columbus's mixed fortunes in the second quarter of the nineteenth century mirrored conditions in Indiana's capital city. Like its Ohio counterpart, Indianapolis relied heavily on the patronage of politicians and their retainers to stimulate the local economy while the legislature was in session. Indianapolis's citizenry soon realized, however, that the continued development of their city required more than just political support and focused increased attention on improving roads and waterways connecting the capital to other populous Indiana cities, like New Albany and Madison, located to the south along the Ohio River. By 1836, this initiative was a statewide concern, prompting legislators to pass "The Mammoth Improvement Bill," providing for eight major public works projects spread throughout Indiana. The financial panic of 1837 put these ambitious projects on hold while irresponsible allocations of sparse funds (catering to local whims instead of agreeing on a coherent, unified, and economically sound agenda) hamstrung building efforts. In spite of the failure of the Mammoth Bill, Indianapolis witnessed moderate population growth in this era as the 726 residents of 1826 became eight thousand by mid-century, passing Madison and nearly equaling New Albany for the distinction of being Indiana's largest city.[5]

Chicago did not incorporate until the 1830s, yet its rise was meteoric. In little more than a decade, the Windy City grew from a "little mushroom town," functioning as a frontier trading outpost dominated by factious surrounding Native American tribes, to a thriving commercial and transportation hub. Between 1837 and 1850, the town's population exploded, increasing from 4,170 to nearly 30,000, due primarily to generous internal improvement funding at both the national and state level. In the early 1830s, Congress voted to appropriate $25,000 to improve the city's moribund harbor, while the state of Illinois financed the construction of the Illinois and Michigan Canal, completed in 1848, locating its northern terminus in Chicago. Railroads, however, ultimately cemented Chicago as the central city of the urban Midwest. Chicagoans chartered the Galena & Chicago Union railroad company, the town's first, in 1836, although it took more than a decade to find sufficient investors willing to complete even the first stages of the venture. By the 1850s, railroads assured Chicago's regional dominance as numerous companies constructed lines around Chicago, transforming the Windy City into a regional, and ultimately national, rail hub. By mid-century there was every indication that the prosperity of Chicago ultimately rested on the influence of the iron horse.[6]

Intending Unity, Harboring Discord

Civic boosters in these maturing cities purposefully composed Independence Day celebrations as uplifting and unifying experiences, showcasing the positive cultural and political attributes of their expanding local communities and promoting ties between contemporary commemorations and those held in the past. Boosters proactively encouraged local citizens to unite in general celebration, free from political and social strife. An Indianapolis editorial written in 1849 poignantly captured this unifying ideal. The Democratic editor made a pointed plea that "the usual avocations of life should be laid aside" on the Fourth of July and that "party and sect should be forgotten, social distinctions and adventitious circumstances obliterated." The newspaperman also called on the "young, old, and middle-aged, rich and poor, the learned and unlearned" to "give way to emotions of patriotism" on the holiday, uniting as upstanding American citizens. Editorials throughout the Midwest during the 1830s and 1840s, regardless of political affiliation, mirrored this desire for short-term political and social détente on Independence Day. In 1839, a Whiggish Columbus editor declared that "party spirit will not be permitted to desecrate the holy recollections which the day calls forth" in the hope that both his party and Democrats could mingle convivially, "in all the kindliness of brotherhood." Three years later, the *Cleveland Herald* proffered the following wish for the city's Independence Day celebration: "May all political, moral, and religious sectarianism be forgotten, and the whole American people be animated by . . . the "Spirit of '76," purposefully employing historical memory as a tool both to unite the populace and delineate the importance of properly commemorating the holiday.These editors and their fellow boosters promoted the potential of the Fourth of July to unite local citizens in a shared glorification of the nation's heritage, temporarily putting aside political, cultural, and social differences to honor the memory of the nation's birth.[7]

Although civic boosters intended Independence Day celebrants to hearken to Fourths of old, when isolated frontier communities pulled together to remember the holiday with a common sense of American patriotism (and nascent regional distinctiveness), most midwestern antebellum celebrations of the Fourth of July were not the well-attended, civic-sponsored, misty-eyed recollections envisioned by civic leaders. Some historians interpret rhetoric extolling patriotic inclusiveness found in newspapers, written primarily by civic boosters, to demonstrate the unifying potential of the Fourth of July. For instance, Mary Ryan, in her examination of New York City, New Orleans, and San Francisco, claims that the Fourth of July brought citizens together "in a short-term commitment to some larger civic identity" while Len Travers, in studying Boston, Philadelphia, and Charleston, asserts that the spectacle of Independence Day festivities masked ethnic, political, and social tension, allowing revelers to forget their disputes amidst the sights and sounds of the day. Although these observations are certainly applicable to the particular cities and eras studied by these and other historians, citizens in the antebellum Midwest often acted contrarily to the ideals promoted by their civic leaders. Most celebrations were not as unifying as boosters intended; the sights and sounds of the day served merely to accentuate the cultural distance between ethnically, socially, or religiously diverse celebrants. Instead, in these midwestern cities, promoting unification often proved to be merely empty rhetoric, employed desperately by city newspaperman to try and unite a populace still struggling with defining their own regional and, by extension, national identity.[8]

In fact, celebrations that seemed to be unifying, and were heralded as such by urban boosters, often hid or masked nascent discord. In Cleveland in 1845, locals gathered in a bipartisan celebration praised by the *Plain Dealer* as "cheering to every patriotic heart." But an anti-immigrant outburst from one reveler marred this idyllic celebration, even after bystanders escorted the instigator from the assembly. The following year, with questions about the fate of the Oregon Territory and the Mexican War dominating local headlines, the editor of the *Cleveland Herald* implored area residents to "assemble as a band of brothers, forgetting all political dissension and family bickerings" on the Fourth of July, an occasion "when Democrats and Whigs, Christian and Infidel, could unite in a common cause." Again, the results failed to match the intent. The orator chosen by Cleveland's civic boosters, rather than praising the bipartisan effort, preached about contentious political issues plaguing the nation—notably questions concerning American designs on Oregon and Texas—while openly criticizing President Polk. Such occurrences were not limited to Cleveland. In 1841, a Columbus newspaper editor, for instance, lamented the fact that local Whigs and Democrats refused to celebrate together, arguing that the factions ought to join in "a meeting and blending of all parties upon that day." The Fourth of July, a day intended to encourage patriotic nationalism and celebrate a collective sense of nationhood, instead witnessed struggles over contested understandings about the proper mode of commemorating the occasion.[9]

POLITICAL PARTISANSHIP

Political partisanship became a primary cause of this internal divisiveness tainting antebellum celebrations of the Fourth of July in the urban Midwest. The demise of the Federalist Party in 1815 (spurred by the ill-fated Hartford Convention) and the subsequent Era of Good Feelings created a political vacuum filled by Andrew Jackson, a charismatic war hero whose political influence became synonymous with the era. Jacksonian America reached its zenith in the early 1830s, engendering a proliferation of party identification and political enthusiasm. The Whig Party emerged during this era as well, consisting of an amalgam of anti-Jackson men favoring Henry Clay's American System promoting a proactive and protective federal government and fearful of the power wielded by King Andrew, as they nicknamed the president. An important by-product of this political upheaval was that the hypernationalism of the Fourth of July magnified the near-incessant politicking of the era, allowing the holiday to increasingly become an opportunity to push political agendas, especially those linked to perceived cultural immorality.[10]

The rampant partisanship dominating Independence Day commemorations in Jacksonian America prompted two opposing reactions from midwestern revelers. One response was enthusiastic, promoting passionate party identification and political exuberance, linking the Fourth of July with uniquely partisan celebrations. Independence Day festivities in Columbus during this era, for example, witnessed especially enthusiastic party identification, as a relatively split populace divided between Whigs and Democrats openly vied for political preeminence on the patriotic holiday. In 1837, Whigs held a nominating convention in the city, drawing over one thousand passionate supporters. They marched in procession to an artificially constructed grove in the city's public square, and leaders provided the requisite Independence Day oration—emulating their vision of old-fashioned Fourth of July civic celebrations. The celebrants then assembled for dinner and toasted their party's leading political figures like Henry Clay and Daniel Webster. Loyal Democrats, not to be outdone by their political adversaries, gathered in a nearby grove (a real one) to support pro-Democratic speeches given by prominent local citizens. Enlivened by the freely flowing alcohol, scores of rowdy Democrats marched up Columbus's High Street searching for the Whigs, but after encountering only a few isolated groups, resumed their drinking in local taverns until the early morning, singing bawdy songs and loudly proclaiming the virtues of the Little Magician and the party of Old Hickory. In 1840, a similar incident occurred in Ohio's capital city. The Whig-published *Ohio State Journal* reported that local Democrats mustered five hundred men and marched, apparently rather pitifully, through the city's concourses. In response, the Whigs hastily assembled their own parade, vastly outnumbering and, in the eyes of the Whig paper embarrassing, their Democratic counterparts.[11]

The second response to antebellum partisanship was complete political disengagement. Instead of enthusiastically celebrating in separate, partisan camps, some men and women avoided civic-sponsored fetes altogether, fearful that, despite assurances from civic boosters, overly politicized events would mar the spirit of the planned festivities. Joel Buttles, a Columbus attorney, civic booster, and leading citizen, best summarized this sentiment in 1845, declaring that "the celebration of this day is evidently done with less and less zeal every year and with less unanimity" due to rampant partisanship. In Indianapolis in 1843, locals could "look in vain for any other symptoms of rejoicing," one newspaper reported, as the Fourth of July resembled "any indifferent day of the year—some day on which nothing had ever occurred either to rejoice at or grieve for." In 1848, Clevelanders captivated by a spirited presidential campaign pitting Zachary Taylor against midwesterner Lewis Cass had "little thought, less soul" for a celebration of the Fourth of July. As the planned civic celebrations characteristic of the early republic gave way to the more loosely organized, politically divided commemorations typifying the antebellum Midwest, some urban residents disengaged from the day's celebrations. In the wake of these declining formal citywide festivities, other issues emerged to help define regional distinctiveness and American nationalism by directly influencing how midwesterners commemorated the holiday.[12]

The Murder of John Tucker

One particular event illuminates many of the contentious social issues emerging in the antebellum urban Midwest and provides tremendous insight into how midwesterners utilized the Independence Day holiday to conceptualize their understandings of American cultural citizenship, regional and ethnic distinctiveness, and patriotic loyalty. At three o'clock in the afternoon of July 4, 1845, several drunken white men brutally murdered an ex-slave named John Tucker in the streets of Indianapolis. Tucker, about 45 years old at the time, was slowly strolling down Illinois Street, enjoying the balmy summer weather when a group of rowdy drunks accosted him. Nicholas Wood, a local ruffian emboldened by liquor, saw Tucker pass and began goading the quiet black man. Several allies quickly joined Wood and surrounded Tucker, berating him with racial slurs. Unable to endure further ridicule, Tucker attacked the white youth and his friends, who responded by beating Tucker with clubs, stones, and pieces of broken brick (known as brickbats). Tucker defended himself fiercely, injuring two of his assailants by hurling brickbats at their unprotected heads. Vastly outnumbered, he fled the scene. But ultimately, he could not outrun his pursuers, who finally stopped him with a blow to the head that would "have felled an ox," according to the local medical examiner, killing him instantly. One local newspaper, the Democratic-controlled *Indiana State Sentinel*, ran an editorial describing the event and lamenting Tucker's death. "It was a horrible spectacle," the article reported, but was "doubly horrible that it should have occurred on the 4th of July, a day which of all others should be consecrated to purposes far different from a display of angry and vindictive passion and brutality."[13]

The events surrounding John Tucker's death elucidate several issues of national and regional importance, highlighting the potency of the Fourth of July in shaping evolving conceptions of patriotic nationalism. Debates about alcohol consumption, increasing violence, race relations, and (although not evident in Tucker's case) the roles of women and religion in antebellum America dominated both national and regional headlines and became especially important and contentious in the hypernationalistic atmosphere of the Fourth of July. As middle-class Americans and civic boosters forwarded their own conceptions of morality, these five issues emerged as core components of the debate over American cultural citizenship and how midwesterners used the Fourth of July to shape the meaning of what it meant to be a "good" loyal American.

ALCOHOL CONSUMPTION

One aspect of Tucker's death that repeatedly appeared in discussions about the event was that his pursuers were intoxicated, while Tucker was not. In terms of per capita consumption, alcohol use in the United States peaked during the 1820s and early 1830s, and its use was nowhere more universal than on Independence Day. With declining community-wide commemorations, young men filled the void left by civic-sponsored parades and patriotic orations by either drinking liquor or rallying against the noxious beverage. Many chose the former. Americans drank liquor on the Fourth of July for numerous reasons. For some, Independence Day marked a rare summer holiday and a break from the monotony of the normal workweek. Other midwesterners invariably linked alcohol consumption with the Fourth of July because both drinking and the holiday connoted freedom—freedom from the usual restraints of middle-class propriety (and sobriety) and freedom to proclaim American superiority on the Fourth of July through uninhibited and unabashed bouts of (often competitive) drinking. Frederick Marryat, an Englishman traveling through the United States in this era, marveled at the drinking proclivity of the Americans he encountered. "I am sure the Americans can fix nothing without a drink," Marryat remarked. "If you meet, you drink; if you part, you drink; if you make acquaintance, you drink; if you close a bargain, you drink; they quarrel in their drink, and they make it up with a drink." Validating his claim, revelers engaging in "a national drunk" dominated Marryat's sole observation of a Fourth of July celebration, spent in New York City in 1837. Summing up his opinion of the events, the Englishman praised intoxication on Independence Day as an appropriate tribute to the nation's free institutions.[14]

Alcohol consumption remained high throughout the 1830s, but by the early 1840s, drinking on Independence Day seemed passé for many

FIGURE 3. "The Times" Clay, E.W. and H.R. Robinson, 1837. Courtesy of the Library Company of Philadelphia.

midwesterners—an aspect of the past preferably forgotten. One Columbus newspaper, for example, noted that drinking on the holiday had "gone out of vogue" among upstanding men. Debates over alcohol consumption became another way to separate good American citizens from those unworthy of cultural citizenship and an opportunity for middle-class midwesterners both to gain greater control of commemorating the Independence Day holiday and set themselves apart as exemplars of true American morality.[15]

TEMPERANCE

Temperance advocates purposefully targeted the Fourth of July in their reform efforts. Paradoxically, just as drinkers argued that consuming alcohol connoted independence from middle-class restraint and sobriety, anti-alcohol forces drew explicit comparisons between King George and King Alcohol, urging freedom from both on the day celebrating the nation's birth. In 1830, Columbus residents listened to an oration delivered by a local physician, Dr. M. B. Wright, concerning midwestern middle-class ideologies of moderation and self-control, especially those pertaining to consuming spirituous liquor. Wright portrayed alcohol as the antithesis of liberty and independence, insisting that true political freedom could only be attained when Americans escaped slavery to the bottle. This theme remained prevalent throughout the decade. Middle-class ideals dictated that celebrating freedom meant celebrating soberly—demonstrating personal *and* political independence. Robert Lowery, a prospective student at liberal Oberlin College, traveled to Cleveland in 1836 for the Fourth of July holiday and articulated this connection in a letter to his father. The throng of people lining the streets and the fervor with which the masses celebrated freedom from the British amazed young Lowery. That a domestic power (alcohol) continued to enslave Cleveland's populace, however, appalled him and he lamented the fact that "their heads frequently landed where their feet should have been."[16]

The American temperance movement began in the late eighteenth-century as northeastern reformers like Benjamin Rush began railing against alcohol consumption and the psychological effects of drinking spirituous liquor. The religious revivalism of the Second Great Awakening, particularly among northern New Englanders and residents of upstate New York's "burned-over" district, transformed the movement. New evangelical denominations blossomed, notably Baptists and Methodists, and embraced the cause of temperance, transmitting the antialcohol message throughout the nation.

Transplanted New Englanders and New Yorkers brought temperance and the accompanying reform impulse to the Midwest in the early 1830s. Despite their efforts, formal temperance movements in the region remained disjointed, as adherents viewed alcohol consumption as a symptom of ethical weakness, rather than a root cause of turpitude. The emerging middle class spearheaded this splintered movement but again placed more emphasis on advancing American Protestantism and ideologies of self-control and restraint than on reforming individual drunkards or closing drinking establishments supporting intemperance. Alfred Crosby typified such single-minded midwestern reformers. Crosby helped establish a Cleveland temperance society on July 4, 1830. For the next four years on the Fourth of July, Crosby regularly attended meetings with like-minded residents, campaigning for a temperate citizenry in northeastern Ohio through moral suasion. Similar efforts took place in Indianapolis, Chicago, Columbus, and Cincinnati during the decade, but despite repeated efforts by midwestern reformers and civic leaders, the fragmented temperance movement could not gain sustained momentum. Instead, the method and message of the anti-liquor crusade necessarily transformed during the 1840s when the nation's first large-scale, well-organized temperance organization brought cohesion to the movement.[17]

Founded in 1840 by six reformed drinkers in Baltimore, the Washington Temperance Society grew rapidly in the northeast, encouraging voluntary abstinence and using moralistic persuasion to discourage drinking. In the midst of the religious revivalism and economic downturn sweeping through the Midwest, transplanted Washingtonians found a ready audience for their reformist message. In 1842 and 1843, nearly all major midwestern cities hosted Washingtonian celebrations of the Fourth of July. In 1842, both Cincinnati and Indianapolis supported large-scale Washingtonian Independence Day fetes, celebrated in a manner similar to the community-wide nonpartisan festivities found in the region 20 years earlier. The Cincinnati program included an oration celebrating independence (this time from drink) as well as rounds of toasting—now done with cold water. Revelers sang patriotic tunes, primarily temperance songs, and listened to a sermon given by Reverend Henry Ward Beecher focusing on parallels between political liberty and freedom from the evils of alcohol. Their counterparts in Indianapolis celebrated in a similar manner, adding a recitation of the "Temperance Declaration of Independence" and wearing blue ribbons on their left lapels to signify membership in the expanding group. Two years later, Cincinnati residents encountered the high point of Washingtonian revelry in their city as thousands attended the "temperately yet zealously" celebrated festivities, again with alcohol-free patriotism at the center of the day's events. On that auspicious anniversary, over one hundred men and women added their names to the rolls of the Washingtonians, pledging both to refrain from drinking alcohol themselves and to encourage others to join them in following the society's teetotal doctrine.[18]

By 1845 the Washingtonian movement faced sharp decline, both regionally and nationally, owing to both a loss of reformist zeal by its earliest adherents and the backsliding of a number of its members. In the urban Midwest, the Sons of Temperance stepped into the sudden void. The Sons of Temperance were a socially exclusive organization charging members both a two-dollar initiation fee and regular membership dues. Local chapters funneled some of these funds to a mutual assistance account, but the expensive dues served primarily to exclude members of lower socioeconomic classes. The Sons of Temperance lasted only a short time in the Midwest, but certainly contributed to ongoing efforts to discourage drinking on the Fourth of July, which did decline both in visibility and sheer numbers by the mid-1840s. In 1845, a cadre of Clevelanders remembered the day "in the antiquated method, with Rum and Gunpowder," drawing derision from middle-class spectators. The following year, a Columbus newspaper confirmed this antiquation, noting that drinking on the holiday had completely "gone out of vogue." Midwestern antialcohol efforts failed to recapture the momentum of the Washingtonians until the emergence of the Women's Christian Temperance Union in the 1870s. Yet temperance remained an important aspect of debating American nationalism in the first half of the nineteenth century. Middle-class morality indicated that "good" Americans did not drink, or at least consumed alcohol only in moderation. Incessant reminders about links between freedom from alcohol and from political tyranny by temperance advocates caused debates over drinking to remain prominent in discussing how midwesterners defined the meaning of being an American.[19]

VIOLENCE

Returning to the topic of John Tucker's brutal murder, another vital aspect of the event was, of course, the actual violence perpetrated by Tucker's assailants. Violent acts on the Fourth of July often received extensive coverage, because of both the visibility afforded by the holiday and because commentators often discussed the paradox of violent actions on a day meant to recall selfless national sacrifice. Most violent Independence Day acts during this period did not end in murder and usually existed in isolation or on a small scale. For example, in 1839, four unidentified Cincinnatians assaulted a young man standing on a street corner. The perpetrators initially eluded capture and barely escaped to Kentucky. Local law enforcers followed the fugitives and returned the foursome to the Queen City to stand trial. A judge found them all guilty of assault. Seven years later, Cincinnatians encountered numerous outbreaks of violence on the Fourth: a pro-Oregon demonstration ending in fisticuffs, volunteers from nearby Camp Washington decapitating turkeys, and prostitutes shooting pistols at soldiers seeking solace in their bawdy establishments. Fourth of July reports also regularly included accounts of unintentionally violent acts, usually perpetrated by youngsters. Fireworks, in particular, often merited attention on Independence Day as young boys used them to frighten horses (causing carriage accidents), set fire to dresses, maim revelers, and cause inestimable property damages. These acts of violence may seem commonplace, but they garnered a great deal of attention because of their ties to Independence Day. Civic boosters continued to stress that the Fourth of July should be a time of solemn recollection, not of drunken brawling or recklessly shooting fireworks, and of regional unanimity, not dispute. Although middle-class civic leaders determinedly foisted inclusive celebrations on the local citizenry, other midwesterners, often unattached young men, resisted their intrusion and continued to act out in outlandish ways on the anniversary of the nation's birth. These acts of violence themselves may have been unremarkable, but the timing was exceptionally important.[20]

Violent acts sometimes ended in bloodshed, or even in maiming, but rarely in loss of life or widespread carnage. Instead, midwesterners considered small-scale violence an unfortunate, if almost expected, by-product of robust and exuberant American patriotism. The aggressive masculinity fostered in the Midwest among young men growing up in urban centers, unfettered by familial ties or the restrictive influence of small-town life, found in the Fourth of July an outlet for energetic if sometimes violent and drunken action, and a forum in which to help define the meaning of American patriotism. When kept on a small scale, local leaders could endure, if not accept, these violent acts. There were rare instances, like the assault of John Tucker, in which violent acts led to murder, but oftentimes the violence was minimal. In Indianapolis in 1841, seemingly innocuous celebrations nearly ended in a riot when the director of the children's Sunday school celebration and leader of the city's Mechanical Societies festivities began yelling at one another. By the end of the afternoon, the Mechanical Societies were firing round after round of cannonade over the heads of the Sunday school celebrants until one of the cannoneers blew his hand off, finally ending the childish standoff. In another event of large-scale violence, in 1836, a group of "turbulent citizens" in Chicago, bored with the complacency of the Windy City's civic leaders (who decided not to hold a community-wide commemoration), commandeered a steamboat and two schooners to take them to Canal Port, a nearby town with an ostensibly more patriotic and lively populace. After a lengthy celebration in Canal Port enlivened by liquor, the revelers aboard the schooners headed back towards Chicago but inexplicably "kicked up a row," and fights broke out aboard both boats. The result was "a number of broken heads and bloody noses." Violent outbursts of patriotism, like those seen in Indianapolis and Chicago, demonstrate that, despite middle-class efforts to promote "good" Americanism through zealously yet temperately celebrating Independence Day, many Americans engendered an entirely separate vision of American liberty—the liberty to defend one's ideals with violence if necessary.[21]

RACE

Although alcohol consumption and violence certainly played important roles in the story of the attack on John Tucker, the central issue on that day in Indianapolis undoubtedly concerned the victim's skin color. The growing presence of free African-Americans in midwestern urban centers, and the appropriation of celebrations of the Fourth of July by some abolitionist reformers (using the holiday as an opportunity to draw parallels between freedom from British tyranny and freedom from the cruelty of slaveholding masters), encouraged debates over slavery in the South and the place of free African-Americans in the Midwest. The Declaration of Independence, dissolving the bonds tying the colonies to the British crown, first broadly linked the concept of slavery with the ideals of American liberty. At the conclusion of the American Revolution, most orators minimized discussions about this aspect of freedom—after all, the war was over and the colonists had emerged victorious. Instead, speakers delineated distinctions between freedom for slaves and for American colonists, claiming that the two were not equally valid. Antislavery advocates quickly pointed out the incongruities of these arguments, recognizing this inherent inconsistency. Having internalized the rhetoric of freedom and independence pronounced in 1776, abolitionists and free blacks used the Fourth of July as a forum to discuss the possibility of emancipation and to protest the lack of African-American independence on an occasion specifically signifying freedom from oppression.[22]

The American Colonization Society (ACS) numbered among the first national organizations to publicly debate the issue of slavery and explicitly link it to the Fourth of July holiday. Founded in 1816 by prominent politicians, including Henry Clay and John Randolph, and religious leaders, such as Reverend Robert Finley, the ACS vowed to return freed slaves to their African ancestral homelands (or at least to Liberia). Ideologically, the society's members comprised a diverse lot; some supported the organization because they deemed relocation the best solution to minimize sectional animosity, while others actively pursued a segregated antislavery agenda, seeking emancipation without the potential for race mixing or African-Americans taking jobs from white men. In the urban Midwest, as throughout the nation, the ACS took full advantage of pointing out the incongruity of promoting American independence while millions of Africans remained enslaved, using the Fourth of July as an opportune time to spread their message of hypocrisy. Slavery and the presence of free blacks presented a problem for the rising middle class, appropriating Independence Day to foist their morality on others, as many perceived the institution as a moral wrong, but were unwilling to allow racial blending.

The American Colonization Society's celebrations of the Fourth of July solved the conundrum of blending patriotism, abolitionism, and latent racism by using the holiday to raise funds for freed slaves to be transported away from the region. The first midwestern Independence Day appearance of the ACS occurred in Cleveland in 1828. On the Fourth of July that year, Clevelanders formed a colonization society chapter and took up a collection to be used to "defray the expense of annually transporting a large number of blacks to Africa." The next year, residents of Columbus encountered a similar message, accompanied by a sermon extolling the morality and positive vision of the ACS. In 1833, the American Colonization Society reached its peak influence in the Midwest, holding a large celebration in Indianapolis that drew hundreds of attendees. Society members solicited funds from local churches to be taken up "on the Sabbath immediately before or after the 4th of July," placing the "dependence of the society . . . entirely upon the liberality of the public." Two local churches, one Methodist and the other Presbyterian, answered the call, contributing $30 towards the cause. The ACS, like many other reform organizations, used Independence Day as an opportunity to stump for change, raise funds, and, especially in the case of the ACS, to claim the holiday "as its own patriotic preserve."[23]

While the American Colonization Society, aided immensely by the efforts of William Lloyd Garrison and other like-minded abolitionists, gained exposure and notoriety by pointing out the inconsistencies in proclaiming American independence while Africans remained enslaved, free African-Americans in the urban Midwest shied away from celebrating Independence Day throughout much of the antebellum era. In these northern cities, the small free African-American populations usually remained invisible on Independence Day, because, in the words of one historian, "with drunken racists roaming the streets, often armed with fireworks, the Fourth was a day better spent indoors." In fact, newspaper accounts, private journals, and letters rarely mention the presence of African-Americans in the day's festivities, except in the negative. For instance, in 1848 a circus traveled through Cincinnati (a common occurrence in the antebellum era around the Fourth) advertising "three prize darkies" and hoping to draw patrons away from competitors promoting their own "darkey of all darkies." In Columbus, white residents derided free African-Americans blacking boots in the city streets for keeping "respectable ladies" from entering nearby stores around the Fourth of July while an African-American man collecting admission fees to a supposedly free Sabbath School celebration corrupted the event. Even in Indianapolis in 1840 when, in a rare moment of inclusion, residents witnessed a biracial Sabbath School parade, organizers relegated the African-American schoolchildren of the city to the rear of the procession, and newspapermen mentioned them only in passing.[24]

Instead of celebrating Independence Day alongside white men and women and facing potential racial retribution, African-Americans created alternative celebrations, often observing the fifth of July, leaving to white antislavery advocates the problem of solving the paradoxical nature of freedom and the Fourth. According to historian Caleb McDaniel, pushing celebrations back one day served dual purposes. First, it allowed African-Americans to remain patriotic and loyal—after all, they still celebrated national independence. Secondly, holding their celebration on a separate day demonstrated their frustration with the hypocrisy of a nation that held slaves yet celebrated freedom. In addition to July fifth, many black communities in the North commemorated March 5— the anniversary of Crispus Attucks's death in the Boston Massacre, or January 1—the date of the abolition of the international slave trade—as more appropriate occasions for African-American nationalistic jubilation. African-American midwesterners doubtlessly celebrated some of these holidays, albeit on a small scale, although there are few mentions of alternative remembrances in newspapers or in the writings of local citizens. By mid-century, with growing African-American populations and the rise of an increasingly militant class of abolitionists, African-American celebrations of the Fourth of July became increasingly difficult to overlook. In fact, during the Civil War era, African-Americans played a prominent if controversial role in celebrating the Fourth of July in the urban Midwest. But during the antebellum era, free blacks mostly stayed away, either fearful of violent retribution, or in protestation of the incongruities of celebrating independence while their brethren in the South remained enslaved.[25]

The Roles of Gender and Religion

The case of John Tucker serves as a starting point for discussions of race, alcohol consumption, and violence, but does not incorporate two other vitally important aspects of early nineteenth-century Independence Day celebrations—the role of women and religion in the day's celebrations. Both gender and religiosity formed key components of developing conceptions of American nationalism central to commemorations of the Fourth of July. Again, the middle-class conception of what constituted a "good" American played a role as it required adherence to Christianity (and, increasingly, to Protestantism) while allowing women increasing participation in moralistic causes. Women throughout the nation drastically increased their public visibility in this era. Famously, in 1848, Lucretia Mott and Elizabeth Cady Stanton led a rally for women's rights in Seneca Falls, New York, that gained international notoriety and lasting acclaim. Not surprisingly, women parlayed their enthusiasm for political and social equality into more visible positions on Independence Day, using the Fourth of July to promote the expanding scope of middle-class morality.[26]

WOMEN

The increased visibility of women on the Fourth of July in the antebellum urban Midwest marked a major departure from earlier Independence Day celebrations, when women participated only symbolically. In the early republic, boosters expected women to remain silent and vigilant on Independence Day, a holiday celebrating the efforts of the Founding Fathers and the republican political institutions conceived and sustained exclusively by men. As was the case in celebrations of the semicentennial, men included women primarily in regular toasts, reserving the thirteenth and final toast to praise the efforts of wives and daughters. For example, in 1827, Clevelanders drank to "the fair sex—the greatest supporters of our happiest institutions, matrimony." In Indianapolis 12 years later, the final regular toast honored "The American Fair," including a chauvinistic promise that "Columbia's brave sons" would always protect them and keep them from harm. Even in parades, women's roles remained primarily symbolic. Floats portraying women as Goddesses of Liberty were common and, in 1830, Clevelanders engaged in a procession led by 24 women dressed all in white, depicting the number of states then in the Union. Frances Trollope, an English novelist living in Cincinnati at the time and notoriously critical of American culture and society, noted disparagingly that "women have but little to do with the pageantry, the splendour, or the gaiety" of the Fourth of July. Instead, women's most important role in these early celebrations involved promoting a virtuous republic while downplaying partisanship—little more than an extension of their ascribed roles as good republican mothers. Historians rightfully downplay women's participation in July Fourth festivities during this era, usually present only as silent parade attendees or recipients of men's boastful toasts. In fact, Ellen Litwicki argues persuasively that women's role remained primarily symbolic until as late as the Progressive Era. But in the Midwest by the late 1830s, in part because of women's increasing activity in reform movements and social organizations, women began playing a much more central part of Independence Day celebrations than they had decades earlier. As such, these women influenced the development of midwestern conceptions of American nationalism and patriotism perhaps more than their counterparts elsewhere in the nation.[27]

During the antebellum era, women never achieved equal status with men in planning or executing civic-sponsored Independence Day festivities in the Midwest. They did, however, serve a much more active, and much less symbolic, role in celebrating the holiday. For example, in Logansport, Indiana, near the state capital at Indianapolis, local women commemorated the Fourth of July, 1839, separately from their husbands and sons, spending the day feasting and toasting. They reserved the final toast of the day to "The Gentlemen," in the hope that "their acts abide their precepts, by teaching as well as toasting us, as their BETTER-HALVES." Elsewhere, women used the Fourth of July as a platform to stump for charitable causes. In 1846, Cleveland women held a dinner and fair at a local church to raise funds to buy the congregation a new bell. The best evidence of this shift towards female activism on Independence Day occurred in Indianapolis in 1843. Women of the city, perhaps inspired by the actions of their Logansport counterparts four years earlier, held an elaborate picnic. Married and single women united to organize the event, inviting their husbands and beaux for a reception in a grove outside the city limits. An article in the *Indiana State Sentinel* bragged that the women consisted "of the very elite, the most beautiful, intelligent, and fascinating," in Indianapolis society. The editor of the *Sentinel* also praised the women for managing to simultaneously care for their children, prepare a prodigious spread, and dance away the evening, "full of the spirit of hilarity and enjoyment." While the position of women in celebrating the Fourth of July remained tenuous and often on the periphery in the urban Midwest, it did improve between 1827 and 1849, providing more evidence of both the changing character of Independence Day celebrations in the first half of the nineteenth century and the ever-evolving gender roles of the era. As women stumped for increasing rights, they stepped up their participation in Fourth of July celebrations, using the holiday as a socially acceptable opportunity to play a role in promoting American patriotism.[28]

RELIGION

Another important issue meriting particular attention in the second quarter of the nineteenth century, especially as it related to developing regional notions of American patriotism and nationalism on the Fourth of July, was religion. Between 1827 and the early 1840s, the Second Great Awakening peaked, forcing Americans throughout the United States to reconsider their denominational doctrines and religious beliefs. To fully understand the influence of this religious transformation on Independence Day celebrations and definitions of American nationalism derived by urban midwesterners, it is important first to differentiate two separate strands of American religion thriving in this era. Organized religion, almost exclusively Protestantism in the antebellum Midwest, revolved around church attendance, camp meetings, and revivals. On Independence Day, organized religion emerged primarily in the guise of Sunday School celebrations and patriotic sermons preached from church pulpits. Civil religion, on the other hand, constituted a much more amorphous aspect of American culture in the 1830s and 1840s and involved venerating national political symbols like the Founding Fathers, the American flag, and the eagle. Midwesterners did not view civil religion as sacrilegious: they firmly believed that worshipping God and revering the Founding Fathers could coexist. As the "great national Sabbath of Freedom," celebrants considered the Fourth of July the political equivalent of attending church. Both Independence Day and church services included solemn remembrances of sacred texts—the Declaration of Independence and the Bible—and heroic leaders—the Founding Fathers and Apostles. While organized and civil religion often overlapped, they must be considered separately to fully appreciate the various ways religiosity spilled over into Fourth of July celebrations and how this influenced the meaning of being a patriotic American in the second quarter of the nineteenth century.[29]

ORGANIZED RELIGION AND SUNDAY SCHOOL CELEBRATIONS

As formal Independence Day civic celebrations declined, cities looked to community-wide, organized religious ceremony (especially in the form of Sunday School celebrations) to fill the void. Sunday School festivities brought together school-aged children from throughout the local community in a non-denominational commemoration of Independence Day, complete with the oratory and refreshments traditionally included in civic-sponsored festivities. Community-wide religious celebrations of the Fourth served three primary roles: uniting the city in an interdenominational remembrance, providing a nonpartisan Independence Day event, and indoctrinating the assembled youth with the patriotic meanings of the Fourth of July holiday—essentially using organized religion to initiate children in the rites of American civil religion.

First, these celebrations marked rare instances of large-scale intercongregational cooperation as the various Protestant denominations in these urban centers assembled together for the festivities, regardless of whether they were Methodist or Baptist, Presbyterian or Lutheran. In Indianapolis, newspapermen referred to the assemblage as the Union Sabbath School Celebration—utilizing the term "union" both to portray the coalition of states comprising the United States and to describe the fusion of thousands of school children across several denominations coming together for the day's events. In Indiana's capital city, the Sabbath School celebration regularly marked "*the* great affair of the day," drawing crowds ranging from less than three hundred in 1831—the date of the first event—to five times that by 1849. Similarly, Cincinnati newspapers praised the behavior of the two thousand local youngsters assembling together in 1839 for an inter-congregational affair while, five years later in Columbus, Joel Buttles estimated that one thousand schoolchildren from a variety of local churches attended the city's celebration and conducted themselves admirably.[30]

The second acknowledged goal of Sunday School festivities involved promoting nonpartisanship, which was, as we have seen, an often unattainable objective for nonreligious, community-wide Independence Day ceremonies in the antebellum era. Instead of political stumping, Sabbath School celebrants listened to pastors deliver simple, patriotic oratory (often referred to simply as "appropriate remarks" by reporting newspapers) intended to uplift both children and their parents. Afterwards, instead of whiskey toasts and gluttonous feasting, parents provided nonspirituous refreshments (often cakes or rusks and lemonade or water). In many ways, Sabbath School celebrations accomplished what civic boosters could not: a nonpartisan, community-wide event that appealed to many local residents and provoked enthusiastic patriotism.[31]

Educating the city's youth about the principles of the republic served as the final purpose of Sunday School Fourth of July festivities. Community leaders intended that Independence Day commemorations both initiate youngsters in the rites of America's civil religion and encourage patriotic loyalty to be passed down to future generations, preserving historical memory as an important aspect of suitably commemorating the holiday. The editor of the *Chicago Democrat* praised the addresses given at one Sabbath School celebration as inculcating "such principles as form the only basis of true Liberty." Similarly in Indianapolis, the editor of the *Indiana Democrat* lauded "this practice of early instilling into the infant mind the duty and necessity of the observance, in a proper manner, of the 4th of July." This editor also remarked that "the most indelible impressions will be made, and when they grow up to manhood, they will cling with tenacity to the customs which they were taught in the spring time of life." These nonpartisan events signaled to civic boosters that their communities could, in fact, pull together without the corrupting influence of party politics, alcohol, or violence marring both eastern commemorations and some in the urban Midwest. Sabbath School celebrations, particularly those including brief, pointed patriotic oratory, indoctrinated area youth in the proper manner of celebrating the Fourth of July, and explicitly linked American Protestantism, American patriotism, and historical consciousness to the birth of the American nation.[32]

Boosters paid particular attention to links between Protestantism and patriotism when the anniversary fell on a Sunday, as occurred three times in this era—1830, 1841, and 1847. Rather than denigrate the Sabbath by setting off fireworks or holding boisterous festivities on July 4, celebrants usually held alternative Independence Day commemorations on Saturday, July 3, or Monday, July 5, attending church meetings as usual on Sunday the Fourth. In 1847 Cincinnatians celebrated twice, on both the third and fifth, although this "double chance of celebrating" proved unsatisfying as neither merited much attention in the Queen City. In Columbus that year, residents conducted Independence Day in "a rather *miscellaneous* manner" as confusion over the proper mode of celebrating a Sunday Fourth resulted in disastrous disorder. Similarly, one Indianapolis resident deemed split celebrations "a complete failure." Pastors, contrarily, took full advantage of the opportunity presented by Sunday Fourths in the 1830s and 1840s. They used the occasion to preach to their flocks about the ties between patriotism and Christianity, imploring congregants to remember the Sabbath of liberty while still solemnly recalling the Sabbath of religion, keeping the days separate in order to give each its proper due.[33]

PROTESTANT PATRIOTISM

The Fourth of July proved an opportune time for middle-class Protestant midwesterners to gain control of commemorations of the holiday and, by extension, to lay claim as the most positive (and, at the same time, most representative) contributors to American culture and, by extension, as the rightful heirs of the revolutionary legacy. In 1829, Cincinnati lawyer Bellamy Storer delivered an Independence Day speech at the city's Methodist Reformed Church. In his talk, Storer discussed the significance of the Fourth of July to both regional understandings of American nationalism and organized religion. "We are assembled to commemorate an event, alike dear to the patriot and the Christian," Storer began, praising the fortitude and morals of the region's earliest European settlers (all, at least in Storer's recollection, Protestant). Storer remained ambivalent about non-Protestants, preferring to let listeners draw their own conclusions, but other orators explicitly tied Protestantism to patriotic loyalty, excluding non-Protestants from the rights (and rites) of full cultural citizenship. In 1847, nearly two decades after Storer's speech, Reverend Charles Boynton delivered an Independence Day oration in Cincinnati conflating Protestantism with "genuine American principles." Unlike Storer, Boynton unequivocally dismissed the efforts of non-Protestants, primarily Catholics, proclaiming that "you cannot build the Temple of American liberty from the drift-wood of European rivers." Marking adherence to Protestantism as a necessary component of inclusion in the American polity became an especially significant aspect of Fourth of July celebrations in the 1850s, as a concomitant rise in Catholic immigration encouraged widespread Protestant rejection of papal authority and spirited reiterations of America's republican (and Puritanical) heritage. Although the second quarter of the nineteenth century witnessed only early indications that Christian infighting could divide the American populace on Independence Day, some holiday celebrations already used Protestantism as a marker for determining loyal patriotism. Civic and religious leaders intended that organized religious Fourth of July ceremonies—notably Sunday School celebrations—unite citizens as Christian and American brothers and sisters, but in effect Protestantism slowly became another means of promoting the exclusionary attributes required of "good" Americans.[34]

CIVIL RELIGION

Organized religion certainly constituted an important aspect of Independence Day celebrations and of self-ascribed definitions of patriotic loyalty conflating Protestantism and patriotism, but it was often overshadowed on the holiday by a different type of veneration, dubbed American civil religion by generations of historians. In newspaper articles and editorials, midwesterners compared the Fourth of July to Christian religious ceremony, referring to the holiday alternately as "our day of Passover," a celebration of "the religion of patriotism," the "Sabbath of

Freedom," and the "Sabbath of Liberty." In fact, celebrants conducted the earliest civic-sponsored Independence Day festivities (first held during the American Revolution and even stretching, in some places, until the mid-nineteenth century) in a manner similar to a church service. After opening the day with a secular flair including cannon fire and parading, revelers marched to the courthouse or church. Services taking place at the latter typically included prayers, patriotic hymns, and an oration (the political equivalent of a sermon) before closing with a benediction.[35]

Over the course of the early nineteenth century, urban midwesterners took part in redefining American civil religion by examining and refining links between American patriotism and American Protestantism. Americans shaped a unique self-image during the early nineteenth century, embracing Puritanism and millennialism (the belief that man could hasten Christ's return by spreading the Christian gospel throughout the earth) as cornerstones of American nationalism and religious culture. As the spiritual, if not physical, descendants of Puritans, midwesterners appropriated John Winthrop's Puritanical ideology of a "city upon a hill" and adapted the concept to the American Midwest. Americans viewed their nation as the New Rome or the New Promised Land, with the Midwest, in particular, representing the promises of geographic expansion and unbound economic opportunity. As historian Ernest Lee Tuveson argues, Americans felt that "Zion could be built only in the United States." And that Zion, Tuveson reiterates, would be located in the vast and developing Midwest. With the growing importance of the Midwest in American civil religion, properly commemorating the Fourth of July in the region took on added significance. The Fourth became, according to historian Sacvan Bercovitch, "the high holy day of American Civil religion," with the Declaration of Independence analogous to Jesus's famed Sermon on the Mount. Contemporaries linked the symbolism displayed on the Fourth of July to this millennialist promise and connections with Puritan religious and cultural heritage, as midwesterners considered themselves God's true chosen people, brought forth from Old World decadence to spread His message— especially evident in Fourth of July orations, which historian Mark Hanley has termed "Protestant political jeremiads"—in the New World.[36]

Grappling with the Past

The so-called first generation of Americans coming into power between 1827 and 1849 (born after the American Revolution) continued to wrestle with their place in America's developing culture. In particular, this "first generation" questioned their worthiness to assume the mantle of the Founding Fathers and to stand alongside that pantheon of luminaries. Contemporaries, well aware of this burden, often used the Fourth of July as a fitting occasion to voice their concerns and uncertainties about their relationships to the memory of the heroes of 1776. "We have felt that a portion of the luster of their names and deeds were cast upon us," remarked the editor of Cincinnati's *Liberty Hall*, questioning whether the conduct of his generation was "worthy of our sires." The contrast, he argued, was "a humiliating one," voicing his fear that succeeding generations would "remember the fourth of July with the deepest shame" because of the poor stewardship of the "first generation." Echoing these sentiments, Benjamin Drake, a Cincinnati lawyer, argued that it was the "solemn duty" of his generation to "make *our* contributions to the great cause." Likewise, Calvin Fletcher, a prominent Indianapolis attorney, spoke of "the mantle of freedom dropped upon the present generation," weighing heavily upon his contemporaries, tentative about their place as successors of their revolutionary forefathers.[37]

Not all Americans were concerned with, or even cognizant of, these comparisons, a point often decried by civic boosters. Despite calls to remember that "we are the lineal descendants of those immortal patriots" and "to celebrate, and to contemplate . . . the virtues of our patriot fathers," midwesterners continued to alter the meaning of patriotic loyalty and the mode of demonstrating American nationalism in the years following the Jubilee celebration of 1826. The passing of President James Monroe on the Fourth of July, 1831—the third of five former presidents to die on Independence Day—merited little attention in midwestern newspapers. Joel Buttles, in his 1842 diary entry on the Fourth of July, noted a similar perceived lack of historical competence concerning the meaning of Independence Day among his contemporaries, arguing that "there is but little comparatively of that patriotic spirit manifested in orations, toasts, songs, and processions which a few years ago was so characteristic." Three years later, Buttles lamented that "the celebration of this day is . . . confined to the common class, very few of the most intelligent and wealthy take any part in it." A letter to the editor of the *Indiana State Sentinel* in July 1843 supported Buttles's claims, alleging that "we have sinned against our forefathers; we exhibit no gratitude for the deeds which they have done." Cleveland's *Plain Dealer* printed an editorial in 1848 summing up this lack of historical consciousness, proclaiming that "amid the fog of political angry controversy, the past is almost wholly forgotten," and adding that "the spirits that rule the hour pay their full devotion to the present—its interest, and passions master their reason and recollection—and they hardly are *willing* to throw their thoughts upon a retrospect of the spirit and manner which guided the fathers of our republic."[38]

Lack of historical consciousness also created a positive by-product, especially in the wake of the deaths of Jefferson, Adams, and Monroe. The demise of these heralded leaders marked, in many ways, the end of the Revolutionary Era and the beginning of an American Era, unblemished by war with Britain and free to grow, expand, and dominate the perceived virginity of the continent's landscape without the specter of the Founding Fathers hanging so perilously close. Many Americans saw the July Fourth deaths of these ex-presidents, therefore, as divine providence and a fitting epitaph to the legacy of the founding generation, allowing the "first generation of Americans" to move beyond pre-Jubilee notions of American cultural citizenship predicated on the shared experience of colonialism and revolution. Midwesterners, perhaps even more than their eastern or southern counterparts, made this potential transformative. But they did not fill this void with patriotic remembrances or solemn recognition of the deeds performed by the founders. Instead, they focused increased attention on moral reform and other concerns haunting the antebellum middle class.[39]

In 1826, the editor of the *Ohio State Journal* penned a typical article detailing the importance of Independence Day celebrations—praising the republican virtue and prosperity of the young nation. However, he included a caveat that came to fruition much sooner than even he could have anticipated. When the Fourth of July should pass "without the manifestations of gratitude and rejoicing," he predicted, "the time will have arrived when the people of the United States shall have become indifferent about their rights, and indeed fit subjects of a tyranny." What he could not anticipate was that in the 1850s, rising immigration, economic downturn, and contested understandings of patriotic loyalty would pit Americans against one another in perhaps the most divisive battle over Independence Day in the nineteenth century. No longer would white skin guarantee entrance into American cultural citizenship and inclusion in the rites of American civil religion on the Independence Day holiday. Instead, perceived ethnic, religious, and cultural differences served as markers of exclusion, while the violence of staunch patriotic loyalty escalated to unforeseen levels as native-born residents and immigrants battled over competing understandings of what it meant to be an American.[40]

2 / "Americans Ruling America": Independence Day Nativism, 1850–1856

To attack and maim adopted citizens has become . . . the par excellence test of Americanism. It is a fashion they have of "Americans ruling America."[1]

—*Cincinnati Enquirer,* July 7, 1855

July 4, 1855, began as a typical Independence Day in Columbus, Ohio, with citizens anticipating parades, railroad excursions, and patriotic oratory. And in fact, the day began innocently enough as a group of German citizens, led by the Turnverein gymnastic society, proudly marched through the city streets, accompanied by two boisterous brass bands and cheering crowds. In the midst of this seemingly innocuous celebration, a local teenager started an argument with several German marchers, inciting stone throwing between young American-born onlookers and their foreign-born counterparts. The situation quickly escalated when several members of the Turnverein pulled out concealed handguns, shooting indiscriminately into the crowd. In the confusion, one bullet passed through the lungs of an American-born blacksmith, Henry Foster, killing him almost instantly. A hastily assembled police force quickly quelled the brief uprising and arrested 24 Germans on suspicion of inciting a riot and murdering young Foster. Within hours of his demise, the dead blacksmith became a poignant regional symbol of a larger battle between native- and foreign-born midwesterners over control of ethnic-American nationalism and cultural citizenship.[2]

The Growth of the Urban Midwest

Unprecedented demographic changes in the middle decade of the nineteenth century altered life in midwestern cities. Immigrants poured into the region from war-torn Europe in unparalleled numbers, fleeing political unrest, famine, and religious turmoil. This influx of European newcomers not only altered life in midwestern urban centers but also remade July Fourth celebrations. Reformers continued to stump for temperance, abolition, and women's rights on Independence Day, and civic boosters remained equally persistent (and equally unsuccessful) in trying to unite local communities. But the overriding issue of Independence Day festivities in the early 1850s quickly became ethnicity. Heated debates over ethnic components of American nationalism tied to control of America's past played out on the Fourth of July, forcing midwesterners to reconsider and reassess the intended purpose of the Independence Day holiday. Immigrants and ethnic midwesterners often celebrated the Fourth of July with great gusto to overtly demonstrate patriotism and loyalty to their adopted nation, overshadowing their native-born counterparts. Native-born midwesterners responded that the holiday was an explicitly American event and that ethnic commemorations disrupted the sanctity of celebrating the birth of the nation.

An immigration-fueled population boom and improved transportation, driven primarily by an expanding railroad industry motivated by an intense and lucrative competition for midwestern markets and agricultural goods, spurred midwestern urbanization. Railroads, already developing as an important industry in the 1840s, dominated the 1850s as railroad mileage in the states carved from the Old Northwest Territory skyrocketed from under 1,300 miles of track to nearly 10,000 during the decade. This growth disproportionately aided Chicago and Cleveland (with access to both rail lines and lake traffic), whereas the economic and demographic growth of Cincinnati (relying on canal and river traffic) began to level off. Columbus and Indianapolis, still primarily political centers, also grew, although at much slower rates than the developing railroad hubs.[3]

Chicago's population more than doubled in the 1850s, nearing 60,000. In 1852, three railroad companies reached the shores of Lake Michigan: the Chicago, Rock Island & Pacific; the Illinois Central; and the Michigan Central. These lines, in turn, encouraged industrial development in Chicago, promoting both in-migration and capital investment. Cincinnati barely held off surging Chicago in the early 1850s for regional supremacy, but still remained the commercial and transportation hub of the Midwest until the Civil War, supporting a population nearing 150,000 and an expanding industrial sector. German immigration further stimulated Cincinnati industry: in 1850, Germans constituted over 20 percent of the city's population, a distinct change from the 5 percent found just 25 years earlier. Cleveland continued its own growth in the 1850s, as the city's population passed 40,000. Part of this expansion was geographic; Cleveland annexed nearby Ohio City to broaden the city's population base and to outdistance nearby competitors like Akron and Canton. Immigration constituted the other part; many of Cleveland's newcomers were of Germanic ancestry—nearing 20 percent by mid-century and rising to almost 30 percent by 1860. Additionally, rail companies took advantage of Cleveland's fortuitous location at the mouth of the Cuyahoga River on Lake Erie, building numerous rail lines to link the city to Pittsburgh, New York City, Chicago, and St. Louis by 1853, making Cleveland one of the leading rail centers in the nation. Columbus, although not growing as rapidly as Chicago, Cincinnati, or Cleveland, nonetheless solidified itself as an important regional and political hub by the middle of the nineteenth century. In the 1850s, Columbus's German community grew dramatically, and by 1860 constituted roughly one-third of the city's population of 18,000. Many of these Germans dwelt in the Fifth Ward, part of which gained repute as German Village, a vibrant ethnic cultural center. Like their counterparts in other midwestern cities, Columbus Germans established German-language newspapers and organized singing societies and other social clubs to preserve their cultural heritage. Indianapolis also witnessed economic and demographic development in the early 1850s, despite the limitations of a subpar transportation network and agriculturally marginal land surrounding the city. During the 1850s, the Circle City more than doubled its mid-century population of 8,091, reaching 18,611 in the 1860 federal census. Local boosters greatly aided Indianapolis's development, successfully promoting the city as the cultural (as well as political and geographic) center of the state, enticing visitors with a state fair (staged in Indianapolis in 1852 and drawing nearly 30,000 visitors) as well as supporting the building of a Masonic Hall, which regularly hosted concerts and lectures.[4]

Midwestern Celebrations of the Fourth Of July

On the surface, Fourth of July commemorations in these growing cities mostly mirrored those of previous decades, focusing on moral reform efforts and partisan politics. Temperance continued to be a predominant issue in this era, its supporters undeterred by numerous setbacks in accomplishing their anti-liquor goals. Ideologically, the movement did evolve in focus as members began to equate problem drinking with lower-class ethnic minorities, but temperate celebrations of Independence Day rarely reflected that change. Religion and political partisanship also remained prevalent issues debated and discussed around the Fourth of July, but they too changed, conforming to larger transformations in American society as anti-Catholicism and sectionalism replaced Sunday School celebrations and posturing between Democrats and Whigs. Abolitionism marked a significant aspect of this political transformation. In 1854, the Democratic *Cleveland Plain Dealer* accused antislavery advocates of making "a party hobby out of a *national* day," unnecessarily politicizing the Fourth of July to "further their *party* aims." On a "*national* day," the paper argued, midwesterners were supposed to celebrate together and lay aside political differences, although by the 1850s, this notion was farcical: urban midwesterners had not spent the holiday in nonpartisan, civic-sponsored revelry for decades. The American Colonization Society also continued to use the holiday to convey its message of repatriation and request financial aid from area churches around Independence Day, though they scaled back their efforts considerably from the society's peak in the 1830s and 1840s.[5]

THE ARRIVAL OF THE IRISH

The influx of immigrants pouring into the urban Midwest (mostly men and women migrating from the Germanic states and Ireland) necessarily altered the cultural landscape of these midwestern cities. Irish immigrants are easily overlooked in this context of the urban Midwest, dominated by the more populous German-Americans. In most eastern cities, Irish formed an ethnic majority and gained well-deserved notoriety for supporting boss politics. Irish in the urban Midwest proved less visible (and less reviled) than their eastern counterparts, avoiding much of the ethnic enmity encountered by Boston's and New York City's maligned Irish populations. Ethnic tension between midwestern Irish- and American-born citizens never reached the level of animosity found in either eastern cities or between German- and native-born citizens in the Midwest. Instead, economic hardship and Catholicism became important points of contention between native- and Irish-born Americans. The potato blight decimating Ireland's staple crop in the early 1840s forced waves of poverty-stricken men and women, dubbed the famine Irish, to flee their homeland. Native-born citizens especially scorned famine Irish, often negatively comparing them to African-Americans as unfortunate blemishes on lily white American society. In addition, many of these impoverished newcomers practiced Catholicism. "Filthy Beggars that swarm through our cities, lying and stealing as they go—they are all-ALL-ALL Catholics!" proclaimed the ethnocentric *Chicago Tribune* in 1855, epitomizing the rampant anti-Catholic sentiment developing in the urban Midwest, and throughout much of the nation, in the mid-1850s. Anti-immigrant advocates also exploited links between the Irish and the papacy, conflating, at least in their minds, Catholicism with political dependence. To these ethnocentric men and women, pledging faithfulness to a foreign entity precluded national patriotic loyalty and threatened the very survival of America so long as the nation remained open to Catholic newcomers. Catholics (primarily Irish in the nineteenth-century urban Midwest) continually found their patriotic loyalty questioned by native-born civic boosters and their tenuous cultural citizenship threatened by nativists, like the editor of the *Chicago Tribune*, explicitly linking popery to dependence, drunkenness, and uncontrollable violence.[6]

Despite perception as dependent, impoverished papists, midwestern Irish celebrated Independence Day as heartily as did most native-born citizens, although their actions rarely merited specific attention in local newspapers. Occasionally, Irish men and women paraded alongside Anglo-Americans in midwestern Fourth of July processions. In 1854, Cleveland's *Plain Dealer* praised the Irish Hibernian Guards as a "patriotic Company" that was "ever on hand to celebrate in American style, the natal day of their adopted country," while, in Cincinnati, loyal Irish regularly lined the streets during Independence Day parades.[7]

GERMANS SETTLE IN THE URBAN MIDWEST

German immigrants arrived in midwestern cities from the earliest period of settlement (two of the first eighteen downtown lots purchased in Columbus went to Teutons). German immigration to the United States peaked in 1854, when over 200,000 Germanic men and women registered in American ports. Swollen by this vast increase in the middle of the decade, the German population of the United States doubled between the censuses of 1850 and 1860. Eager to replicate their European lifestyles in North America, many of these immigrants settled in the Midwest, seeking similar climate and terrain, as well as German-speaking neighbors, to ease their transition to the United States.[8]

Midwestern Germans used language and social organizations to promote their cultural heritage. In Ohio during the 1840s, the state legislature printed laws in German, because, as American-born William Dean Howells of Columbus acknowledged, "there was a common feeling that we ought to know their language." However, it soon became apparent to many German newcomers, especially in midwestern cities, that mastery of the English language constituted an important requirement for economic and social advancement. "The first 2 year, I didn't like being here too much," Chicago's Gotthilft Willig remarked in 1852. "The greatest handicap was, that we could not speake English. Now we know what is necessary; an my children speak English as well as German."[9] While some Germans, like Willig, willingly gave up their linguistic heritage, most Teutonic immigrants clung tightly to German social and cultural institutions and even expanded the role of these societies in evolving German-American culture, establishing singing groups like the Mannerchor and gymnastic organizations like the Turnverein throughout the urban Midwest. The Turnverein (or Turners), in particular, fostered masculine Germanic culture in midwestern cities. Founded in 1811 in Berlin, as Napoleon ravished Prussia, the Turnverein served as a tool to instill a sense of German national pride during that tumultuous time, in much the same way that it gave rise to conceptions of German-American nationalism in the 1850s. Cleveland's *Plain Dealer* reported in 1856 that "it is a sort of religious duty with the Germans to spend a portion of his time in the gymnasium." Indeed in many ways, the Turnverein approximated German-American civil religion—indoctrinating youths in the importance of moral virtue, healthy living, and cultural awareness.[10]

Language and social organizations formed important aspects of German culture in these midwestern communities, but ethnic celebrations played an even more vital role in shaping conceptions of patriotic loyalty and American nationalism for immigrants in the urban Midwest. The first Sangerfest in America, a competitive contest of German singers, met in Cincinnati in 1849. The program included numerous German folksongs as well as overtures and operas like Handel's *Messiah* and Mozart's *Magic Flute*. Other German festivals, catering to locals on a much smaller scale, offered revelers the opportunity to "indulge in the old-time style" reminiscent of Old World celebrations, showcase their proud Teutonic heritage, and spend time with family and friends in a comfortably German (yet not anti-American) atmosphere.[11]

ASSIMILATION AND ACCULTURATION IN MIDWESTERN CITIES

Generations of historians have debated the extent to which immigrants, particularly Germans, assimilated into American culture, and the relationship between this assimilation and developing notions of American nationalism. Some have argued that immigrants almost immediately traded many of their Old World customs for the benefits of American citizenship, pointing in particular to linguistic developments and adopting American customs as evidence of this acculturation. Other historians point to aspects of cultural retention as evidence of minimal assimilation to (or outright rejection of) Anglo-American culture, utilizing terms like cultural mosaic and stewing pot to describe cross-cultural interaction rather than conforming to the Anglo-dominated myth of the American melting pot. In the urban Midwest, neither model adequately describes the complexities of the cultural exchange between immigrants and native-born Americans. Instead, recent studies of assimilation, instead of focusing on immigrants' surrendering their cultural identity to that of a dominant "Anglo-American core" or desperately clinging to remnants of their Old World culture, debate the merits of an "invention of ethnicity" in which ethnic identity is culturally constructed and bidirectional. In this model, native Anglo-American society integrated and appropriated European immigrant traditions just as newcomers adopted and adapted to New World customs. Invented ethnicity, discussed by pluralist immigration historians Kathleen Conzen and David Gerber, gives great weight to the give-and-take facilitated by cross-cultural contact found throughout the urban Midwest and serves as a template for understanding how Fourth of July celebrations reflected newly developing conceptions of patriotic loyalty among ethnic Americans.[12]

In this model of invented ethnicity, German immigrants in the urban Midwest assimilated and acculturated on their own terms, usually for economic or social benefits and coupled with developing notions of ethnic Americanness, rather than due to successful pressure from the hegemonic native-born society. This cultural exchange began in earnest in the urban Midwest in the 1840s. "Being German-American is a very personal thing," Johann Bernard Stallo, a Latin teacher and lawyer from Cincinnati, declared in 1848. "We build our houses the way Americans do, but inside there is a German hearth that glows," Stallo continued. "We live according to what is customary in America, but we hold dear our German customs and traditions. We speak English, but we think and feel in German." American cultural citizenship, Stallo decided, was appropriate only for social or economic betterment, not as a replacement for Old World traditions, and should form an exterior shell, visible to outside observers but not indicative of one's true persona. Native-born Americans, on the other hand, saw only the exterior façade, the appearance of assimilation in these early newcomers. An 1843 guide promoting immigration to the Midwest noted that, "emigrants from Europe have brought the peculiarities of the nations and countries from which they have originated, but are fast losing their national manners and feelings, and to use a provincial term, will soon become 'westernized,'" assuring native-born readers that, in fact, the newcomers would easily and willingly melt into the preexisting social structure.[13]

By the 1850s, this dual identity became increasingly difficult for ethnic immigrants to maintain as nativist fervor intensified, focusing most intently on visible signs of cultural retention like German language, social organizations, and ethnic celebrations (especially those on the Fourth of July). Bernard Stallo's ideal of layering the trappings of American citizenship over German character and intellect became an arduous (if not impossible) task. In the urban Midwest, German culture continued to thrive throughout the early 1850s as immigrants insisted that American patriotism could include an ethnic component, arguing that the two were not mutually exclusive. Thus German immigrants could profess to be both committed carriers of Teutonic culture and loyal American citizens, proudly marching in July Fourth parades without the taint of European decadence and monarchism.[14]

GERMAN CELEBRATIONS

Germanic celebratory culture stood in sharp contrast to the holiday calendar of American-born citizens in the 1850s. Germans in the urban Midwest celebrated holidays much more regularly and much more heartily than their native-born counterparts. In *Domestic Manners of the Americans*, Frances Trollope quoted a German woman who claimed that Americans "do not love music. Oh no! and they never amuse themselves." Only Independence Day, Thanksgiving, Christmas (and occasionally New Year's and George Washington's birthday) warranted extensive commemoration in the mid-nineteenth-century Midwest among Anglo-Americans.[15]

Celebrations of the Fourth of July presented rare opportunities for German immigrants to visibly display their patriotism and proclaim loyalty to their adopted nation while adhering to their traditional exuberant German festive culture. In Columbus in 1853, one newspaper reported that the city's south end, encompassing the Fifth Ward and German Village, "monopolized all the sport, and parade, and patriotism of the day." Captain Schneider's German militiamen, several fire companies, and the local Mannerchor paraded through the city streets, winding their way to a local beer garden where the company spent the afternoon listening to a brass band and drinking copious quantities of cool, crisp, lager beer. This was a common event—Germans participated in nearly every Fourth of July in each of these five cities during the early 1850s. The Turnverein often paraded alongside members of American fraternal lodges and clubs and regularly accompanied German bands and singing societies while families picnicked in local groves. In fact, Germans dominated so many early 1850s Independence Day celebrations in Cleveland that the editor of the *Plain Dealer* conceded that they could teach "a lesson to Yankees how to enjoy some of the solid comforts of life in a sociable and sensible manner." In 1850, Jakob Mueller, a recently arrived German immigrant in Cleveland, confirmed the editor's claim. "The procession on the Fourth of July, which was observed annually by the Americans in a mechanical and spiritless manner, was so unworthy of the historic nature of the event that we [the Germans] parted ways with the Americans," Mueller recounted, "holding our own celebrations in nearby groves in keeping with the esthetic style of the free men, abandoning ourselves to the happiest of patriotic moods." Germans notoriously commemorated Independence Day with great Gemütlichkeit—celebratory spirit—toasting American political leaders and institutions, along with figures from the Old World, and drinking lager until late in the night.[16]

Nativism

Immigration and increasing ethnic appropriation of the Fourth of July combined with a myriad of other issues (including antislavery, sectional animosity, economic recession, and temperance) to set off a virulent anti-immigrant backlash—later dubbed nativism. Most adherents to this doctrine, called nativists, were white, American-born, Protestant men. These men (at least in their own minds) served the United States as white knights, defending the honor of American national identity from the degraded, poverty-stricken monarchists and papists threatening the nation's political and cultural institutions. Defending the Fourth of July took prominence, as controlling celebrations of Independence Day not only allowed nativists to dictate inclusion in the American cultural polity, but also to more stringently define for the region the acceptable boundaries of loyal patriotism.

Mid-nineteenth-century nativism was not a coherent social movement. Instead, it constituted an amalgamation of oppositional opinions drawn together by an intensely ethnocentric American patriotism. Some nativists promoted temperance while others drank freely; some foreswore slavery while others embraced perpetual African servitude; some were virulently anti-Rome while a small minority practiced Catholicism; and some were anti-immigrant while others were, in fact, foreign-born themselves. Thus nativism cannot be understood simply as spontaneous xenophobic reactions to increasing numbers of immigrants threatening the economic livelihood of native-born Americans. Instead, nativism relied on developing notions of American cultural superiority intensified by (but not resulting solely from) moral reform efforts, spikes in immigration, economic downturn, and ongoing debates about American nationalism. While not necessarily xenophobic, nativism was distinctively ethnocentric, promoting exclusivity based on American conceptions of cultural preeminence preferencing patriotic character and loyalty over birthplace, social class, or political persuasion.[17]

The roots of nativism, intended to limit, or even exclude, access to American political and cultural citizenship, can be traced to the 1840s when eastern native-born Americans first saw fit to more stringently define conceptions of loyal American patriotism. The economic downturn of the late 1830s and early 1840s combined with the changing character (and peak numbers) of European immigrants to create a native-born citizenry less accommodating in their dealings with ethnic newcomers. Their ethnocentric efforts can be divided into two categories: social and political nativism. Social nativism marked the first organized wave of anti-immigrant activity. It formed initially in the late 1840s in the guise of secret societies, functioning as bastions of anti-radical, anti-Catholic, and, perhaps most importantly, pro-native-born sentiment. Native-born Americans founded the Order of the Star Spangled Banner and the Order of Red Men, among the first social nativist organizations, in New York City. Their ideology was not new. In 1751, Benjamin Franklin famously declared that, should Germanic immigration continue unabated, Teutons would be "so numerous as to Germanize us instead of our Anglifying them." Social nativism promised that this would not happen, promoting, in the words of one historian, "a return to the early republican virtues of hard work, piety, and mutuality, all supposedly mocked by loose-moraled foreigners." Protestant revivalism emerging out of the Second Great Awakening spurred social nativism just as it had ignited temperance, abolition, and women's rights—urging the midwestern Christian middle class to embrace moral reform efforts and supposedly American virtues. Advocates of American reformist middle-class culture focused on implementing and defending their ideals against the supposedly lazy and destitute foreigners, proclaiming the superiority of native-born American society and its republican institutions. Nearly a century after Franklin's anti-Teutonic diatribe, Anglophilic nativists like Cincinnati's Orestes A. Brownson considered Franklin's fears unfounded. "No nationality here can stand a moment before the Anglo-Saxons," Brownson proclaimed in an 1854 July Fourth oration, boasting that "it is the all-absorbing power."[18]

NATIVISM IN THE MIDWEST

In the 1830s and 1840s, native-born midwesterners, unlike their eastern counterparts, generally encouraged immigration to the region because in-migration stimulated local economies by providing inexpensive labor for internal improvement projects and fledgling industry. Prominent Cincinnatian Daniel Drake reported that "there is much to admire in the German character," in a speech he presented in 1835. The Democratic *Cleveland Plain Dealer*, four years later, lauded the "indomitable love of freedom" of German immigrants. In 1844, one Columbus newspaper lauded the local German and Irish as being "all *American*" due to their hardworking and generally affable natures.[19]

But by the mid-to-late-1840s, native-born midwesterners began to reconsider their once-positive perception of immigrants. Historical memory stood at the center of this dispute, causing tension between immigrants and militantly ethnocentric native-born Americans over access to the legacy of the Founding Fathers. Midwesterners still, in many ways, considered themselves uniquely representative of the American nation and staunchly defended that position in the face of a perceived attack by unworthy outsiders. In 1844, Indianapolis nativists formed the American Republican Association (ARA), determined to resist "the encroachments of foreigners upon the rights" and protect the "privileges of the *native born* citizens." The Association further vowed that "Americans can and will protect the Flag of their country" from immigrants ostensibly seeking to co-opt and defile the symbols of American civil religion. The formation of the ARA incensed the Democratic editor of the *Indiana State Sentinel*, who argued that German-Americans were at least as patriotic as any nativist. The editor, Jacob Page Chapman—recently arrived from Massachusetts—directly challenged the nationalist loyalty of the Association, asking if they recalled that "in that noble band . . . of the memorable 4th of July, 1776 . . . there were many foreigners." Using memory to invoke the role of foreign-born citizens in securing American independence became an important point of contention between nativists and immigrants. In 1845 in Cleveland, a group of rowdy nativists interrupted a

FIGURE 4. "Dr. Daniel Drake," engraved by A.H. Ritchie, date unknown.

community-wide assemblage of both foreign- and native-born citizens, causing one local Democrat broadsheet to scold "Native Americans" who forgot "that our liberties were achieved by the blood of foreigners mingled with that of our own countrymen." In 1847, Reverend Charles Boynton of Cincinnati spoke on the incompatibility of foreign-born and native-born Americans, typifying the growing nativism of the urban Midwest. Perpetuating American liberty, Boynton argued, required that the United States regulate immigration. He reminded listeners that "you cannot build the Temple of American Liberty from the drift-wood of European rivers." This tension between immigrants and nativists over historical memory marked only the beginning of a long, drawn-out feud over the role of ethnicity in developing conceptions of American nationalism that reached its apex in the mid-1850s.[20]

By 1854, with German immigration at its peak, midwestern nativists intensified their attempts to limit the influence of immigrants—both politically and in commemorating American national festivals like the Fourth of July. In Columbus, nativists organized themselves into contentious societies like the "Washington Lodge" and the "Mount Vernon," carefully cultivating the image of George Washington to fit their pro-native-born agenda. In Chicago, nativists called themselves simply "Law and order," or "Sam" (as in Uncle Sam), again proclaiming their patriotism and vigilance while implying native-born control of America's national symbols. In Indianapolis, they referred to themselves as the American Republican Association, similarly invoking the specter of the nation's founders. By the mid-1850s, midwestern nativists feared that combating the influence of foreign-born newcomers could not be accomplished through these clandestine societies alone, which relied solely on moral suasion and nativist cultural dominance. Instead, vitriolic native-born citizens turned to the most American of institutions in their quest: appropriating democratic government as a vehicle for their ethnocentric anti-immigrant crusade.[21]

POLITICAL NATIVISM AND THE KNOW-NOTHING PARTY

Political nativism, inextricably linked to the short-lived Know-Nothing Party, first emerged in the 1840s and was spurred, as was social nativism, by Protestant revivalism and evolving midwestern middle-class conceptions of what constituted a good American. But until 1854, political nativism remained the bastion of a small native-born minority, manifest in secret social fraternal organizations like the Order of the Star Spangled Banner, the American Republican Association, and the Sag Nichts, a popular Columbus society. In 1854, with immigration at its peak, the once-secret societies publicly proclaimed their opposition to foreign-born influence in American politics and formed coalitions throughout the nation expressly intended to preserve Anglo-American political and cultural hegemony.

The nativist political platform, though intentionally amorphous so as to cater to its broad, diverse coalition, loosely rested on four basic tenets. First, American society was defined exclusively by Protestantism. Nativists denounced Catholicism as incompatible with American values and fundamentally at odds with notions of independence because parishoners proclaimed fealty to a foreign entity. Second, Catholics, whether Irish or German, attempted to gain undue political influence and power over their native-born betters through corruption and illicit means—Tammany Hall in New York City was an oft-cited example. Third, traditional political parties (in this case Democrats and Whigs) were ineffective vehicles for social change, refusing to address major political issues (notably slavery) in the interest of maintaining cordial sectional relationships, necessitating a grassroots organization (nativism) to deliver the message of native-born superiority to the masses. And finally, political nativism sought broadly to limit both the extension of liquor consumption and slavery, generally supporting Maine Laws and the American Colonization Society in their respective efforts to rid the nation of alcohol and African-Americans.[22]

As political nativism spread from eastern cities to midwestern urban centers, adherents to these basic tenets (having originated in clandestine societies) refused to publicly acknowledge their organization's political efforts, claiming to "know nothing" about the movement. From this term, mid-nineteenth-century political nativism gained its lasting moniker: the Know-Nothing Party. In the urban Midwest, many frustrated native-born citizens responded positively to the Know-Nothing message of limiting foreign influence in American institutions, and membership in the Know-Nothing Party increased dramatically.

Nativist Backlash

The urban Midwest was not alone in inciting ethnic animosity. Nativist riots in Philadelphia and St. Louis in 1844 and Know Nothing riots in Baltimore and Washington, D.C. in 1856 and 1857 demonstrated that intense ethnocentrism transcended regional boundaries. The Philadelphia riot, in particular, included many characteristics of the ethnic turmoil facing the Midwest in the mid-1850s. Although Independence Day celebrations were not at the heart of the conflict (even though the riot occurred around the Fourth of July), native-born Philadelphians staunchly defended national symbols and their place in the pecking order against foreigners whom they perceived to be both appropriating American nationalism and taking their jobs—threatening both their cultural and economic freedoms.[23]

Three events in the urban Midwest highlight the profound influence of nativism on developing conceptions of American nationalism and patriotic loyalty in the 1850s. The events themselves are somewhat atypical, but all are indicative of the ethnic tension permeating mid-century society and the way in which both native- and foreign-born midwesterners appropriated symbols of American nationalism and patriotism to define what it meant to be a loyal American. First, the Chicago Lager Beer Riot of 1855 pitted native-born citizens against German brewers in a battle over both Sunday drinking (an important German cultural import) and cultural assimilation. Second, Cincinnatians in 1855 argued about how to best celebrate the Fourth of July as local citizens rebuffed repeated appeals for a nativist-only celebration and countered by calling for a more ethnically inclusive commemoration of the holiday. And finally, the outbreak of violence on July 4, 1855, in Columbus, Ohio, dubbed the Bloody Fourth, involved German-born and American-born citizens in a life-and-death struggle over patriotic loyalty to the American nation on Independence Day.[24]

THE CHICAGO LAGER BEER RIOT

In Chicago, in the fall of 1854, the Know-Nothing Party focused on the upcoming mayoral contest to flex its newfound political muscle. Many Chicagoans, especially the editor of the *Chicago Tribune*, Joseph Medill, warmly embraced the party because of its strong moralistic stance in the face of increasing crime rates accompanying rapid urbanization (and, ostensibly, immigration). Know-Nothing Mayor Levi Boone encountered ethnic animosity in April 1855, just one month after gaining office, when a test case brought against several immigrant saloonkeepers charged with selling liquor on Sundays (a common target of Know-Nothing reform in the 1850s) went to trial. Word spread quickly throughout Chicago's immigrant population and scores of Germans gathered around the city courthouse, anxiously awaiting the verdict. The crowd soon grew restless and Mayor Boone called in his nativist police force to disperse the gathering mob. Police drove the crowd back, using handcuffs as brass knuckles, while leaders of the riot vowed to return. Mayor Boone immediately deputized an additional 150 men and sent spies to the German sections of town to gauge potential recourse. Informants brought word that five thousand North Side Germans were armed, preparing to burn City Hall and hang the mayor. The mob, actually numbering closer to six hundred, marched toward City Hall and met staunch police resistance. In the ensuing riot, a recently deputized nativist shot and killed a German cigar maker while police arrested another 60 rioters for disorderly conduct. After an hour, the rioters slowly dispersed, carrying their wounded back to the city's North Side. The police, wary of alienating Chicago's growing and influential German population base, officially charged only two rioters with perpetrating the uprising—both Irishmen.[25]

NATIVIST EXCLUSIONISM IN CINCINNATI

In Cincinnati, an explicitly Know-Nothing Independence Day celebration in 1855 proved to be an important battleground for defining American patriotic loyalty in the Queen City. Cincinnati had its fair share of ethnic violence. In 1855 and 1856, election-day riots witnessed nativist mobs bent on keeping immigrants from voting for Democratic candidates. The mobs also destroyed ballots before marching with fife and drum through the city streets. Their actions intentionally invoked memories of the American Revolution, reminding foreign-born citizens of bonds linking Anglo heritage and American patriotism. The Fourth of July that year was just as heated. In June 1855, local nativists issued a call for participants in "an *exclusive* celebration of Freedom's Anniversary," requiring adherence to Protestantism and specifically barring Catholics, citing their lack of "American feeling." Their political opponents, primarily Democrats, condemned the Know-Nothing stance, accusing them of exhibiting "narrow mindedness and selfishness hitherto unknown in any celebration in this city," and of using religion as "a passport to all the honors and distinctions of civil life." During late June and early July the *Cincinnati Enquirer*, an overtly Democratic organ, denounced nativist actions, blaming Know-Nothings for placing religious and partisan interests above civic well-being. Editors of the *Enquirer* decried the nativist stance as a "discreditable effort to desecrate that great day" and a mean-spirited example of "sectarian exclusiveness." In response to the restricted Know-Nothing commemoration, opponents of nativism formulated their own celebration, "without distinction of party, religion or nativity," calling for "Democrats, Know-Nothings, Protestants, Catholics and Jews" to "unite as Americans in one common celebration." On the Fourth of July, five to ten thousand Cincinnatians (estimates varied widely) gathered on Court Street to listen to the nonpartisan oration of Charles Anderson, who spoke at length about cultural tolerance and religious freedom, exhorting his listeners to practice acceptance and inclusion rather than bigotry and exclusion. By contrast, less than one hundred members of the local "American Protestant Association" turned out for the Know-Nothing celebration, drawing nine wagons full of children to swell their numbers. Although it did not result in bloodshed, the fervor citizens displayed in planning the 1855 Cincinnati Independence Day celebration underscores the tension prevalent in these urban centers during the nativist era.[26]

COLUMBUS'S BLOODY FOURTH

The pivotal event of this era in terms of demonstrating the ethnic component of American nationalism occurred in Columbus in 1855 and gained repute as the "Bloody Fourth." As in the 1840s, when the city encountered intense political partisanship between Whigs and Democrats, Columbus remained a contested area in the 1850s as Democrats and Know-Nothings vied for preeminence. Columbus's journalistic scene reflected this division: two newspapers, the nativist *Ohio State Journal* and the Democratic *Ohio Statesman*, split the English-language readership in Ohio's capital city. "We have no knowledge of the 'Know Nothings,'" the *Ohio State Journal* claimed in July 1854, apparently trying to distance the paper's anti-immigrant stance from a particular political party, although they allowed that "the result of their movements seem to be wholesome, and apparently designed to sustain good order and an impartial administration of the laws." By October of that year, 2,500 Columbus residents (nearly one-third of the male population of the city) belonged to Know-Nothing lodges. In addition to the rapid growth of these nativist organizations, there were also portents of ethnic conflict. In May 1855, native-born residents clashed with a group of Turners as the latter marched to a picnic, arguing about a flag decorated with German script (which, reportedly, read "Fresh—Merry—Free"). Although there were no deaths and just a few minor injuries as a result of this confrontation, there were obvious undercurrents of anti-immigrant sentiment aimed at a perceived ethnic appropriation of American symbols of patriotism, in this case a flag leading a parade. With political identity and control of patriotic loyalty so central to Ohio's capital city, both because of its status as the capital and the relatively equal divide between Democrats and nativists, the city was primed for an explosion of ethnic backlash—all it would take was a spark to set the entire city ablaze with nativist fervor.[27]

On July 4, 1855, German Turners marching in an Independence Day parade provided that spark. They clashed with native-born onlookers, resulting in the death of a young blacksmith, Henry Foster. The actual event, described at the beginning of this chapter and quickly dubbed the Bloody Fourth by local newspaper editors, lasted only a short time. Columbus policemen arrived on the scene swiftly after hearing about the shooting, although their heavy-handedness may have actually added to the general mayhem rather than solving any problems. They rounded up 24 German suspects and sent them to jail, despite dubious evidence.

Many of the police actions that day, including pulling Germans indiscriminately from their homes, hinged on preexisting ethnic stereotypes, namely their refusal to submit to the hegemonic middle-class Anglo-American culture. Perhaps attempting to justify the haphazard collection of suspects, and to reinforce entrenched ethnic stereotypes, the local nativist broadsheet reported that, "reeking with the fumes of Lager Bier, and nearly crazed under its demoralizing influence, the shouts and yells of the prisoners could be heard a square's distance."[28]

Coverage of the events from the German perspective, found in the German-language newspaper *Der Wesbote*, differs notably from reports issued by the English-language press and provides an interesting perspective into how Columbus's German community conceived of American nationalism and reacted to the Bloody Fourth. The nativist *Ohio State Journal* placed all culpability with the Turners for inciting the riot, while the Democratic editor of the *Ohio Statesman* merely defended the Germans' actions but refused to alienate potential supporters among the city's population by blaming all native-born Americans. But the editor of *Der Wesbote* blamed not only the entire Know-Nothing population of the city, but the dead blacksmith and Columbus's small African-American population as well, arguing that nativists (including Foster) harassed the Turners for the entire length of the otherwise peaceful procession and that blame for the haphazard roundup of suspects rested with the city's free black population. Several of the hastily deputized nativists were, in fact, African-Americans, but there is little evidence, or reason to suspect, that they had any role in the escalation of violence or in deciding whom to arrest. Nonetheless, in the days following the Bloody Fourth, the German community unsuccessfully tried to cope with the brutal melee, haphazardly placing blame and trying to defend the patriotic loyalty of the accused. "There was once a time," the editor of *Der Wesbote* lamented, "when the Americans and Germans of our city lived with each other happily as good neighbors." Indeed, German-born citizens, in each of the previous two years, initiated discussions for a community-wide celebration, but elicited little support from their native-born counterparts. But by 1855, a July Fourth détente became seemingly impossible in the face of equally stubborn nativists and Germans and a hegemonic middle-class Anglo-American political and cultural community in Columbus bent on using the Fourth of July to suppress ethnic peculiarities, using the pretext of defending the boundaries of what it meant to be a good American.[29]

The events of the Bloody Fourth illuminate many of the characteristics of contested celebrations marking the early 1850s and, perhaps better than any other single event, highlight the ongoing debate between midwesterners about the proper way to celebrate the holiday and to participate in the Sabbath of American civil religion. Germans regularly marched through Columbus's streets on the Fourth of July, parading with the Stars and Stripes at their head. Yet in 1855, native-born citizens, incensed at perceived German appropriation of American Independence Day, attacked German marchers. It was no coincidence that the clash between nativists and immigrants occurred on the Fourth of July, as Americans of all creeds used the holiday to define themselves and others through patriotic bravado and parading. On July 4, 1855, in Columbus, this posturing reached an unfortunate outcome: full-scale ethnic violence. This sentiment is perhaps best summed up by an editorial published in the Democratic *Cincinnati Daily Enquirer* which lambasted the Know-Nothings, claiming that "to attack and maim adopted citizens" on the Fourth had become "the par excellence test of Americanism" and "a fashion they have of 'Americans ruling America.'"[30]

THE DECLINE OF NATIVISM

The fallout from these incidents of ethnic violence was far-reaching. Due to the Philadelphia Riots, the Bloody Fourth, and the numerous incidents of ethnic hostility throughout the nation, Know-Nothings faced bleak political prospects after 1855, having instigated, or at least fueled, intense ethnic animosity. In retrospect, 1855 marked the apex of Know-Nothing influence at both the regional and national levels. The party lost mayoral and gubernatorial bids throughout the nation in 1856 despite Know-Nothing momentum just two years earlier, while Millard Fillmore, the Know-Nothing presidential candidate, amassed just over 20 percent of the national vote (and only 332 of 11,000 votes cast in Chicago) in his unsuccessful bid for the presidency.[31]

THE EFFECTS OF NATIVISM ON LATER
INDEPENDENCE DAY CELEBRATIONS

Although incidents of nativist violence greatly influenced the direction of local politics, they had an even more significant impact—at least in the context of defining American patriotism and nationalism—on subsequent Fourth of July celebrations. Rather than confront the meanings of contested celebrations and parse out underlying ethnic tensions, residents in these midwestern cities took a decidedly different approach, acting as though the events never occurred.

In Chicago, following the April Lager Beer Riot, revelers prepared for the coming holiday in "beer saloons and doggeries," drinking copious amounts of lager and then stumbling through the Windy City in what the Republican *Tribune* enthusiastically termed "an exercise of liberty!" Unlike its violent predecessor, July 4, 1856, in Columbus passed without mention of the Bloody Fourth. Despite a conscious effort on the part of Columbus's citizens to move past the event, it could not have been far from their minds when the editor of the *Ohio State Journal* implored his readers to "hearken to a regular old fashioned Fourth of July time" in recalling the day. In 1856, Cincinnatians—still smarting over the exclusivity of the previous year's celebration—pleaded with municipal leaders to fund a community-wide, nonpartisan commemoration. The tightfisted authorities refused, and support for the unified celebration collapsed. One newspaper reported that the day could be summed up as follows: "crackers went off, rockets went up, and lager went down in comfortable quantities," while another editorial poignantly commented on the lack of civic commemoration in the Queen City in 1856, noting that "the rage of faction and the jealousies of section" dampened patriotic enthusiasm for the Fourth of July. The editor even raised the question as to whether "the Union [shall] continue to triumph" amidst the "designs and schemes of conspirators and factionists" seeking to ruin, or compromise, the meaning of the nation's birthday. Conspiring to taint the remembrance of the nation's birth, the specter of sectionalism descended on the Queen City, as it did in many urban centers, as the 1860s approached.[32]

The anniversary of the nation's birth, and, by extension, evolving understandings of American nationalism, faced incredible ethnic division between 1850 and 1856. On the Fourth of July, ethnicity became a defining factor in determining what constituted a good midwestern American. Civic boosters and other members of the middle class, especially those supporting nativism, opposed foreign-born appropriation of Independence Day, while immigrants embraced the holiday as an opportunity both to practice their boisterous Old World festive culture and to publicly proclaim their patriotic loyalty to their adopted nation. A holiday intended to bring together disparate factions of American society instead deepened the fractious ethnic relations plaguing the mid-century Midwest. After 1856, however, the nation confronted a greater problem than the ethnic troubles promulgated by nativists and immigrants. By the 1860s, the United States faced rampant sectionalism that not only threatened the future of the nation, but also the very essence of the nationalism celebrated on the Fourth of July.

3 / "We shall still celebrate, but not as of old": Independence Day and the Civil War, 1857–1865

"Henceforth the anniversary of American Independence will never dawn meaningless."[1]

—*Chicago Tribune*, July 4, 1864

The Civil War transformed American life in the mid-nineteenth century, putting to rest the supposition that sectional political concessions could be achieved through military action or secession. But the war also drastically changed midwestern perceptions of nationalism and patriotic loyalty. As soldiers gave their lives on far-away battlefields, citizens on the home front fought to keep patriotism alive in the face of divisive sectional animosity and lost loved ones. The actions of patriotic midwesterners on the Fourth of July mirrored prevailing attitudes about the war and forever altered the role of Independence Day and definitions of American nationalism. Before the Civil War, midwesterners watched military parades, argued for (or against) reformist calls for social change, debated ethnocentrism, and hailed the sacrifices of Revolutionary War heroes. After Appomattox, a culture of avoidance stressing recreation, leisure, and commercialism on the Fourth of July reigned supreme while commentators favorably compared the efforts of midwestern Union veterans to those of their ideological eastern forefathers struggling for independence from the British.

The Coming of the Civil War

Fighting the Civil War was a watershed event without parallel in American history, but it must be understood in the context of larger social, cultural, and political issues. Historian Peter Parish cogently argues that the Civil War "should be used as a powerful lens through which to observe the structure and development of nineteenth-century America." Examining the Fourth of July during this era adds an even stronger focus, illuminating changing midwestern conceptions of American nationalism wrought by the war effort. Commemorations of the Fourth of July and midwestern conceptions of the meanings associated with the holiday continued to evolve in this period, reflecting ongoing community-wide debates about what constituted a "good" American and how regional identity confirmed an entitled sense of patriotism.[2]

As sectional discord overwhelmed nativist concerns in the late 1850s, national political parties devolved into little more than sectional factions. At the same time, slavery replaced immigration as the nation's greatest political and social issue, fracturing the populace along regional lines. The Know-Nothing Party crumbled in 1856, decimated by political infighting, as antislavery fervor subsumed anti-immigrant, anti-liquor, and anti-Catholic sentiment. Harriet Beecher Stowe's *Uncle Tom's Cabin* (1853), Justice Roger B. Taney's majority opinion in *Dred Scott v. Sanford* (1857), and John Brown's 1859 raid on Harper's Ferry (among other key events) dominated national headlines and prompted the rise of an explicitly antislavery party to battle the forces of perceived southern tyranny—vilified by northerners as the shadowy Slave Power. The Republican Party, founded in 1854, filled this void and emerged as a dominant northern sectional party by 1857, drawing support from former Whigs, disillusioned Democrats, and reformed Know-Nothings (many of whom dropped their nativist stance to induce immigrants to join their moral crusade against slavery). These Republicans, however, approached nationalism differently than their predecessors in combining what Peter Parish terms the "institutional" and the "psychological," embracing both a political American nation and an ideological one relying heavily on symbolism and historical memory. Many of these Republican leaders came of age in the early Republic and, imbued with the ideals of the American Revolution, created, in the words of George Forgie, a "post-heroic cohort" that relied on sentimental nationalism to preserve the Union. For Republicans, Union-evoked familial affections passed from (founding) father to (metaphorical) son: the latter was responsible for preserving the nation created by the former. Democrats also faced sectional divisions, but evolved quite differently. Instead of uniting the party, post-heroic sentiment caused an ideological split along the Mason-Dixon Line, with northerners flocking to the popular sovereignty platform of Illinois's Stephen Douglas and southerners rallying around Fire-Eaters like Robert Rhett and William Yancey, who insisted that they followed the true path laid down by the Founding Fathers.[3]

"Old-Fashioned" Celebrations and Independence Day

In the midst of this sectional political breakdown, Independence Day celebrations and the underlying associations of these festivities changed as well. Civic boosters, clearly cognizant of the changing national culture, focused increased attention on carefully shaping and planning wartime holiday commemorations. By controlling the Fourth of July, community spokesmen focused on their shared revolutionary legacy and tried to impart the importance of political, social, and cultural unity to a fragmented populace.

Between 1857 and 1860, midwestern civic leaders promoted military parades and processions in an attempt to revive interest in "old-fashioned" Fourth of July festivities. Military parades had constituted a regular part of Independence Day celebrations in the early nineteenth century, but between the 1820s and 1850s they had fallen into disuse as large-scale civic commemorations gave way to private celebrations, reformist calls for social change, and debates about ethnic character. In the late 1850s, militarism instigated by the coming Civil War inaugurated a brief revival of interest in military processions. Community leaders convinced war veterans to march in parades or participate in sham battles, glorifying America's shared martial past as the nation battled dire sectional turmoil. In 1857, the Cincinnati city council organized Mexican-American War volunteers in a parade through the streets of the Queen City. Cincinnati's civic leaders urged the populace to participate in a "regular old-fashioned Fourth of July," marked by "the largest liberty of fireworks, jollification, hurraing, parading, and everything but fighting and drinking." The following year, Clevelanders raised nearly $3,000 in private subscriptions to fund a citywide, though not civic-sponsored, military parade, drawing thirty-five thousand strangers to the city. One newspaperman hailed the procession as "the most magnificent and imposing ever witnessed in Cleveland," while the appearance of Jared Farrand, a 102-year-old Revolutionary War veteran, drew thunderous applause from the assembled crowd. In 1859, Cincinnati's Independence Day parade included many of the city's militiamen, artillery, and benevolent societies, displaying a patriotic spirit reportedly exceeding that of all past demonstrations. In Columbus that year, planned events included a community-wide parade, a picnic, and fireworks, concluding with a "grand Sham Battle." The pseudo-conflict pitted city residents shooting Roman Candles at one another, drawing extensive participation from the city's young men and enthusiastic crowds eager to watch their neighbors engage in a mock battle.[4]

The scope of these military parades paled in comparison to the encampment held near Battle Ground, Indiana on July 4, 1859. The citizens of Lafayette, Indiana (located roughly halfway between Chicago and Indianapolis), planned a huge event attracting 25 companies from throughout the Midwest, including militiamen from Chicago, Cincinnati, and Indianapolis. In Indianapolis, perhaps encouraged by the militaristic display of their Lafayette counterparts, veterans of the War of 1812 paraded through the streets carrying at their head "a revolving wheel, on which . . . was inscribed the names of the different battles in which our country had been victorious." The wheel presented a visible symbol of the nation's martial past, reminding citizens of the bloodshed and unity required to establish and maintain the American nation. Joseph J. Bingham, the editor of the *Indiana State Sentinel* and a staunch Democrat, expressed his desire that the celebrations in Lafayette and Indianapolis would together spur Independence Day patriotism, stating that "we hope that these Fourth of July celebrations on a grand scale, may soon be as common in our country as they once were," again invoking historical memory to urge citizens to be more cognizant of how exuberantly celebrating the Fourth of July demonstrated patriotic loyalty.[5]

Civic boosters like Bingham stressed that displays re-creating the elusive old-fashioned Fourth of July could help pull the nation together by reminding citizens of their common past. But despite these calls for national unity, it was becoming increasingly evident that the nation faced disaster. The *Indiana State Sentinel* of July 4, 1859, asked pointedly, "what shall be our future?" The burning question, the paper proposed, was, would the country "remain a united nation" or would it, "through a sectional spirit, engendered by sectional interests, be broken up into contending States?"A series of events that culminated in the election of Illinois lawyer Abraham Lincoln to the presidency in 1860 all but guaranteed the latter.[6]

1860: Inaugurating a War

By 1860, sectional concerns dominated midwestern commemorations of the Fourth of July. "The hearts of the people are with and for the Union," promised an Independence Day editorial published by Joseph

Bingham in 1860. Bingham anticipated "divisions and disputes and dis-sentions" but reminded his readers that "one love has united the great mass of the people—the love of the union of these States, and it burns as pure to-day in all hearts" as much as "when the Union was formed." The editor remained confident that, despite sectional turmoil, "the old ship Constitution will ride gallantly through every gale." Similarly, in the same year, Cincinnatians read an editorial asking that all Americans "make a solemn vow of allegiance and fidelity to the Union," pledging to oppose any entity attempting to weaken the bonds of the nation. Even as the nation moved closer to war, civic boosters remained insistent that the Fourth of July could pull together an increasingly split populace for a day of national remembrance and reconciliation.[7]

Scholars have debated the causes of the American Civil War for gen-erations. Most historians today, at least, can agree on one point. The Civil War was fought over slavery. Americans in 1860 heatedly debated the extension of slavery into territories won from Mexico, the possibil-ity (however remote) of slavery returning to northern free states, and the potential annexation of Cuba to further the southern slaveholding empire. But the war also involved changing perceptions of American political and cultural citizenship. As Peter Parish argues, antebellum northerners "hijacked American nationalism and changed its charac-ter dramatically," shaping it into a "greater New England," supporting reform impulses and moralistic piety. As southern conceptions of Amer-ican nationalism evolved into southern particularism (later dubbed southern sectionalism), northerners tried in vain to impose their visions of national identity onto the South. Northerners sought to replace Jef-ferson's ideal of virtuous, independent yeoman farmers with the holy crusaders of Protestant evangelicalism, decrying the backward agrarian Slave Power prevalent in the antebellum South and determined to fulfill America's millennial destiny by cleansing the nation of the foul stench of slavery.[8]

MIDWESTERN CITIES DIVERGE

To this point, differences between the five midwestern cities have been minimized. Before 1860, midwestern urban centers faced many of the same political, cultural, and social circumstances: antebellum life in Cincinnati approximated existence in Chicago, Cleveland, Columbus, and Indianapolis. In addition, legislators carved Indiana, Illinois, and Ohio all out of the Northwest Territory, while a roughly equivalent amal-gam of New Englanders, migrants from the Upper South, and European immigrants defined the characteristics of their residents. But the Civil War tremendously magnified the geographic and cultural differences between residents of these five cities. For instance, the war forced many residents of Indianapolis to choose between their slaveholding Kentucky ancestry and status as citizens of a free state. Upon hearing the news of the attack on Fort Sumter, the Democrat-controlled Indianapolis *Daily Sentinel* decried the "Abolition War of Seward, Lincoln and Company." Governor Oliver P. Morton forcefully quelled discussions of secession in and around the state capital, although some Indianans continued their Copperhead ways throughout the war, supporting the Confederacy economically, morally, and occasionally with manpower. In Ohio, Cincinnatians merely had to look across the Ohio River to observe Kentucky's state government debating whether to remain loyal to the Union or follow their southern brethren in secession. Tellingly, one resident of the Queen City remarked that many Cincinnatians wished "Lincoln and all political parties were in hell" for causing the war. Contrarily, the New England character of Cleveland and the strong ethnic makeup of Chicago and Columbus, as well as their relative distance from Confederate strongholds, brought those cities even closer to the North and Union.[9]

Newspapers in the mid-nineteenth century reflected the sectional partisanship and diverging interests of midwestern cities in this era, as the outbreak of war exaggerated the already political nature of the press. Columbus supported two main newspapers, the *Statesman*, a Democratic paper, and the *Ohio State Journal*. The *Journal* resolutely backed the Republican Party, regularly accusing leading Democrats, particularly Samuel Medary, a rival newspaperman, of disloyalty. Cincinnati faced a similar situation; the *Enquirer* and the *Gazette* supported the Democrats and Republicans respectively. The *Enquirer*, under the editorship of Michael Faran and the ownership of Washington McLean, became a well-known Copperhead broadsheet, regularly attacking Lincoln's policies and sympathizing with, if not publicly endorsing, the plight of the seceded Confederacy. In Cleveland, the *Plain Dealer* maintained the widest circulation, having been founded in 1842 by Joseph Gray, a strong supporter of Stephen Douglas. Under Gray's editorship, the paper served as a Democrat organ in a Republican city and gained widespread notoriety as an anti-Lincoln broadsheet, although it was not as sympathetic to the South as some of its brethren. Similarly, Indianapolis's *Indiana State Sentinel* ranked among the most outspoken Copperhead newspapers in the entire nation at the beginning of the war. Editor Joseph J. Bingham regularly printed articles condemning Republican leadership in the state and openly supported Stephen

FIGURE 5. "Portrait of Joseph Medill," artist unknown, 1850. Courtesy of the Chicago Historical Museum.

Douglas in the 1860 presidential election. In fact, residents of Indianapolis questioned Bingham's political loyalty to the extent that, in August 1861, a Union mob forcibly led him to Indianapolis's mayoral office to publicly swear allegiance to the United States government. Bingham defended his patriotism, retorting that he was not treasonous, but merely exercising his First Amendment rights to freely criticize the party in power. Yet after that event, the *State Sentinel* became increasingly moderate, calling for peace rather than espousing any sentiment that could be considered seditious. Chicago's *Tribune*, published by managing editor Joseph Medill, stood in stark contrast to the *State Sentinel*. Medill, a Radical Republican, purchased an interest in the *Tribune* in 1854 and, after a brief flirtation with political nativism, became a loyal ally to Abraham Lincoln in his bid for the presidency six years later.[10]

Through their newspapers, midwestern editors continued to serve as civic boosters, but they began to provide vastly different outlooks on the war effort and interpretations of American nationalism and patriotic loyalty. Editorials from all sides conflating Independence Day with the Union cause began in earnest around the Fourth of July 1861, and typified the intense patriotism at work on the urban Midwest home front. In Indianapolis, the *State Sentinel* published a feature about this connection, describing the roots of the Civil War and, surprisingly for a Bingham-edited paper, accusing Southern apologists of only supporting the Declaration of Independence when it proved convenient. In this editorial, Bingham also addressed the changes in American patriotism wrought by the insurgency, noting that news of the war replaced the "festivities, bonfires, and illuminations" typically found on Independence Day. The only hope for the nation, he insisted, was American patriotism, "the ark of freedom to the oppressed of all nations, and the beacon light of liberty to the whole world." Bingham's imagery evoked a common Fourth of July theme: historical memory. The "city upon a hill" ideology espoused in this Independence Day editorial reminded midwesterners of both their duty to win the war and the long-standing links to their puritanical, millennialist heritage. Antebellum orators recalled the glories of the Founding Fathers and the need for contemporaries to assume their mantle. Civil war made the call much more urgent and much more real.[11]

FORT SUMTER

On April 12, 1861, Confederate forces led by General P. G. T. Beauregard attacked Major Robert Anderson's garrison at Ft. Sumter, South Carolina, officially inaugurating the American Civil War. News of the firing on Ft. Sumter solidified tenuous northern support for armed conflict as thousands of young men eager to bask in the glory of war answered President Lincoln's initial call for 75,000 volunteers to battle the Confederacy. Lincoln's request included the formation of 13 regiments from Ohio, prompting William Dennison, Ohio's governor, to confidently respond that "without seriously repressing the ardor of the people, I can hardly stop short of twenty." Neither the nation—nor the celebration of the anniversary of its birth—would ever be the same again.[12]

Americans greeted July 4, 1861, in a state of warfare, although the first major battle (Bull Run/Manassas) remained two weeks away. Midwesterners welcomed Independence Day 1861 with the exuberant patriotism of a people newly at war as communities rallied around the anniversary of the nation's birth. Perhaps most importantly, the day marked the first opportunity for midwesterners to publicly demonstrate patriotic loyalty and allegiance on a national holiday since the secession of Confederate states. On July 13, 1861, *Harper's Weekly* printed a Fourth of July oration succinctly describing prevailing opinions regarding the first Civil War Independence Day by using an unflattering comparison between the Revolutionary War heroes of 1776 and the Confederate villains of 1861. "The patriots of '76 built their house upon the rock of Justice, and the winds and rains have not and shall not prevail against it," the orator reminded his audience. But the rebels of 1861 "build their house upon the sands of injustice," and the orator promised that "the floods are coming, the winds are blowing and beating upon that house, and great will be the fall of it." This is powerful imagery, juxtaposing the prudent strength of the founders with the fleeting temerity of the rebels, decrying evolving southern conceptions of American nationalism and building up the legacy of the Founding Fathers and their progeny defending the Union.[13]

MIDWESTERNERS FIGHTING THE CIVIL WAR

The most famous military events in the American Civil War took place in the Eastern Theater, covering Virginia, Pennsylvania, Maryland, and coastal North Carolina. Extensive media coverage and their proximity to major eastern urban centers guaranteed that troop movements and battles gained widespread attention. The Western Theater, encompassing the area between the Mississippi River and Appalachian Mountains, gained much less notoriety at the time but was of at least equal importance in determining the outcome of the war. Many of the troops fighting in the major battles on this front, like Shiloh, Chickamauga (where Ohioans comprised half the Union forces), and Vicksburg hailed from midwestern states. Of the Union's three million troops, 750,000 (nearly one-quarter) left behind families in Illinois, Indiana, and Ohio to fight. Many of the Union's storied leaders also hailed from the Midwest. Abraham Lincoln was Kentucky-born but later moved to Indiana before settling in Illinois. Generals Ulysses S. Grant, Phillip Sheridan, and William Tecumseh Sherman were all Ohio natives, as were Secretary of War

Edwin Stanton and Secretary of the Treasury Salmon P. Chase. Although the Midwest encountered little actual military action in the Civil War, midwesterners played a tremendous role in securing Union victory.[14]

INDEPENDENCE DAY MILITARISM

Midwestern celebrations of the Fourth of July in this era reflected an internal struggle between martial spirit and the harsh reality of war, as enthusiasm for the holiday ebbed and flowed according to results on the battlefield and larger political, social, and cultural truths emerging during the conflict. One immediate result included a steady rise in Independence Day militarism in the late 1850s and during the early years of the Civil War. Just as eager volunteers anticipated a glorious (and most importantly, a short and decisive) victory, their compatriots on the home front, stirred by emotive orations like the one printed in *Harper's* in the summer of 1861, expected no less. In Cincinnati, civic boosters planned an extensive parade for Independence Day in 1861 and called for all available area militiamen to participate. The *Cincinnati Enquirer* deemed it "the finest military display that has taken place in this city for many years," drawing thousands of cheering onlookers. "Several companies" of area schoolchildren, who had spent earlier Independence Days in somber Sunday school gatherings, followed the troops. These youngsters (instead of singing solemn patriotic hymns as in years past) dressed like soldiers, carried miniature guns, and marched in procession, mimicking their full-grown counterparts. Similarly, in Indianapolis, boosters planned an extensive military parade through the city concourses. Ironically, the proposed parade lost 2,500 participants to an actual wartime military action when Gen. George B. McClellan ordered a forward movement of several of the companies scheduled to march in the procession. In Cleveland, artillerists prepared for the July Fourth holiday by firing rounds of cannons into the bright morning sky. Following the cannonade revelry, Clevelanders watched a long military parade led by 30 war veterans (25 from the War of 1812 and 5 from the more recent conflict with Mexico). In Columbus, marching local militia companies appeared in each of the several small processions winding through the city. Just as the Battle Ground encampment drew crowds in 1859, two years later Chicago attracted droves of militaristic revelers with celebrations at Camp Douglas. Crowds gathered early in the day at the camp as soldiers received their friends "by the thousands."[15]

Benevolent society commemorations of Independence Day also underwent a transition during wartime. Instead of using the Fourth of July to promote social reform, as they had in the 1830s and 1840s, these societies utilized Independence Days during the Civil War to raise money for charitable causes related to the war effort. Hundreds of Chicagoans attended a ball hosted by the Seaman's Benefit Society on July 4, 1861, to raise funds for injured sailors and their families. Windy City residents also raised money by subscription for a fund to aid the families of fallen soldiers and held numerous "old-fashioned" celebrations to remember their loved ones on faraway battlefields. Chicago benevolent societies took the lead at the beginning of the war, but soon other cities followed suit.[16]

As war broke out in 1861, midwestern conceptions of American nationalism reflected a very optimistic, pro-Union sensibility. Before the Confederacy routed the Union army at First Bull Run, the enthusiasm in midwestern cities was palpable. On Independence Day, military bravado inspired celebrants while civic boosters employed commemorations to unite a nation fragmented along sectional, racial, class, and ethnic lines. Despite earlier attempts to draw the populace together in celebrating Independence Day in the first half of the nineteenth century, it took a civil war to finally—but temporarily—bind communities on the Fourth of July.[17]

1861: Enthusiasm for the Cause

In 1861, at the beginning of the Civil War, optimism reigned supreme. Midwesterners anticipated a quick victory and spent the July Fourth holiday accordingly, marching in parades glorifying armed conflict, raising money to benefit soldiers and sailors lost to fighting (probably minimal since they expected the war to be short and victorious), and reading editorials proclaiming the superiority of northern society and regional visions of American nationalism. Just three days before the holiday, the *Cleveland Plain Dealer* estimated that July 4, 1861, would be spent "whipping the rebels" and "driving in rebel pickets." In Cincinnati, despite the oppressive heat, citizens exuded an "aspect of peace and happiness," secure in the imminence of northern victory. Columbus residents, as they had in years past, marveled at John Kinney's grand fireworks exhibition on the Fourth. But in 1861, onlookers not only cheered Kinney's usual array of pyrotechnics, but also the grand finale entitled the "Flight of the Rebels," which drew resounding cheers from the patriotic crowd. Silas William Blizard, living outside Indianapolis, commented that it was "a beautiful 4th" in 1861, marked with "great preparations made at

Indianapolis for the occasion." Although stung by the loss of thousands of soldiers called to the front by McClellan, residents of Indiana's capital city rebounded with a formidable parade demonstrating their resolve to celebrate the holiday with all the trappings of patriotic loyalty. Chicagoans also remained optimistic, though some chose to respond with prayer rather than patriotic bravado as area YMCA members met on Independence Day to pray "in remembrance of the perils that surround our beloved country."[18]

Not all midwesterners believed with such certainty that the war would be a short, decisive Union victory. Even in the midst of brash patriotic celebrations, Independence Day celebrations glorifying militarism rang hollow to some observers. "It is no time for vaporings of the rostrum [long-winded speeches], mock parades, and banging away with blank cartridges," a *Chicago Tribune* editorial began, arguing that, "we have sterner work for powder to do, this year, than to coruscate in Rockets and glare in Roman Candles." The editor of the *Tribune* seemed to sense that the surge in militarism represented a short-term by-product of the beginning of the war and that children (and men) haphazardly parading the streets, shooting off firecrackers and pistols, and participating in sham battles could only distract residents for a brief period of time before they must face the harsh reality of war. An editorial in the Democratic *Cincinnati Enquirer* acknowledged that even the sound of cannon seemed different than in years past. No longer did it designate the beginning of a day spent listening to droning orators or singing patriotic hymns. Instead, cannons in 1861 sounded as "iron messengers, scattering death and destruction," and served as a vivid reminder of the conflict taking young men from their homes and families in the urban Midwest and placing them in harm's way on battlefields hundreds of miles away.[19]

1862: Decline in Enthusiastic Militarism

The days separating Independence Day celebrations in 1861 and 1862 witnessed numerous bloody conflicts between the Union and Confederacy. Despite northern optimism and southern resolve, neither side gained a substantial advantage that year—Confederate victories at Bull Run and Ball's Bluff offset Union triumphs at Shiloh and Forts Henry and Donelson—and the war, supposed to be a brief, decisive Union victory (at least in the eyes of most optimistic midwesterners), raged on. Decisive Union triumphs occurred most often in the western theater where midwestern troops (of whom nearly two-thirds hailed from Illinois, Indiana, and

Ohio) comprised nearly all of General Grant's army. Despite the martial successes of midwestern soldiers, their friends and families anxiously awaited letters and news, becoming increasingly disillusioned about the lengthy and bloody war effort. In this milieu, militarism began to lose its luster and the reality of fallen soldiers and lost loved ones tempered the glory of battlefield heroism.[20]

Patriotic displays by urban midwesterners continued to reflect prevailing national moods as July 1862 approached. For one, certainty that the war would end quickly and decisively subsided. In Cincinnati, an editorial written by Michael Faran lamented the prolonged war, declaring that "it is melancholy to those who have seen so many happy Fourths of July—when . . . North and South, East and West, vied with each other in doing honor to the anniversary." Faran, an antiwar Democrat, remained tentatively optimistic, adding his hope that, by the Fourth of July 1863, "peace will smile upon the land, and the anthems of Union and Independence forever be chanted from Portland to New Orleans, Baltimore to San Francisco." Similarly, in Cleveland, the *Plain Dealer*'s Joseph Gray anticipated that "we may yet be able to celebrate the Fourth and rejoice over the capture of Richmond at the same time this year." Elsewhere, cracks in northern unity showed all too clearly. Confidence in Union efforts remained high, but inconclusive results on the battlefield pushed back the timetable for victory.[21]

Allusions to militarism on the Fourth of July, like unbound midwestern confidence in Union victory, eroded between 1861 and 1862. The sham battles and troops of children emulating grown soldiers subsided, replaced by both an increase in benevolent society work on the Fourth (aiding the families of dead or wounded soldiers) and more solemn remembrances of the holiday. In Chicago, the Ladies' Hospital Relief Society planned a basket picnic and excursion for the Fourth of July, promoting dancing and "strawberries cream" in return for the 75-cent ticket and distributing the proceeds to the families of injured soldiers. Other Chicagoans came together for a nonmilitary parade, drawing numerous local ethnic, fraternal, and benevolent organizations in a communitywide procession attracting thousands of onlookers. Columbus residents ventured to nearby Camp Thomas for their own festivities, intended to be the grandest seen in the city for many years. The camp drew thousands of visitors from Ohio's state capital, and only a premature cannon discharge that blew off the hand of an unlucky artillerist marred the otherwise jubilant celebration. The soldiers did not parade, drill (except to shoot off cannons—not loaded with live ammo), or provide speakers expounding the importance of a vigilant military or lauding America's free institutions. Instead, Columbus residents spent a relaxing afternoon socializing with soldiers, providing the latter with a respite from days of drilling, weeks of waiting, and incessant combat preparation.[22]

In Cincinnati, residents chose from a variety of events (none militaristic) including fireworks shows, concerts, and "the greatest of all charities," an "Orphans' Union Picnic." The most discussed celebration in Cincinnati in 1862, however, was the Pioneer Reunion, open only to those residents having lived in Ohio each of the past 50 years. The pioneers spent much of the afternoon chatting idly, discussing their lives and the changes wrought by technology, population growth, and industrialization as they gazed upon a banner flown above New Orleans in 1815, recalling memories of Andrew Jackson's heroism in the War of 1812. As the festivities came to a close, conversation invariably turned to the Civil War and a sense of melancholy descended on the assembled group. As their thoughts turned from the glories of the past to the "mournful spirit" of the present, the pioneers quieted their idle chitchat and left the assembly to deal resolutely with the overwhelming reality of war.[23]

The example of Cincinnati's Pioneer Association demonstrates an important aspect of how the war distracted from Independence Day celebrations. This soon became a regional trend not limited to the Queen City. Indianapolis resident Silas William Blizard spent Independence Day 1862 plowing corn and "did not celebrate the 4th." His rationale was "not because that we disapprove of the practice, but are highly in favor of it." Instead, feeding his family and providing supplies for Union troops took precedence. Residents of each of these midwestern cities bemoaned a general lack of civic commemoration (Chicago's effort notwithstanding). Michael Faran noted a decided "melancholy" in Cincinnati's celebrations, reminding readers that, "two years ago the Fourth of July was celebrated as it ought to be" with military parades, speeches, dinners, fireworks, and bonfires. But in 1862, "the public mind did not feel like indulging in such manifestations," and was "too absorbed in our national calamity" to be bothered with planning an extensive Independence Day celebration. Even the outward signs of patriotic loyalty could not mask apprehension about celebrating American freedom while in the midst of a civil war. "The Union flag was displayed upon almost all our public buildings," Faran remarked. "But the *heart* appeared to be absent, the *real* spirit of the thing was lacking."[24]

This melancholy spirit descended upon Cleveland as well. Three weeks before Independence Day, Joseph Gray inquired whether residents would celebrate the holiday at all with no preparations having yet been made for the day's commemoration. "Are we to pass the Fourth of July contemptuously by this year, as though it was an ordinary day?" the Democratic editor rhetorically asked his readers. Even in times of war, he argued, citizens should brush off the "dust and cob-webs" of patriotism on Independence Day and celebrate "so that the present generation can look upon the scenes they depict, and be stimulated to still greater exertions, in the present trying hour." Once again, the specter of the Revolutionary War generation loomed large, and civic boosters invoked historic memory to spur citizens to action. In Cleveland in 1862, using the past to spur celebrations in the present failed miserably. Despite repeated calls for action, Independence Day in Cleveland passed without civic-sponsored revelry. "There will be no oration, no reading of the Declaration of Independence, no parades, no ginger-bread and beer, no fireworks, and no jolly time generally," Gray declared in the pages of the *Plain Dealer*. Rationalizing why there was no general celebration, the editor decided that, "we have all been so much absorbed in thrilling and exciting war news of late, that the Fourth of July has stolen upon us almost unawares this year," despite repeated attempts to organize a community-wide celebration.[25]

The tension of the war effort began to grate on already frayed nerves as the fate of the nation seemed to hang in precarious balance. Most tellingly was a fight in Cleveland between an African-American and an intoxicated native-born man. At a Cuyahoga County Fairgrounds horse race, the white man accosted the African-American, demonstratively berating him as an unwelcome presence at the racetrack's bar. The white man pushed the African-American and challenged him to fight. The African-American, not intimidated by the liquid courage and swaying pugilism of his attacker, responded by thrashing the instigator unmercifully. Police arrested, and later released, both men without charging either. Joseph Gray, a staunch Democrat in the Republican-dominated city, tapped into both his party's frustrations with the ongoing war and the racism of the era by assessing that "no one can say *this* war was waged for the nigger!"[26]

Midwesterners generally spent July 4, 1862, quietly and without the militaristic bravado of previous years. Instead of staging sham battles and parading veterans, celebrants were distracted by news from the battlefields, and festivities that year lacked the traditional upsurge of Independence Day patriotism. Clearly, conceptions of American nationalism and patriotic loyalty underwent a significant transformation in the first full year of the Civil War. The war's events caused Midwesterners to be far less optimistic than they had been just a year earlier. By 1862, patriotic loyalty required supporting the Union cause and evolving midwestern conceptions of nationalism even as victory no longer seemed imminent, or even certain.

1863: Turning the Tide of War

July 4, 1863, ranks among the most significant days in American history with the near-simultaneous Union triumphs at Vicksburg and Gettysburg. Together, these victories steeled Union resolve and turned the tide of the war in favor of the northern forces. But midwesterners, yet to hear the news of the Confederate setbacks, celebrated Independence Day as they had the previous year, with heavy hearts and restraint. Notable differences, however, are shown in vitally important incidents occurring between the summers of 1862 and 1863.

Several events, far too close to home for many midwesterners, affected numerous borderland communities. First, in September 1862, Confederate forces under Brig. Gen. Henry Heth marched on Cincinnati. Twenty-two thousand Union troops and fifty thousand volunteers poured into the hills surrounding the Queen City and erected batteries and forts to defend the besieged city. Upon reaching the Union barricades, General Heth reconsidered the decision to attack and instead retreated, saving Cincinnati from actual armed combat but certainly bringing the reality of war to southern Ohio. The second occurrence involved John Hunt Morgan and his Confederate raiders terrorizing southern Ohio and Indiana in the summer of 1863. Although not venturing as far north as Indianapolis or ranging close to Cincinnati, Morgan's Raid undeniably affected the psyche of urban midwesterners. In July 1863, John Hunt Morgan crossed onto free soil, harassing small towns along the Ohio River. Evading Union cavalry, Morgan zigzagged across the Midwest into northeast Ohio before being captured and sent to Ohio's state penitentiary in Columbus. The surviving raiders tunneled out and escaped back to Tennessee. Before 1863, the Civil War had existed as an abstract, if ever-present, concern. Major battles had taken place in Tennessee, Maryland, Virginia, and along the Mississippi River, but not in the Midwest. Morgan's Raid brought home the reality of war to midwesterners like few events before.[27]

The preeminent event of the year, and among the most important in American history, took place on September 22, 1862, when Abraham

FIGURE 6. "Oliver P. Morton," engraved by Alonzo Chappel, 1860. Courtesy of the Indiana Historical Society.

Lincoln issued his long-awaited preliminary Emancipation Proclamation—effective January 1, 1863. While Radical Republicans praised the
president for his humanitarian efforts, Lincoln's detractors greeted the
proclamation with scorn. In Indianapolis, the state legislature declared
that Indiana would "never voluntarily contribute another man or dollar"
until Lincoln withdrew the proclamation, while Governor Oliver Morton feared that the document would incite an uprising among southern
sympathizers. At the same time, many Cincinnatians also found Lincoln's proclamation repugnant, siding with their brethren in southern
Indiana and Kentucky in alleging that Lincoln was "false to his pledges,
his position, and his country."[28]

Lincoln's Emancipation Proclamation (whether praised or reviled)
also raised the visibility of African-Americans on the Fourth of July in
these communities, forcing race relations to the front of patriotic com-
mentary about 1863 Independence Day celebrations. Lincoln's proclamation, historian Leonard Sweet argues, "allowed blacks their first real
look at July 4 as a day of honor rather than hypocrisy." In the urban
Midwest in 1863, African-Americans visibly celebrated the Fourth of
July for the first time, parading and recruiting volunteers to aid the
Union cause. In Cincinnati, the presence of African-American troops
constituted the grandest spectacle of the day. Perhaps emboldened by
the Emancipation Proclamation, in effect for only six months, African-
American soldiers spent the holiday parading through the city streets
and informally "drumming up recruits" for the Union army. The small
African-American population of the Queen City (only 4,000 of the more
than 200,000 residents of Hamilton County in the 1860 census were of
African descent) turned out en masse, cheering their patriotic brethren.
Despite the close encounter with Confederate forces in September of
the previous year, Queen City residents scoffed at the ragtag Union procession; the Copperhead-edited *Cincinnati Enquirer* reported that the
maneuvers of the soldiers afforded white onlookers "a great amount of
amusement" and resulted in few successful recruits. Cleveland African-
Americans also celebrated Independence Day 1863 with great gusto. Mr.
Greene, an area barber and African-American militia leader, used the
holiday to drum up support for raising a volunteer company in the city,
adding to the 64 regiments already formed in northern states. African-
Americans assumed a much greater role in commemorating the Fourth
of July in 1863 than in years past when they had either celebrated alternative holidays or remained invisible in the face of an overly patriotic (and
often inebriated) white populace on the Fourth.[29]

Independence Day 1863 also marked a newfound northern resolve to win the war which, many midwesterners believed, would inaugurate a new era in American history and allow the Civil War to eclipse the Revolutionary War as the nation's preeminent event. In these celebrations, a fundamental shift in the larger historical narrative emerged as commemorations came to reflect a reformed American patriotism, focused on the meaning, rather than the rote recitation, of the Declaration of Independence. "We have entered upon a new age, and opened a new page in our national history," an editorial in the *Chicago Tribune* began. The Civil War (dubbed "the greatest of human contests" by the *Tribune*) initiated this transformation, as old-fashioned celebrations, including "their citizen-military pomp and parade, the burning of peaceful powder," and readings of the Declaration of Independence, were "gone forever." Seeing sons and neighbors die fighting for the United States revolutionized American patriotism and nationalism. This sentiment is perhaps most clearly articulated in Columbus's Republican *Ohio State Journal*, which argued that this "new baptism of blood" would cause Americans to arise "regenerated and disenthralled." This sentiment transcended political bounds as Democratic stalwart Joseph Medill proclaimed that Independence Day "is the most appropriate of all occasions, for fresh vows of fidelity to the Union," expressing his hope that "this anniversary be the birthday of new vows, and fresh hopes of a brighter day to dawn upon our rescued and re-united land." Although the fighting on the battlefield was far from over, midwesterners were already looking ahead to how the memory of the Civil War would rekindle the fire of patriotic nationalism and perhaps even surpass the American Revolution in defining what it meant to be an American.[30]

MIDWESTERN REACTION TO GETTYSBURG AND VICKSBURG

Efforts to revitalize Independence Day and awaken the latent patriotism of revelers were validated when, on July 7, midwesterners learned of the concomitant Union victories at Gettysburg and Vicksburg. Lee's defeat at Gettysburg caused widespread spontaneous celebration. In Columbus, Republican revelers descended on a Democrat loudly downplaying the significance of the victory and damning the Lincoln administration, forcing the Copperhead to flee the festive scene. Residents of Ohio's state capital greeted the news of Vicksburg's capture just as heartily. Citizens quickly collected money for a bonfire and fireworks, setting off a spontaneous celebration commemorating the valiant efforts of General Grant's Army of the Tennessee (again, comprised almost exclusively of midwesterners). Similar spontaneity energized other midwestern urban centers. "Vicksburg has fallen!" Cleveland's *Plain Dealer* exclaimed, adding, "glory to Grant and to the soldiers of his command." The newspaper further encouraged citizens to publicly demonstrate their patriotism by putting out flags, shooting off cannons, and shouting "till you are hoarse." Clevelanders answered the call. Fireworks, bonfires, and an effigy of Jefferson Davis (complete with crude tombstone) "about to give up the ghost, from the effect of Vicksburg's fall and Lee's defeat," enlivened the festivities. In some locales, residents celebrated the seventh and eighth of July even more heartily than the Fourth in 1863, with extensive civic commemorations and spontaneous patriotism exploding in the form of fireworks and Roman candles throughout the two-day-long festivity. The symbolic power of Vicksburg and Gettysburg on commemorations of Independence Day was tremendous. In 1864, a Chicago editorial promoting the Fourth reminded readers that "the Fourth of July is at hand, rendered doubly memorable by the fall of Vicksburg on that time honored day."[31]

1864: Midwesterners Tire of War

Northern momentum won in July 1863 did not carry troops through the following year. Union triumphs at the Wilderness and in the Shenandoah Valley, the transfer of General Grant to the eastern theatre, and Lincoln's strong reelection campaign eroded Confederate resolve, but were tempered by Sherman's inability to capture Atlanta and Grant's stalling at Petersburg. Midwestern boosters seemed desperate to quell Copperhead dissension, consciously constructing Fourth of July celebrations in 1864 to quiet opposition by reminding citizens of what lay ahead if peace were achieved on Union terms. Independence Day commemorations in 1864 included repeated requests for fund-raising to support the families of troops and orphaned children and a continued decline in the day's militarism (ebbing since the war's beginning) as citizens sought refuge from the brutal realities of war.

Benevolent societies often used Independence Day commemorations to raise money for their various social causes, primarily orphanages, churches, and asylums. But in 1864, these societies gave the war effort their full attention. Chicagoans celebrated the Fourth of July that year with events sponsored by a local branch of the Sanitary Commission, founded in 1861 to send medical personnel and supplies to the warfront. Residents attended picnics, excursions, and balloon ascensions to raise funds for a variety of war-related charitable causes. Sanitary Commission

representatives also urged Chicagoans to participate in the "free will offering of the people permitted to dwell at home in peace while the boys in the
front suffer and die." An editorial in the *Chicago Tribune* promoted the
Commission-sponsored events, using memory of the victories at Vicksburg and Gettysburg to spur renewed pro-Union efforts on the Fourth.
The fund-raiser earned the Sanitary Commission nearly $500 and praise
from local citizens for demonstrating the proper patriotic spirit. Joseph
Medill asked rhetorically if the goodwill offering, "deepened in you, a love
of country unknown to you in the past when 4th of July was a noisy holiday," and promised a tenfold return for a people "purified, as if by fire."
Many Cincinnatians spent the day similarly, celebrating with an orphan's
picnic (by 1864 an annual event) sponsored by the city's Catholic Societies. Despite its papist backing, the picnic welcomed citizens of all religious
creeds, raising money for destitute children and providing residents with
an escape from the humdrum of the Queen City, which did not host a
large-scale civic celebration. Also in Cincinnati, a contingent of women
provided dinners for invalids on Independence Day, serving warm meals
to wounded soldiers in Seminary Hospital. In Columbus, groups of citizens left the city for fund-raising picnics. Among those who fled the state
capital for cleaner climes was a sizable contingent of African-Americans.
In fact, most of Columbus's small African-American population escaped
the city in 1864, holding a picnic in a nearby grove with proceeds ear-
marked to benefit their own "Colored Soldiers Aid Society."[32]

Militarism also continued its steady decline in 1864, no doubt abetted
by war fatigue plaguing both midwestern troops and their families on
the home front. In Chicago, boosters did not announce a public celebration because, as Joseph Medill explained, "we have enough of the reality
of war to be able for once to dispense with its artificial semblance." By
1864, the devastating physical and psychological cost of war clearly resonated with urban midwesterners. In the first years of the war, citizens
lauded children mimicking military movements as patriotic actions of
Young America. In 1864, mock battles between well-intentioned youths,
according to Medill, "pale[d] in significance before the light of the ter-
ribly actual conflict now waging."[33]

While pretending to be soldiers no longer attracted acclaim in 1864,
respect and recognition for actual Union soldiers increased. Clevelanders honored the Seventh and Eighth Ohio Regiments (noble "war-worn
veterans") with a parade. Residents of Cleveland, conscious of the numerous parallels between the Revolutionary and Civil Wars, hoped that the
celebration would "express our veneration for the heroes of '76" as well

as "our love and veneration for the heroes of '61 and '64." Linking the Revolutionary War generation to their Civil War counterparts was certainly not a new tactic for enhancing northern morale. As an 1861 article in *Harper's Weekly* reminds us, northerners strongly believed they carried the mantle of the founding generation, defending the Union (and by extension, the nation) from the usurping Confederates. As boosters intended, the revelry in Cleveland was a decided success, capped by the appearance of the color-bearer of the Ohio Eighth, James Conlan, a veteran of 42 battles and 17 engagements. The wounded veteran "sped out in front of his regiment" during the procession and proposed three cheers for his comrades, drawing spirited praise from the assembled on-lookers.[34]

THE BEGINNINGS OF ESCAPISM

Commemorations of the Fourth of July during the Civil War marked a major turning point in both the meaning of celebrating the nation's birth and the actual events promoted on Independence Day. By 1864, midwestern revelers tired of seeing loved ones return crippled (or not return at all) began to convert the holiday into a day of escape, a respite from the pain and suffering brought about by the Civil War. Rail companies promoted excursion trains to isolated destinations (often nearby groves for picnics or, in the case of Chicago and Cleveland, lake islands), encouraging residents to flee the din and dust of the city and the tumult of wartime life. In Chicago, balloon ascensions outside the city drew an estimated ten thousand spectators. Chicagoans also attended horse races at the driving park, a minstrel show, a museum—promoting exhibits portraying "Uncle Tom's Cabin" and "Christ's trial with Pontius Pilate"—and beer houses, extensively patronizing each one. Chicago resident Elisabeth Gookin lamented the way her day was wasted in the kitchen preparing meals for her family instead of relaxing and spending the day outdoors. "It is not the most desirable manner of celebrating the National holiday," she confided in her diary, "but such seems to be my fate." In Columbus, numerous residents celebrated the nation's birth by leaving for the countryside while boys, left to their own devices in the city streets, purchased piles of fireworks, shooting them off throughout the day. In Cleveland, despite the patriotic appearance of regiments of returned war heroes, many residents "put an enemy in their mouths to steal away their brains," imbibing liquid patriotism at bars and causing a number of drunken brawls in the city square—all aspects of this rampant culture of avoidance developing alongside patriotic loyalty to Union forces.[35]

In many ways, 1864 marked a transitional year in Independence Day celebrations. Militarism continued to decline—although it still found an outlet in Cleveland—while many revelers instead practiced escapism. By July 1864, midwesterners sought an end to the long and brutal war, looking forward to eventually reuniting a fragmented nation or, at the very least, welcoming home their loved ones fighting on far-away battlefields. But the harsh realities of war tempered even this enthusiasm as midwesterners constantly perceived reminders of wartime sacrifice visible on the faces (and crippled bodies) of returned veterans and injured soldiers.[36]

1865: Celebrating Victory

Eighteen sixty-five witnessed several key events preceding the exuberant festivities of the Fourth of July that year—the first celebrated by a country at peace in nearly five years. General Lee's surrender at Appomattox Courthouse on April 9, 1865, essentially guaranteed Union victory. The following day, upon hearing the news of Lee's demise, Cornelius Madden, a corporal in the 102nd Ohio Infantry stationed in Columbus, penned a letter to his father in Shelby County. "This is the glorious day that we have been looking forward to," he gushed, "the Nation is ablaze with bonfires, and drunk with enthusiasm." Most tellingly, however, Cornelius likened the celebration to those typically found on Independence Day. "These are memorable days—*fourths of Julys*, every one of them—and will be considered so by the coming generations, who will appreciate the greatness and grandeur of this Struggle much more than we of the present day."[37]

Northern jubilation proved short-lived. Less than a week after the triumph at Appomattox, news reached midwesterners that a disgruntled actor and Confederate supporter from Baltimore named John Wilkes Booth had assassinated President Lincoln in his box at Ford's Theater. Houses draped in stolid black bunting, a symbol of a nation in mourning, replaced red, white, and blue drapery celebrating Union victory. Lincoln's death left the North not only bereft of leadership, but also struggling to reacquire a national identity after losing their most prominent and visible symbol of northern American nationalism. Finally, on April 26, Gen. Joseph E. Johnston surrendered his forces to Ohio native Gen. William T. Sherman, all but ending the American Civil War.[38]

Midwestern celebrations of American independence in 1865 ranged widely: residents of some cities burst forth in exuberance, honoring returned war vets, while others faltered, as if even the energy of planning

FIGURE 7. "Peace—Fourth of July 1865," *Harper's Weekly*,
July 8, 1865.

a Fourth of July parade was too taxing for an emotionally and physically
drained populace. Despite the loss of Lincoln and controversy regarding national reconciliation (or, perhaps, because of it), citizens began
planning Fourth of July celebrations early in the month of June 1865,
intending the festivities to both commemorate the end of the war and
the reconstitution of the once-fragmented country. Chicagoans hastily
assembled a Citizen's Committee, charged with making "great preparations of a grand celebration of the day," calling on local residents for
donations. Funds poured in to the committee ($4,500 in total) sponsor-
ing an extensive fireworks show intended to surpass any other in the
entire nation. In Cincinnati, the Republican editor of the local *Gazette*

promised that "no anniversary of our American Independence has been celebrated to such an extent as will be the coming 4th of July." The efforts of local citizens validated the editor's claim as Cincinnatians planned an event including both returning soldiers and area youths in a lively Sunday school celebration. As in Chicago, Cincinnatians canvassed the city for donations (to pay for both fireworks and ornate arches commemorating Union victory). Clevelanders, not to be outdone by their Queen City counterparts, also planned with great energy, proposing a procession made up of Sunday school children, benevolent societies, fire companies, trade unions, and a citizen's brigade. The procession would be further enlivened by a miniature gunboat (fully manned by returning veterans) placed in a wagon drawn by six horses and concluding in a sham battle marked by "all the pomp and circumstance of war." The day would end, as was typical in most large midwestern cities, with a fireworks show and pyrotechnic display. Clevelanders donated more than $1,200 for the cause, as citizens solicited contributions for several weeks to raise the necessary funds. In Ohio's capital city, residents planned with less structure and met with less success. A citizen's meeting elicited minimal enthusiasm for a large public celebration; Columbus residents settled for balloon ascensions, recreational sports, dancing, fireworks, and a festival to raise money for an area orphan's home. Indianapolis residents proved even more apathetic—only two attended a meeting called to plan a civic commemoration of Independence Day. "The people are tired of displays and parades," reported one local newspaper, arguing that, "the best way is for every family to make their own arrangements for enjoying the Fourth as they think most proper." The end of the war meant constant reminders of patriotic sacrifice and boisterous patriotism. Some residents of the Midwest grew tired of the pomp and parading and merely sought a quiet respite from the din and bustle promised by the Fourth of July, while others sought closure through exuberant festivities marking the end of the brutal war.[39]

COMPARING 1776 AND 1865

In both the planning and execution of Independence Day celebrations in 1865, midwestern revelers drew parallels between the eastern heroes of 1776 and their own victorious armies of 1865. Making these ties explicit not only connected war veterans to their Revolutionary War kindred, but also linked the rebirth of American nationalism and patriotic loyalty brought forth by the Civil War to the battles faced by the Founding Fathers in building a national identity nearly a century earlier. Some of

FIGURE 8. "Washington and Lincoln, the Father and Saviour of Our Country," Currier and Ives, 1865. Courtesy of the Indiana Historical Society.

the editorials and orations proved so sycophantic that midwestern Civil War heroes seemed to eclipse their colonial counterparts. In Chicago, the *Tribune* urged readers to remember not only "the noble deeds of the old heroes of 1776," but also "the brace and daring heroes of 1865," reminding them that "the former created, but the latter preserved and maintained our government by their heroic valor." The editor referred to 1865 as "the second birth of the nation," standing alongside 1776 as one of the two most important years in American history. Not to be outdone, Cincinnatians erected gigantic arches along Fourth Street, ornamented with portraits glorifying Civil War heroes. Images of Union Generals Grant and Sherman (both Ohio-born), Sheridan, and Hooker decorated the arches, but larger pictures depicting Abraham Lincoln (another native midwesterner) and George Washington—heralded as the co-fathers of the country—overwhelmed the arches. As if that juxtaposition was not evidence enough of symbolic ties between the founding generation and the Union efforts, the arches also included one side emblazoned with the years 1776 and 1865, making the connection complete. The Civil War did not create American nationalism, but it certainly altered it, forcing a narrative shift in commemorations of the Fourth of July. The Civil War, as Peter Parish argues, was the "culmination of the first chapter in the building of the American nation." Midwesterners connected nationalistic celebrations of America's first birth on the Fourth of July and the heroes of the Civil War inaugurating the nation's rebirth to re-create an American nationalism in which they played a vital role, this time using the recent struggle for Union as a basis for loyal patriotism and irrevocably linking the heroes of 1776 and 1865.[40]

Citizens on the home front hailed returning troops as heroes and defenders of a nation reborn. If the holiday belonged to anyone in 1865, it was midwestern Union soldiers flush from their hard-fought victory over the Confederacy. Chicagoans invited returning veterans to turn out "*en masse* and receive the loud huzzas of admiring citizens." If soldiers preferred a quiet respite on the Fourth, ladies of the Windy City obliged, arranging a huge dinner (waited on by more than one hundred local women) attended by 1,500 veterans. In Cleveland, area women prepared a celebration dinner for hundreds of returned vets to honor their wartime sacrifices. In Cincinnati, returning soldiers were greeted by a procession in their honor and the aforementioned arches. In Columbus and Indianapolis, lacking the enthusiasm for a civic celebration of the holiday, residents remembered their war heroes through inspired oratory, as area speakers lauded the efforts of those who suppressed "the awful rebellion," while "good martial music" set the auditory tone of the day.[41]

Above all, Independence Day celebrations in 1865 marked both the beginning of a new era in American history and a transition in commemorations of the nation's birth. Union troops put down the southern rebellion, American (or midwestern conceptions of American) nationalism won the day, and patriotic loyalty was "strengthened by the blood of patriots; redeemed, regenerated." Historians of the nineteenth century often (rightfully) mark the Civil War as a significant point of transition in American history. But the Civil War also marked a turning point in understandings of American nationalism portrayed on and evinced by July Fourth celebrations. As historian Melinda Lawson argues, "by war's end, a 'union' of states had become a 'nation' of Americans." After the big blowout in 1865, a war-ravaged people longed for peace, tranquility, and escape from the brutal realities of war rather than the pomp and circumstance of military parades and sham battles. The end of the Civil War was the last time, at least until the Spanish-American War, that American troops engaged the enemy in full-scale armed combat. It also concluded a short-lived era of militarism on the Fourth of July as commercialism (which allowed crafty capitalists to exploit the ties between patriotic loyalty and commercial opportunity—the nineteenth-century version of "Buying American"), recreational pursuits, and leisurely release on the midsummer holiday came to define postbellum Independence Day celebrations.[42]

THE ROLE OF AFRICAN-AMERICANS

African-Americans were, not surprisingly, absent from these final Civil War celebrations of freedom because, as was exemplified by Indiana's declaration in 1862, many white midwesterners had convinced themselves that they did not fight the war to free the slaves. Chicago's chosen orator in 1865, Henry Winter Davis, spoke at the Great Sanitary Hall on the Fourth of July, greeting listeners on a date "now celebrated with additional joy, additional heartiness, and overflowing exultation at the second founding of the American Republic." But Davis, despite being a Radical Republican and antislavery advocate from Maryland, concluded his lecture with a reminder that he was not "convinced of the intellectual superiority of the negro over the white," deriding efforts to grant equal political and social standing to African-Americans. Davis's declaration echoed a troubling sentiment in parts of the postwar Midwest (and indeed the entire North); African-Americans remained unworthy of American citizenship, whatever political rights the Fourteenth Amendment might confer. In much the same way that nativists denied Irish Catholics or pro-liquor Germans the full rights of cultural citizenship in the antebellum era, skin color dictated the terms of African-Americans' exclusion from full recognition as part of the reconstituted American nation. Davis's speech included an important caveat; despite their perceived laziness and lack of intellect, the votes of black men were of the utmost importance. "It is numbers, not intelligence, that count at the ballot box," Davis concluded. Republicans recognized the need for African-American votes in the Reconstructed South. But in the Republican-dominated Midwest, their votes mattered less and Davis's statements seemed more apt. Davis's oration marked a rare mention of African-Americans on the Fourth of July, 1865 in these midwestern cities. After increasing visibility in previous years, including soldiers seeking volunteers and parading noisily through the city streets or African-American picnic fund-raisers, African-Americans once again became invisible after Union victory. This too proved to be a harbinger of ill-fated Reconstruction efforts.[43]

How the Civil War Transformed the Fourth of July

In the years following the Civil War, contemporaries commented at great length about the transformative effect of the war on Fourth of July celebrations. An article in the *Chicago Tribune* in 1870 argued that celebrating freedom from Great Britain was not nearly as important as the "cause of free government and human equality" won by "the defeat of Lee at Gettysburg and the surrender of Pemberton at Vicksburg, which occurred on the same day seven years ago." The *Cincinnati Enquirer* lamented this transformation, arguing that "there exists a disposition to exaggerate the importance of the late civil war by making its events the great date of every thing instead of the old era of 1776." The Democratic editor of the *Enquirer*, Michael Faran, of course blamed the whole ordeal on the Republicans who would "throw the Fourth of July into the shade in the hope of obtaining by it some other anniversary of a more recent date." The war so dominated nationalist and patriotic discourse that Margarethe Winkelmeiner of Indianapolis wrote to her parents in Germany that "on the 4th of July no one has to work, the day is a holiday because that's the day the war ended and they made peace." The Civil War cast its lengthy shadow on the Fourth of July long after Confederate soldiers surrendered at Appomattox. For decades, if not generations, the war generated regional discussions about American nationalism, the past and the present, forgetting and remembering, and the relative merits of the eastern heroes of 1776 and their midwestern counterparts of 1865.[44]

Huge parades, extensive soldiers' dinners, and laudatory speeches proclaiming the reformation of the United States dominated Independence Day celebrations in 1865. The Civil War ended with Union victory, and soldiers returned home to greet missed loved ones while revelers welcomed the resumption of Independence Day in a reconstituted nation. But not everything went back to normal—too much had changed. The bloody battles at Antietam, Shiloh, and Gettysburg not only transformed the American nation, but also midwestern conceptions of American nationalism. The Civil War inevitably altered the Fourth of July, and its role in reflecting and defining patriotic loyalty. Midwesterners initially responded to armed conflict through civic activity and mimicking the trappings of war. But as the war dragged on, militarism declined and escapism, fund-raising, and picnicking flourished, along with a new sense of American patriotism's rebirth. By war's end, midwesterners welcomed the Fourth of July as an opportunity to celebrate the end of a long and bloody conflict and immortalize the valiant Union victors. But after that initial outburst of patriotism, the holiday became more about blissful forgetfulness and less about truly remembering the reasons for the holiday at all. In the postbellum world, issues of sectional reconciliation, commercialism, and the commodification of the day overwhelmed the Fourth of July. Independence Day would never be the same. In the prophetic words of Joseph Medill as he looked toward the future of the holiday in 1864, "we shall still celebrate, but not as of old."[45]

4 / "The Fourth Celebrates Itself": Recreation, Historical Memory, and the Commodification of Independence Day, 1866–1875

"The observance of the [Fourth] was unmarked by anything extraordinary in our city, unless we may call extraordinary the spectacle of 400,000 people entirely given over to recreation."[1]
– *Chicago Tribune*, JULY 6, 1875

In 1866, Chicagoans kicked off the Fourth of July with pistol fire and a cannonade revelry, using armaments that, the *Tribune* reminded readers, had recently "hurled death and destruction" at Confederate troops. Fireworks sellers and bars remained open that day, the latter selling "whiskey and enthusiasm for a dime." Many Chicagoans escaped to the countryside, picnicking and enjoying "dancing, flirting, reading, chatting, eating, drinking, singing, and music" in the various groves scattered around the Windy City.[2]

These Independence Day festivities typified the postbellum era, reflecting a fundamental shift from antebellum commemorations and revealing the importance of the Civil War as a turning point both in remembrances of the national anniversary and in evolving regional definitions of patriotic loyalty. Celebrants before 1860 often invoked remnants of the revolutionary era, venerating easterners like Washington, Jefferson, Adams, and the heroes of 1776. Postwar revelers, on the other hand, usually recalled the more recent efforts of midwesterners such as Grant, Sherman, Lincoln, and the Union troops in preserving the Union. Prewar celebrations revolved around military parades, social and moral reform efforts, ethnocentric debates over cultural citizenship, and constant comparisons between contemporaries and the founding generation. Postbellum Independence Days centered on recreation, commercialism, struggles over the meaning of the past, and the place of African-Americans in the newly reconstituted nation. After the Civil War, urban midwesterners reinvented the Fourth of July as a commercialized leisure holiday and reclaimed the day from civic boosters, transforming it into, in the words of the editor of *Harper's Weekly*, "the People's day."[3]

Postbellum Independence Day Celebrations

Postbellum urban midwesterners celebrated the Fourth of July in variable fashions. In order to comprehend the breadth of these Independence Day commemorations, it is helpful to take inventory of the festivities marking the holiday between the end of the Civil War and 1875, briefly touring the celebrations typical of the postwar Midwest. Clearly, there was no one way to celebrate the Fourth of July in this era, but from this compendium, certain generalities and trends emerge.

Chicagoans celebrated the Fourth of July much as they had in 1866, with some noteworthy exceptions. In 1869, when the holiday fell on a Sunday, the city celebrated on July 5, as a local militia company and the Chicago "Merchants' and Commercial Travellers Association" cosponsored a celebration that included military drill, footraces, baseball games, cricket, dancing, and a picnic, enticing 20,000 participants to the festivities. In 1871, a baseball game pitting the home White Stockings against their archrivals from nearby Rockford served as the day's biggest draw. After the game, most spectators stayed at the stadium to watch a magnificent fireworks display that could be seen by citizens throughout the Windy City. Summing up postbellum Independence Day commemorations in Chicago, the editor of the *Tribune* remarked in 1875, somewhat tongue-in-cheek, that "the observance of the [Fourth] was unmarked by anything extraordinary in our city, unless we may call extraordinary the spectacle of 400,000 people entirely given over to recreation."[4]

In Cincinnati, Independence Day celebrations followed a similar pattern as recreation and leisure dominated the day's events. In 1868, the St. Louis Unions and Cincinnati Red Stockings played a baseball game to decide the mythical "championship of the West." In 1870, African-American Cincinnatians planned a gathering outside the Queen City on July Fourth, while their white counterparts attended baseball games and picnics. Also that year, four thousand revelers traveled to Parlor Grove and twelve hundred attended the "Merry Young Bachelors Dancing Association" gala. The following year, the editor of the *Enquirer* argued that "the day has degenerated into an occasion for social parties and for private dissipations," as Cincinnatians, overwhelmingly, spent the day at picnics and in preparations for the elaborate fireworks show marking the conclusion of the day's festivities. In 1875, the Marietta and Cincinnati

Railroad company sponsored numerous excursion trains, charging half-price fares to induce rail travel to picnic destinations, promising "all variety of popular amusements, picnic excursions, social parties, theatrical entertainments, terpsichorean hops, fashionable concerts, and rich fun generally, to divert the public mind during our great National holiday."[5]

Informal celebrations also took center stage in Cleveland between 1866 and 1875. Pistol fire and firecrackers welcomed the 1866 Independence Day, as thousands of celebrants prepared for a balloon ascension by the acclaimed Professor Steiner. In 1869, the holiday fell on the Sabbath, causing controversy in Cleveland. Local Germans determined to celebrate on Sunday, provoking members of the local YMCA to decry their actions as "a desecration of the day and a sin against God, a violation of the moral law." In response, American-born Clevelanders hastily assembled a celebration scheduled for Monday, July 5, complete with fireworks and numerous private picnics, demonstrating that ethnic differences remained important, if greatly subdued, in the postbellum era. In 1872, the most prominent event included a rail excursion to Baker's Grove highlighted by a military drill given by the Detroit Light Guards and Cleveland Grays. This was, one editor gushed, "the first time in several years Cleveland . . . celebrated the Fourth of July in the old fashioned way."[6]

Germans dominated postwar Independence Day celebrations in Indianapolis. In 1866, Germans congregated in woods outside the city for an oration (given in their native tongue), patriotic singing, and Turner gymnastic exhibitions. The Mannerchor singing society and the Turners, cosponsoring the event, equally split the proceeds (primarily from beer sales). In 1869, American-born residents joined their German-born brethren in a celebration at Moore's Grove. Citizens "comprised of all nationalities" loaded into rail cars, which toted revelers to and from the festivities every hour, on the hour, throughout the day. In 1870, with no general celebration, one newspaper reported that "numerous society and private picnics had to answer for what used to be grand demonstrations joined in by everybody."[7]

Many Columbus residents also found Independence Day an opportune time to escape from Ohio's capital city. In 1868, Columbus residents celebrated "very generally, and in what may be termed a sort of miscellaneous manner," as some citizens went to a baseball tournament featuring area squads while others cheered on a military procession. In 1871, John Kinney constructed a Temple of Liberty, paid for by private subscriptions. One paper predicted that "different railroads leading into the city will be taxed to their utmost capacity to carry the mass of people who expect to come here on that day to witness the numerous sights," as, in addition to Kinney's display, a baseball tournament "for the championship of Central Ohio" pitted clubs from Delaware and Lancaster against a team from Columbus. The next year, one editor laid out the day's program in great detail. "People will tramp through the dusty streets in procession; exhaust the soda fountains and lemonade stands to the profound astonishment of the stomachs," he began. They will "gulp down flies, bugs, worms, and other trifles in their picnic coffee, and shout themselves into sunstroke over the Star Spangled Banner." The editor also predicted that "private pic-nics will probably abound in Goodale Park, and the owners of fast horses will possibly indulge in a little competition as to speed on the course at the Fair Grounds," while many others "will shed their garments as far as propriety will admit, and lay themselves out for a day of complete relaxation in their homes, and cultivate the acquaintance of their families."[8]

SHIFTS IN MIDWESTERN URBANIZATION
AND REGIONAL IDENTITY

As river transportation yielded to railroad travel, location on or near the Ohio River seemed less enticing to eastern investors and transportation magnates. The Ohio River ceased even to be the most important waterway for regional development, surpassed by the Great Lakes, which connected eastern cities like New York City with rich midwestern agricultural hinterlands. At the same time, railroad transportation overtook both canal and river travel, benefiting certain cities at the expense of others. Cincinnati, in particular, lost its role as the preeminent urban center in the Midwest in the postwar era, passed first by St. Louis and then Chicago. Although Cincinnati boasted a population surpassing 200,000 in 1870, its economic influence declined relative to other midwestern cities. Chicago, located at the southern tip of Lake Michigan, took over as the regional centerpiece, witnessing astonishing population increases of 58,000 during the Civil War and an additional 100,000 in the four years following Appomattox. Other cities also benefited from the ascendancy of the Great Lakes and the birth of a booming rail industry as, by the turn of the twentieth century, Cleveland replaced Cincinnati as Ohio's leading manufacturing and population center. Even by 1870, nearly 93,000 called Cleveland home—many of them first generation immigrants, a definite shift from the city's earlier predominantly New England Yankee character. The transition from river to rail travel did not affect all midwestern cities equally, although most did reap demographic benefits from continued industrialization. Columbus remained little more than an important regional political center in the 1860s, despite a population increase from 18,000 to 31,000 in the decade. Geographic centrality remained Columbus's largest and most exploited advantage, guaranteeing the city's continuation as the state capital and ensuring connections to the state's industrializing regions. Likewise, Indianapolis grew rapidly between 1860 and 1870, more than doubling its prewar population of 18,611 to reach 48,244. But like Columbus, the success of Indiana's capital city continued to rely heavily on its political and geographic centrality.[9]

This period also witnessed the continued maturation of midwestern regional identity. Midwestern regionality can be traced to the late antebellum period, when the Northwest Territory finally disappeared into a well-defined collection of states. By the mid-1870s, the romanticized notion of an American frontier had long since passed Ohio, Indiana, and Illinois. In this context, the Midwest became, somewhat paradoxically, both representative (embodying what was morally right and good about the United States) and unique (attempting to ideologically distance itself from the troublesome racial and class conflicts that seemed to plague other regions of the country). Midwesterners and regional commentators positioned the region to represent the very best qualities of the nation while remaining the sole location that could suitably achieve these qualities. During this era, loose notions of what it meant to be a midwesterner in the early republic gave way to a well-defined regional identity.[10]

Civic boosters played a vital role in this emerging regionality, even as their roles in reshaping midwestern conceptions of American political and social culture by using July Fourth commemorations declined. Postwar politics encouraged raucous partisanship and witnessed record turnouts for elections, as politicians of both parties replaced antebellum issues of sectional animosity and nativism with party identification and partisan loyalty. This political enthusiasm did not transfer to Independence Day celebrations as, instead of attending civic-sponsored parades or politically charged orations, most revelers escaped to the countryside or participated in diverting recreational pursuits.[11]

Commercializing and Commodifying the Holiday

The modes of celebrating the July Fourth holiday and the associated meanings of these commemorations reflected these larger political and cultural trends and can be divided into three distinct categories: commercialism, leisure and recreation, and historical memory. By 1864, midwesterners already started to shift attention on the Fourth of July away from the pressing events of a war-torn nation. Leisurely picnics and commercial amusements replaced benevolent society fund-raisers. Vendors hawking cool beverages and hot snacks supplanted orations reminding Americans about their duty to the nation, while military parades (already in decline by the middle of the war) gave way to baseball games and horse races. These developments mirrored larger cultural changes as postwar consumption patterns and labor concerns merited debate about the role of leisure and play. As historian Matthew Dennis argues, the "commercialization, even trivialization, of the holiday offered Americans a pleasurable escape." To take this one step further, midwesterners not only commercialized or trivialized the Fourth of July: they commodified the event. Between 1866 and 1875, midwesterners transformed the Fourth of July from a patriotic anniversary promoting remembrance to a commercialized event encouraging blissful forgetfulness and purchasable patriotism.[12]

Midwestern businessmen took the lead in commercializing and commodifying Independence Day in this decade. Historically, employers gave employees a well-deserved day off on July 4, marking a rare summer holiday. After the war, this practice became less uniform, particularly in service and retail sectors. In the antebellum era, taverns and saloons often remained open on the holiday, much to the consternation of teetotal reformers. In the postbellum era, restaurants and shops selling patriotic accoutrements or fireworks joined drinking establishments in exploiting the potential profitability of the Fourth of July.

The experiences of Andrew Manning, a young clerk in Cleveland, provide a firsthand account of the growing commercialism and commodification of the Fourth of July. In 1867, 19-year-old Manning inaugurated Independence Day by joining three acquaintances at a local theatre. One young female friend reportedly could not enjoy the show because she "was in fidgets about her new bonnet," purchased especially for the holiday. When the performance was over, the group removed to a nearby parlor for a dinner of ice cream before traveling to a relative's house to shoot off firecrackers. After depleting their supply of pyrotechnics, they reconvened downtown, purchasing more fireworks (as well as soda water and lemonade) before spending the balance of the evening leisurely strolling around the streets of Cleveland and setting off firecrackers. In 1869, Manning again found a group of like-minded associates and spent the day drinking soda, playing billiards, and passing out fireworks to residents of the nearby Orphan's Home. In 1870, young Manning drank champagne and wine and spent the afternoon attending a baseball game. Two years later, his only diary entry was that he ate cherries, smoked, and fiddled.[13]

On its own, Andrew Manning's diary details simply the Independence Day experiences of a single young Clevelander. But Manning was certainly not alone in being swept up in the regional commercialization and commodification of July Fourth. The editor of the *Cleveland Plain Dealer*, in both 1871 and 1872, printed long editorials promoting the confluence of commercial interests and patriotic remembrances of the holiday. In 1871, the editor encouraged area businessmen to raise funds to support a community-wide celebration of the Fourth of July, arguing that sponsors would be "richly repaid" for their patriotism, clearly linking commercial enterprise with nationalistic celebrations. "People would have flocked to Cleveland," the newspaper estimated, "and naturally would have dropped a very considerable amount of money here" if local businesses "would have something on that day worth seeing." The following year, the editor again reminded area businessmen, particularly owners of hotels, restaurants, retail stores, and railway companies, how much they stood to gain from patriotic entrepreneurism, promising that "for every dollar they invest in this way they will receive ten or more from the crowds which will come from the country if something grand is prepared for the entertainment of the populace." He estimated that, with the right promotion, visitors would spend upwards of half a million dollars, and he encouraged residents to "open their purses and try the experiment." Area businessmen did contribute over $4,000 for a large civic celebration in Cleveland that year, with much of the funding fronted by railway companies which, naturally, stood to benefit from attracting rural visitors. The results were astounding, as newspapers unanimously recognized Cleveland's celebration as the state's most jubilant. The *Plain Dealer* estimated that more than 30,000 strangers came to Cleveland for the day's festivities while "the hotels, restaurants, saloons, bakeries and temporary eating and drinking stands . . . were taxed to their utmost capacity to supply the demands of the hungry and thirsty." Cleveland's resurgence demonstrated, in strict economic terms, what the Fourth of July could mean for commercial interests in the urban Midwest. Proprietors found that keeping their stores open on the holiday could be quite profitable for their businesses and that they could deflect discussions about their own commercial successes by maintaining that they provided their patrons with a valuable patriotic public service by selling cold drinks, hot meals, and goods at reasonable prices.[14]

To promote business on the Fourth of July, entrepreneurs consciously and purposefully commodified American patriotism, insisting to potential customers that buying fireworks, food, flags, or other goods reflected patriotic loyalty. Whether their intentions were noble or if, in fact, they simply recognized the advertising potential of purchasable patriotism, certain consumer goods sold quite well on the Fourth of July. Firecracker sales, in particular, soared on and around July 4. In the early republic, young boys celebrated Independence Day by firing pistols into the air. After the Civil War, in part due to increased Chinese immigration on the west coast and better transportation networks to ship incendiaries east, fireworks replaced pistol fire as the preferred Fourth of July noisemaker. In 1873, the editor of the *Cincinnati Enquirer* explicitly tied patriotism to the fireworks industry, asking, "how can a man be willing to fight for his country, who did not when a boy fire crackers in honor of the Liberty of '76?" Soon, youngsters came to consider shooting off fireworks on July Fourth an essential part of commemorating Independence Day. James L. Davis, a Cincinnati youth, wrote in his diary that on the Fourth "juveniles are rejoicing," firing crackers beginning on the evening of July 3. Davis himself often spent the day setting off fireworks, recalling in his diary in 1870 that he was disappointed with his purchase as "the stuff burnt up" before he could even set them off.[15]

Fireworks merchants, however, often had to contend with disapproving city authorities, fearful of a large-scale conflagration and concerned with the safety of their community. Specifically, city officials pointed to the events in Portland, Maine, in 1866 when a stray firework started a fire that consumed much of the town. In addition, newspaper accounts following July 4 regularly described in gruesome detail incidents of boys blowing off fingers or blinding themselves with defective, or improperly used, incendiaries. Some cities in the 1860s and 1870s lifted fireworks ordinances for the holiday while in others, youths simply ignored the ban. In Chicago, in particular, residents and city officials feared another blaze like the Great Fire of 1871. Before Independence Day 1872, local authorities in the Windy City enacted anti-fireworks legislation, entirely outlawing the use of incendiaries, although, as was often the case, officials loosely enforced the law. In response to the ordinance, a young boy named George wrote a letter to the *Tribune*, complaining about the unfairness of the law. "I think it real mean of Mr. Medill [the mayor] not to let us boys have any fun on the Fourth of July," the letter began. The reason, George proposed, was that he had frugally saved his money for weeks "and bought fireworks, and now can't fire them." The most important contribution of the young man's plea, however, was his rationale for firing crackers. George asked rhetorically, "What was the Fourth of July made for if we can't fire crackers?" Clearly young boys like James Davis and George associated Independence Day with commercial endeavors far more closely than with patriotic sacrifice and remembrances of 1776.[16]

Besides selling fireworks, businessmen promoted other consumer goods as necessary features of properly commemorating the Fourth of July and, by extension, of being a patriotic citizen. In particular, midwesterners purchased and hung flags and other red, white, and blue decorations to visibly display their patriotism. In Indianapolis, one newspaper office sold flags of all sizes; 25 cents bought a "cheap edition" while a flag "bound in cloth, with speeches" cost one dollar. During the Civil War, midwesterners decorated their businesses and homes to honor both troops fighting on distant battlefields and the struggle to rebind the Union. The tradition remained and expanded in the postbellum era. "Buildings, public offices, and private residences, by a common impulse, had been profusely decorated with the American flag and other patriotic devices," the *Indianapolis Journal* crowed in 1866, concluding that "to find a building without these decorations was a rare exception." In Cleveland in 1873, the *Plain Dealer* reported that "the whole city was in holiday attire," and that residents even decorated the Perry Monument, commemorating Oliver Hazard Perry's victory in the Battle of Lake Erie during the War of 1812, with patriotic bunting.[17]

Other businessmen utilized the holiday to promote their own goods with a patriotic twist rather than sell explicitly nationalistic items like flags or decorative bunting. These examples, perhaps even more than shopkeepers' selling flags or red, white, and blue fabrics, demonstrate the pervasiveness of commodified patriotism. A Cleveland milliner named McGinness promoted himself as the one man in the city "who is determined to make the people happy on the Fourth of July," promising low prices to fashion residents with affordable headwear. The partnership of Boutall & Doolittle, also of Cleveland, recommended buying their shirts as the "most sensible" choice for "celebrating Uncle Sam's day." Similarly, Indianapolis's J. P. Gramling advertised his "Ready Made Clothing" as a good investment "on the Fourth of July, or any other day," making otherwise mundane items seem patriotic. Also in the Circle City, Davis & Wright promoted a furniture sale "in order that the 4th may be properly celebrated," although the proprietors failed to mention how buying a new dining room table exemplified patriotic loyalty.[18]

Several historians have capably demonstrated this trend toward increased commercialization in celebrations of nationalistic holidays in the wake of the Civil War. Scott Martin, for instance, argues quite cogently that postbellum "commercialization, fragmentation, and privatization of leisure" pervaded American society. But in the urban Midwest, Fourth of July sales were more than just a by-product of commercialized recreation. Independence Day also became a valuable commodity, advertised by businessmen trading in American patriotism. Some entrepreneurs showcased their goods as exemplars of true patriotism and patriotic loyalty while others lauded their amusements and spectacles as the basis of a resurgent and reunified American culture. Postbellum businessmen peddled patriotism, promoting their goods and services by using nationalism and underlying associations between American national identity and the Fourth of July to spur sales and link their particular products to true-blue American patriotism.[19]

CHANGING COMMERCIAL PRACTICES

While many midwesterners seemed to embrace the commercialization and commodification of July Fourth, others debated the propriety of businesses' being open on the day at all, a once solemn holiday that seemed to be devolving into a soulless day of commercialism, recreation, and leisure. "All public offices and many business houses and manufactories were closed during the day," the *Ohio State Journal* reported of Columbus's Fourth in 1871. But the newspaper reminded readers that "some of the leading dry goods emporiums kept open doors until noon." Brash commercialism and businesses open on Independence Day caused a mixed reaction from urban midwesterners. On one hand, open stores were a convenience; on the other, it seemed unpatriotic to force workers to spend the day commemorating America's birth behind a counter hawking the accoutrements of patriotism. Their sentiment about this commercial transformation is most poignantly summarized in an editorial printed in the *Chicago Tribune* in 1868. That year, "the shops and stores were closed at an early hour," as was typical of the era. "But many made amends by charging exorbitant prices for what they sold," the paper lamented, "and when remonstrated with, cheerfully observed that it was the Fourth of July and that the purchaser could either take it or leave it alone." This was an isolated, atypical event, but debates about the propriety of mixing commercial interests and Independence

Day resonated throughout the Midwest in the 1860s and 1870s as mass-distributed and mass-produced consumer goods flooded the market and the postwar economy exploded, predicated on distinctive economic agendas promoted by national political leaders.[20]

In the 1860s and 1870s, a well-defined set of businesses remained open on the Fourth of July. Public offices, banks, courts, and most factories closed entirely on Independence Day, while the service industry ramped up operation to sate public demand. In particular, restaurant owners, saloonkeepers, and other salesmen of food and drink took advantage by remaining open. In Cleveland in 1872, temporary eating and drinking stands "which were numbered by scores . . . were taxed to their utmost capacity to supply the demands of the hungry and thirsty" according to one newspaper account. The next year, the *Cleveland Plain Dealer* reported that these businesses "did a brisk trade," taking advantage of a heat wave to peddle icy cold beverages to holiday revelers. In Columbus in 1872, newspapers advertised "Orange Ice," "Pine Apple Ices," wine, cigars, ale, porter, and beer on Independence Day to appeal to celebrants. Sometimes, in order to afford employees the opportunity to celebrate the Fourth of July, a conglomeration of businessmen self-regulated their industry. In Columbus in 1867, area dry goods merchants signed an accord in which they agreed to all keep their places of business closed on the Fourth, ensuring that no single enterprise would reap the economic benefits of remaining open on Independence Day.[21]

Postbellum Independence Day celebrations also embraced citizens' love of commercial spectacle. In 1875, the *Cincinnati Enquirer* alliteratively advertised July Fourth as promoting "Pageants, Processions, Picnics, Patriotic Parades and Promiscuous Pleasantness." These actions, the editor promised, would "divert the public mind during our great National holiday." Commercial promoters planned extravagant events to draw large crowds, constantly reminding potential customers that displaying their American patriotism depended on patronizing commercial amusements (as well as purchasing the necessary accoutrements). Circuses constituted an important aspect of the holiday in many communities, as the traveling extravaganza often timed visits to large urban areas around Independence Day to benefit from an idle populace. In Columbus in 1868, the Heming, Cooper and Whitbys Circus advertised tumblers, jugglers, and a menagerie on the holiday while a circus traveling to their city in 1874 promised Clevelanders an aviary, Roman hippodrome, and Egyptian caravan. Perhaps most ironically, circus promoters urged Chicagoans to validate their patriotism and American cultural identity on Independence Day in 1872 by attending a "Great Roman Exhibition" pitting "Romans, Greeks, and Wild Arabs" in mock battle. In addition to this "Terrible Conflict" was a "Great Indian Battle, Japanese Bare Back Riding, [and] The Great Comanche Chief and Daughter."[22]

One midwestern businessman, in particular, epitomized the rampant commodification and commercialism of the July Fourth holiday. John M. Kinney was Columbus's answer to P. T. Barnum, constantly promoting his exhibitions, his shows, and himself. In 1871, Kinney planned an exorbitant patriotic spectacle. He erected a "Temple of Liberty" for display on July 4, accompanied by a "Union Fountain." The structure included 13 columns, bearing an equal number of paintings depicting the signing of the Declaration of Independence, decorated garishly with the coats of arms of the 37 states. The dome on top of the edifice was blue and studded with a thousand stars, topped by a carved golden eagle clutching an American flag. Inside the patriotically named Temple stood the coup-de-grace, 37 fountains lit up by gaslights known collectively as the Union Fountain. Kinney estimated the total cost of the construction at $6,000, which he hoped to recoup by selling tickets to the amusement. On July 1, Kinney wrote to the local newspapers, imploring readers to do their duty "as patriotic citizens" and visit the structure, reminding them that a single ticket entitled them not only to the exhibition of the Temple and Fountain, but also to a picnic, balloon ascension, and fireworks held concomitantly on the fairgrounds. Kinney's fountain typified the paradoxical use of nationalism in postbellum commemorations. He made extensive use of national symbols, prominently featuring the eagle, American flag, Declaration of Independence, and national colors. But he utilized these symbols to increase commercial patronage, not solely to remind viewers of America's rich history. This demonstrates a changing mentality about what it meant to be a loyal patriotic American during the 1860s and 1870s—garish amusements and the trappings of patriotism elicited more reaction than debates over patriotic loyalty and inclusiveness, which had been so central to earlier commemorations.[23]

Independence Day celebrations involving amusements, spectacles, and consumer goods replaced the old-fashioned commemorations of antebellum America in which oratory, public dinners, civic processions, and the reading of the Declaration of Independence served to entertain citizens. Urban midwesterners recognized this transition and often tried to reconcile tradition and innovation, just as earlier generations wrestled with their place alongside the nation's founders. In 1866, Chicago boosters did not plan a formal celebration of the Fourth of July, although the

Tribune reported that "those who desire to hear orations can easily be gratified by joining any chance party around a lager beer table" where "the spontaneous oratory which one hears in this way is often quite as instructive as the labored public harangues before the multitude." At Haas Park in Chicago in 1868, the program included both "an old-time celebration," complete with oration and a reading of the Declaration, and "an ascension and performances on the tight rope, and four trained geese . . . made to draw a wash-tub over the Aux Plaines River." That year in Cleveland, the editor of the *Plain Dealer* reported that "it matters little whether the municipal authorities take steps to insure a formal celebration of the Fourth or not," as they had in the past, assessing that "the Fourth celebrates itself, and fire crackers, guns, pistols, patriotism, noise, good feeling, lemonade, etc. are sure to be its characteristics under any circumstances." Instead of seamlessly meshing old-fashioned celebrations with newly emerging conceptions of the proper mode of commemorating Independence Day, these hybrid festivities seemed awkwardly constructed, revealing the important disconnect between memorializing the past and celebrating the present.[24]

LEISURE AND RECREATION

Leisure and recreation served multiple purposes in postbellum Fourth of July celebrations. They provided diversions to keep celebrants from dwelling on the horrors of war (which were, in many ways, linked to conceptions of American patriotism espoused on the Fourth of July) and the failings of America's social and political agendas. Leisure and recreation could also simply provide much-needed respite from the tedium and monotony of industrial work in the postbellum era, as celebrating the Fourth of July became central to arguments about the benefits of the eight-hour workday and other labor demands and an important symbol of freedom—in this case, freedom from the oppression of tyrannical bosses and an industrializing workforce.[25]

Only through relaxation and leisurely endeavors could citizens "refresh mental and physical energies wearied or unstrung by the monotony of the past year's steady toll," an editor for the *Cincinnati Enquirer* argued in 1875. Independence Day served to break up the long, sultry summers in midwestern cities as entrepreneurs and other commentators encouraged workers, afforded a rare holiday, to enjoy the event rather than recall the sacrifice of fallen soldiers (as civic boosters once hoped). A Columbus newspaper remarked in 1869 that the people, "whose leisure movements meant rest and pleasure," thronged the city streets, while the following year it reported that Americans needed to enjoy themselves more, rather than "work so many hours in the day, or so many days in the year." Working-class midwesterners could celebrate the holiday with a relaxing picnic or excursion to an outlying grove instead of following the pattern set forth by middle- and upper-class civic boosters. Leisurely pursuits on the Fourth of July also reminded midwesterners of another American freedom: the freedom to do absolutely nothing in honor of the nation's birth.[26]

Many midwesterners spent leisure time on the Fourth of July with their families, reinforcing the primacy of family groups. Many examples exist of this movement in the Midwest toward familial Independence Day festivities. Elvira Sheridan Badger, a Chicagoan, typified this development, celebrating the holiday exclusively with her family in the years following the Civil War. In 1866, the Badgers had "a fine fourth at home," firing crackers and sipping tea. In 1873, she spent the holiday "at home very quietly," with her children while the next year she again "staid [sic] at home" with her two boys, who spent much of the day shooting off fireworks in the front yard. Similarly, Elisabeth Gookin, also of Chicago, passed most Fourth of July holidays as she did in 1869, "quietly at home," after a brief trip to get ice cream. The *Chicago Tribune* praised this sense of familial togetherness, arguing that celebrating the day as a family was "quite as patriotic" as listening to long-winded orations, shooting firecrackers, and commemorating the "spirit of '76." Likewise, in 1872, one Columbus editor praised local citizens who "lay themselves out for a day of complete relaxation in their homes, and cultivate the acquaintance of their families" on Independence Day. July Fourth served as a respite from everyday life, an opportunity for family and friends to congregate, and, perhaps most importantly, a true reflection of changing American attitudes toward what constituted the proper mode of celebrating of the holiday. Civic-sponsored parades and patriotic oratory were no longer the only ways to properly commemorate Independence Day.[27]

Picnicking on the Fourth of July for families preferring a psychological *and* physical escape from city life became another popular postbellum pastime. In fact, picnics were probably the most oft-mentioned and well-attended events on Independence Day in the 1860s and 1870s. Some affairs involved simple private gatherings, including little more than families or friends meeting in a shaded grove outside the city for a day of eating, relaxing, and togetherness. The *Chicago Tribune*, in 1871, praised this type of commemoration, urging readers to "take your family off all by yourself in the woods" on Independence Day for a relaxing picnic, promising that "in this way an enjoyable Fourth may be spent." Similarly, the editor of the *Columbus Morning Journal* recommended "fresh air and exercise" for July 4, so as to build an appetite for the mounds of fresh berries, ice cream, and lemonade sure to accompany the picnic. Other picnics were more elaborate, requiring revelers to purchase tickets and sometimes including thousands of picnickers. Railroad companies often cross-promoted these more extensive celebrations as rail executives recognized this pent-up urban desire for the countryside and offered half-price fares for Independence Day excursion trains to rural destinations. In this way, rail companies stimulated business both from the city to the countryside and vice versa as urban residents left the cities while their country cousins poured into town.[28]

SPORTING CULTURE AND THE POSTBELLUM FOURTH

While thousands of urban residents fled midwestern cities for quieter and more relaxing picnic quarters on the Fourth of July, numerous amusements in town still attracted patrons from both the city and countryside. Many of these events relied upon the emergence of an American sporting culture blossoming in the postbellum era. The growth of American sports represented part of a larger trend tied to conceptions of muscular Christianity, burgeoning commercialism, and changing definitions of amateurism and professionalism. As historian S. W. Pope argues, "between the mid-1860s and mid-1870s, sports proliferated, and were transformed from local and regional contests into nationally standardized and commercialized ones." Baseball and horse racing, in particular, flourished in this era and shared many characteristics. Both pitted competitors in athletic feats of strength, speed, stamina, and skill. Both took place outdoors in the summer months and, most importantly in this context, horse races and baseball games both became vital aspects of July Fourth celebrations by reflecting and encouraging the growing commodification of the holiday and its accelerating transition toward recreation and leisure.[29]

In 1866, the *Chicago Tribune* reported that "the American people are fast becoming infatuated with a love of the sports of the turf." After the Civil War, horse racing emerged as a popular pastime in the Midwest, brought from Britain and, like many British imports, readily adapted to the American culture and climate, placing speed above pageantry and mainstream culture above the high society of the sport of kings. Horse racing first took root in places like Saratoga Springs in upstate New York, soon the most famous resort and horse racing venue in the

United States. The Saratoga Race Course opened in 1863—in the midst of the Civil War—and became especially popular among eastern elites. But midwesterners also quickly became intoxicated by the allure of the track. In 1867, Chicagoans opened the Dexter Driving Park on July 4, enticing racing enthusiasts and trainers with a $1,000 purse for the park's very first heat. The next year, the purse was larger, with stakes up to $1,500 for a race deemed the "American Independence Post" in honor of the national birthday. By 1871, one purse, for a trotting match, reached $5,000, drawing thousands of spectators to witness (and bet on) the high-stakes race. Other midwesterners also promoted and patronized horse races on the Fourth. In 1872 at the Buckeye track in Cincinnati, an estimated 25,000 spectators gathered for a series of trotting races while Cleveland's *Plain Dealer* regularly provided details about the stakes in that city. Summing up the ties between the Fourth of July and horse racing, James Comly, the editor of the *Columbus Ohio State Journal*, reported that the races "constituted the main feature of the celebration of Independence Day, and the sport was good."[30]

Although horse racing became a popular Independence Day spectacle and amused thousands of itinerant young men, it paled in comparison to the popularity of baseball, a sport that quickly became America's national pastime. Baseball was an ideal match for the postbellum Fourth of July, promoting recreation for participants, leisure and family togetherness for spectators, and commercial opportunities for promoters. Additionally, baseball emerged in this era as an important symbol of developing postwar understandings of American nationalism, patriotism, and cultural identity tied to the Fourth of July.

A compendium of historical inaccuracies and folk history cloud the origins of baseball. In 1905, a dispute between rivals Henry Chadwick and A. G. Spalding led to the creation of the Mills Commission, charged with determining the historical roots of the game of baseball. Seeking an American origin story to distance the sport from its European cousin of rounders, the Mills Commission attributed the invention of the game to a former Civil War general, Abner Doubleday, locating the game's roots in Cooperstown, New York. Despite solid evidence that Doubleday was hundreds of miles from Cooperstown in 1839 (when he supposedly invented the game in a cow pasture) and obvious links between baseball and English bat and ball games, the Doubleday myth stuck and baseball was granted its American origin. As historian S. W. Pope argues, "the Doubleday myth created a fertile framework within which the game could be used to extol the virtues of the American character."

Baseball epitomized and rewarded the Protestant, individualistic, rural values that symbolized early American society and continued to influence midwestern ethics in the 1860s and 1870s. In many ways, baseball functioned on the same level as Independence Day, bridging the past and present by connecting a popular modern sport with a creation tale exuding patriotic nationalism.[31]

Baseball quickly gained popularity in eastern urban centers in the late antebellum era, representing "part pastoral country game and part scientific, rational urban amusement," in the words of one historian. Eastern gentlemen lauding the game's healthfulness and social interaction became its earliest promoters, transforming the voluntary associations of the 1830s and 1840s promoting temperance and social activism into organized baseball clubs just a decade later. During the 1840s and 1850s, the game grew in popularity, especially among blue collar workers and immigrants, who, shut out of more respectable clubs, formed their own squads. In 1858, the *Atlantic Monthly* described "our indigenous American game of baseball" and how it suited the national character with its "briskness and unceasing activity" as opposed to the slothful pace of cricket. During the Civil War, members of eastern baseball clubs joined the Union army and brought with them their love of the game, prompting Charles A. Peverelly to write in 1866 that "the game of Base Ball has now become beyond question the leading feature of the out-door sports of the United States."[32]

Soldiers disseminated baseball throughout the midwestern frontier and formed their own teams modeled after eastern clubs. In 1866, young men returning from the war formed three baseball clubs in Columbus: the Buckeyes, Capitals, and Excelsiors. In Chicago, the White Stockings began play in 1871, joining the Continental and the Actives, both established in 1867. Clevelanders formed the Forest City team in 1866 and the Railway Union club in 1868, while Indianapolis's principal team was simply named "The Indianapolis Team." These were all ostensibly amateur teams (though top players regularly received cushy jobs from discerning owners), often comprising clerks and other young businessmen who regularly competed against other area and regional squads for recreation, social interaction, and community bragging rights. These teams, however, paled in comparison to the most famous club in the region, which began play in Cincinnati shortly after the end of the Civil War.[33]

A group of attorneys established the Cincinnati Red Stockings in 1866. The Red Stockings remained an amateur club until 1869 when Harry Wright, the team's star pitcher, brought overt professionalism to baseball, recruiting better players by paying regular salaries and expecting to turn a profit from ticket sales. To increase revenue, the now-powerful Red Stockings barnstormed throughout the nation, finishing their first season as professionals an undefeated 57–0. Baseball clubs in New York, Boston, and Philadelphia quickly countered, paying players to compete with the Red Stockings. From then on, baseball functioned on multiple levels: from professional to amateur to sandlot. The professionalism of baseball built on the consumerism and commercialism rampant in the postbellum era, further entrenching the growing sport as an American pastime and reflecting the evolving cultural identity of the urban Midwest. A London newspaper, *The Field*, covering a barnstorming tour by teams from Boston and Philadelphia, perhaps best described this phenomenon. "Base-ball with the Americans is the sport-of sports," the paper reported. "Its influence is unbounded and its supremacy preeminent over the American continent," the reporter gushed, concluding that "it is essentially suited to the American disposition."[34]

Links between baseball and the Fourth of July emerged during this era of professionalization. Promoters quickly recognized the potential profitability and visibility provided by combining the leading national holiday with the emerging national sporting phenomenon. To best profit from the holiday's associations with baseball, clubs often reserved the Fourth of July for particularly engaging contests. Sometimes social societies played friendly matches on Independence Day. In 1867, in Indianapolis, the local YMCA sponsored an intramural baseball game on the Fourth, enticing potential members to their picnic grounds with promises of lively recreational activity. In Chicago in 1870, rival lodges of the Odd Fellows played baseball after a combined picnic celebration. The following year, the *Chicago Tribune* estimated that there would be "fifty or sixty 'snipe' games" between young men as well as a match between boys at the Reform School. Other holiday games pitted rival cities or towns battling one another on the baseball diamond, giving players important bragging rights predicated on the game's outcome. In 1868, the Capital Base Ball Club of Columbus spent the Fourth of July playing in a tournament in nearby Gallion against squads from throughout the area. The villages of Delaware and Lancaster regularly sent teams to the state capital "to compete with our Columbus boys for the championship of Central Ohio," while the Indianapolis squad often welcomed the Kekionga Nine from Fort Wayne for a holiday match. Cleveland teams regularly played Detroit clubs for regional dominance, often incorporating the day's games into larger-scale festivities centered on the baseball field and including fireworks and picnicking to further entice spectators. The Chicago White Stockings and Rockford Forest Citys, the latter led by future Baseball Hall of Famers Cap Anson and A. G. Spalding, had regular matches on the Fourth. In 1868, the Unions of St. Louis challenged the Cincinnati Red Stockings for "the championship of the West" in a contest lauded as "the game of the season," won easily by the still-amateur Cincinnati club.[35]

Baseball and the Fourth of July became inseparable during the post-bellum era. The nationalization and universal appeal of baseball brought together rural and urban participants and members from all socio-economic classes while promoting regional and intercity rivalries. In this context, debates about the place of baseball on Independence Day became part of a larger cultural discussion about properly commemorating the holiday. Some civic leaders "saw frivolous amusements as being the bane of patriotism and national unity," one historian argues, while "an emergent generation of educated, middle-class individuals saw the opposite"—insisting that mass culture and enthusiastic recreation could assist the creation and implementation of "new civic standards," changing, but certainly not eliminating, conceptions of patriotic loyalty. By the mid-1870s, a "good" American could, perhaps, play or watch baseball on the Fourth of July, regardless of socioeconomic class or ethnic background.[36]

The Role of Historical Memory

Divergence between adherents of the emerging sporting culture and midwesterners striving to keep the Fourth of July as a sacred holiday of remembrance prompted debates about the role of historical memory, the third component of postbellum Independence Day celebrations. As recreational and leisure pursuits replaced militia procession and patriotic oratory, midwesterners contorted the significance of the Fourth of July. "It was the universal practice until within the last few years," the *Cincinnati Enquirer* reported, for every town to have a formal celebration, including the reading of the Declaration of Independence and an oration. But that practice, the newspaper explained, had fallen into disuse. It was regrettable, the editor lamented, because "it seemed to keep in the National heart the remembrance of 1776," and served to educate "the youthful mind in patriotic principles that governed them through life." The editor of the *Chicago Tribune* agreed, arguing that "very few . . . have the slightest idea of the causes which led to the Fourth of July." As the

Centennial celebration of 1876 approached, the American Revolution seemed increasingly remote. Nearly a century had passed since the Founding Fathers signed the Declaration of Independence, and major events in the succeeding decades clouded the story of 1776. These transformations caused the editor of the *Tribune* to conclude that "the old Fourth of July has become mouldy with age."[37]

Sweeping changes in commemorations of the Independence Day holiday and in conceptions of American culture led some midwesterners between 1866 and 1875 to wonder why, indeed, they celebrated the holiday at all and, more alarmingly, to question the need for a day losing its immediacy and potency. Independence Day signified American freedom from British tyranny, but, by the 1860s, internal turmoil seemed far more dangerous to the nation's future than foreign invasion. The holiday glorified the heroes of the American Revolution—Washington, Adams, Jefferson, and Franklin—but the postbellum generation had its own pantheon of luminaries—Lincoln, Grant, Sherman, and Sheridan. Should they be less venerated than the Founding Fathers? Or did they deserve equal (or even greater) acclamation for saving in 1865 the nation the founders had created in 1776?

The rise of Memorial Day and other holidays of remembrance compounded these issues, further diminishing the historical role of the Fourth of July as it vied for patriotic attention on the American social calendar. Memorial Day originated in the Confederacy, but was copied by northerners and dubbed Decoration Day, designed as an opportunity to decorate the graves of fallen Civil War soldiers. Although Joseph Medill, the editor of the *Chicago Tribune*, acknowledged that there would be "some disinclination" by Unionists to decorate Confederate graves, and vice versa, he predicted that this would "fade as the passions of the war disappear" and that Americans would "generally render the same tribute to the fallen dead of both armies." Above all, Memorial Day would serve as a "festival common to whites and blacks, Unionists and rebels, Democrats and Republicans," aided immeasurably by support from the Grand Army of the Republic. It was to be universal and without the cultural and historical baggage of the Fourth of July, linked irrevocably to both the Union army and the heroes of 1776, who seemed irrelevant, antiquated, or too polarizing in the postbellum nation.[38]

In 1867, the *Chicago Tribune* ran an editorial arguing that midwesterners celebrated the Fourth of July with less and less enthusiasm every year, concluding that although the day "must forever remain distinguished as the anniversary of the Declaration, the people will turn to some other day in the calendar," which "commemorate other national events of more recent date." The result, the editor argued, would "hereafter divide with this anniversary the favor and enthusiasm of the American people." In 1870, an article published in the *Cincinnati Enquirer* served to inculcate readers as to the purpose of the Fourth of July and to justify its continued celebration. "The Fourth of July originated some distance back," the editorial began vaguely, "when holidays were few, and the means of amusement limited." With increasing possibilities for enjoyment on the Fourth (as more celebrants preferred commercial and recreational endeavors than somber remembrances of the Founding Fathers), and the advent of less politically contentious holidays, revelers paid less attention to the traditions historically associated with Independence Day. The editor of the *Enquirer* reported that, since the first Fourth of July in 1776, "great events have intervened which have not destroyed the memory of our beginning as a nation but have given it less relative importance." In 1874, a writer for the *Chicago Tribune* argued that soon "the day will scarcely be recognized except as a general holiday," lacking the distinctive nationalistic features defining earlier Independence Day commemorations. Military parades, cannonade revelry, and boisterous oration were things of the past, according to one editor who lamented that "the Fourth of July has lost its pristine significance."[39]

Occasionally, midwesterners even seemed to forget what they were commemorating. One editor claimed to overhear an Irish servant contemptuously remark that July Fourth was celebrated with more enthusiasm in Ireland than in America, obviously ignorant of the origins of the holiday. A letter from Margarethe Winkelmeiner of Indianapolis to her parents in Germany demonstrated a similar lack of historical knowledge. Margarethe reported to her parents that, "On the 4th of July no one has to work, the day is a holiday because that's the day the war ended and they made peace." Perhaps to combat this lack of historical consciousness, the *Columbus Morning Journal* recommended that adults tell their children the story of the history of the Fourth of July so that they "may not be wholly in ignorance of the import of the term."[40]

THE TRANSFORMATIVE POWER OF THE CIVIL WAR

The Civil War dramatically altered this historical memory, particularly influencing how race and regional identity fit into prevailing conceptions of what it meant to be an American. On the Fourth of July, midwesterners vigorously debated how to explain the events leading up to the war and to rationalize newly constructed conceptions of race. One argument revolved around how to reintegrate the South into the American nation. Much of this debate concerned memorializing the past. How would the former Confederate states be received if allowed to reenter American society? What would be the role of newly freed African-Americans? Northerners addressed these questions gradually over time, but followed one general trend. As historian David Blight contends, northerners welcomed former Confederates back with open arms, while African-Americans faced vilification and cultural disenfranchisement. Instead of a biracial coalition of northerners and freed blacks, the North, by and large, left African-Americans out of their developing visions of America's future. Northerners replaced their Civil War allies with members of the newly reconstructed South in an alliance of white men in which race trumped past sectional and political indiscretions.[41]

A series of editorials printed in the Republican *Chicago Tribune* between 1866 and 1869 traces the intersection of sectional reconciliation, midwestern conceptions of American nationalism, and their relationships to the Fourth of July. In 1866, the *Tribune* included a piece attempting to properly portray the sentiment of Windy City residents immediately following the war. The Fourth of July that year began with a cannonade revelry, leading the editor of the newspaper to remind his readers that those same ordnances had served the Union effort faithfully when "facing the nation's foes," hurling "death and destruction" at the rebel forces. Sectional reconciliation was in its earliest stages in 1866 when the editor, Joseph Medill, expressed his desire that the next anniversary of American independence would dawn on a people "who have but one aim, one thought, one heart, and that centered upon the cause of freedom, liberty, and everlasting Union," although even Medill acknowledged that the chances were slim. In 1866, as he realized, most midwesterners believed that the South had not yet earned the right to be reintegrated back into the United States—at least not on terms equal to those of the states that had remained loyal to the Union cause—and that the wounds cut too deep to already be fully healed. In 1867, despite the desire for reconciliation expressed the previous year, Medill conceded that the Fourth would "for many years" only "serve to remind [the South] that they are involuntary dwellers in a land where all men have the inalienable right of liberty," lamenting the fact that "the Fourth of July has lost character" because of Southern odium for the holiday. Yet in 1868, he argued that finally "the traces of a terrible, intense war have been obliterated," and that the states of the former Confederacy had, at least on the surface, adopted Reconstruction measures and prepared to "ensure order and freedom within their boundaries." Most importantly, he noted, Democrats and Republicans from all areas of the reconstituted nation busily prepared for the presidential contest between Ohio-born Ulysses S. Grant and New Yorker Horatio Seymour. Medill promised that the contest, unlike the election of Lincoln eight years earlier, would be "a peaceful one" with results "accepted peacefully" by men from both the North and the South. By 1869, sectional reconciliation was, at least in the eyes of the Republican editor of the *Tribune*, almost complete, even at the expense of celebrating the Fourth of July. "Two new festivals have arisen out of the painful events of the recent war for the Union and for social freedom," the editorial proclaimed. One was Memorial Day, while, according to Medill, the other was "mainly for the colored race only," commemorating both the Emancipation Proclamation and the fall of Richmond. Medill predicted that together these two holidays would out-pace Independence Day and that the Fourth would "pass gradually and slowly, but certainly into disuse."[42]

Many midwestern newspapers echoed similar sectionalist sentiments during the late 1860s, although not predicting the doom of Independence Day quite as certainly as the *Tribune*. In 1866, the *Cincinnati Enquirer* printed an editorial arguing that the Declaration of Independence would "sound queerly to those of our fellow-citizens who are in the South," and questioned how the nation would "get over these ugly reminiscences on the coming Fourth." In Cleveland, the Democrat-dominated *Plain Dealer* printed an anti-Republican rant, blaming that party for ruining Independence Day and causing the holiday to lose all "sacredness in their eyes," adding that "negro emancipation and suffrage are considered of greater interest and value than the freedom and rights of white men." The *Plain Dealer* also speculated that Republicans were "ashamed and even afraid to have the Declaration of Independence read on the Fourth of July," because it reminded them of "their mis-government and tyranny exercised over these [Confederate] States." By 1869, the *Plain Dealer*, like its counterpart in Chicago, estimated that the South was fully integrated into the American nation. "We are all One now," the paper crowed, predicting a "future of unexampled splendor" in the reconstituted nation.[43]

AFRICAN-AMERICANS

The most visible reason for paying greater attention to sectional reconciliation on the Fourth of July involved the growing presence of free African-Americans in the urban Midwest. Thousands of newly freed African-Americans poured into midwestern towns, escaping postbellum sharecropping and tenant farming (only slightly preferable to slavery) and viewing the region, as had their ethnic American predecessors in the antebellum era, as a land of unbridled economic, political, and social opportunity. The three states considered in this study—Ohio, Indiana, and Illinois—witnessed widespread African-American migration in the 1860s. The number of African-Americans in Ohio rose by 72 percent, from 36,673 to 63,077. In Indiana, their population more than doubled its prewar total of 11,428, and in Illinois it quadrupled to nearly 29,000 (from 7,628) during the decade. In general, these migrants faced terrible poverty, escaping the South with little more than the shirts on their backs, and moved as family units, hoping to scratch out a meager existence on midwestern soil.[44]

Many African-Americans chose to relocate to midwestern urban centers, drawn by economic opportunity, industrial expansion, and already settled black communities. What they found, however, was an entrenched white population unwilling to concede jobs, neighborhoods, political rights, or economic opportunity to free blacks. Only the lowest, most menial jobs incorporated African-Americans, and housing remained intensely segregated. The percentage of blacks in these cities remained small—less than 4 percent in every case—despite raw population increases. Even as African-Americans increased in number, they were overwhelmed by waves of immigrants much more likely to be included in American cultural citizenship than were blacks. Instead of finding their elusive dreams of freedom, African-American migrants encountered black codes and racial exclusion laws designed to restrict them to the lowest rungs of midwestern society.[45]

Despite relatively low percentages of African-Americans in the urban Midwest, their visibility on the Fourth of July increased dramatically in the postbellum era. In many ways, there was a shift in focus from ethnicity to race as white-skinned immigrants gained the benefits of cultural citizenship that had been withheld from them decades earlier when the region battled nativism and virulent ethnocentrism. But African-Americans, due to their skin color, remained outside the cultural polity. On Independence Day, free blacks faced one of the strictest tests of American cultural and political citizenship—participating in July Fourth celebrations historically dominated by white men. In Columbus in 1867, the Republican Party held a nominating convention on Independence Day. The committee endorsed Phil Sheridan for president, and then called for Frederick Douglass "and other colored orators" to "canvass the State," stumping for the former Union general. In Cleveland, the city's black

population regularly celebrated the holiday with great exuberance, especially in 1873. In that year, African-Americans gathered at Garrett's Hall
to hear a patriotic address delivered by J. M. Gregory of Howard University, an all-black institution established just seven years earlier. After the
address, celebrants listened to other speeches or danced, congregating
together without fear of white intrusion or discrimination.[46]

Cincinnati's sizable African-American community, in particular,
publicly celebrated Independence Day with great exuberance after the
Civil War. To these free men and women, the Fourth of July symbolized the hope of freedom and equality for all. Lockland, a village just
north of the Queen City, hosted a "grand demonstration on the Fourth"
in 1870 for area African-Americans, celebrating both Independence Day
and the ratification of the Fifteenth Amendment, completed earlier that
year. Peter Clark, one of the nation's leading black abolitionists, joined
"other colored celebrities" to give orations at Lockland, drawing thousands from Cincinnati's growing African-American population. In 1872,
African-American Cincinnatians planned their greatest Independence
Day festival to date, a July Fourth picnic held just outside the city limits.
The *Cincinnati Enquirer* reported that it was "a huge affair, numerically
considered." Revelers spent the day eating, drinking, and "rolling and
tumbling," joyously celebrating Independence Day in a racially segregated setting.[47]

Most white midwesterners did not view increased African-American
visibility on Independence Day in a positive light, retaining aspects of
their prewar racism. The *Cincinnati Enquirer*, remarking on the 1872
African-American picnic, accused the festivity of being no more than "a
political mass colored meeting," spent praising General Grant's corrupt
administration. In 1868, the *Indiana State Sentinel* reported that "three
Irishmen and five darkies engaged in a free fight" on the holiday, though
the paper provided no additional details. In 1875, multiple outbreaks of
violence involving African-Americans occurred on July 4. In Columbus,
a notorious white vagabond, Pete Truitt, picked a fight with a black man,
Walter Lyon, at an area saloon. The situation grew tense as Truitt called
Lyon vulgar names before stabbing and killing him in cold blood. Lyon's
acquaintances tried to intercede on behalf of their friend, but Truitt
attacked them as well before authorities could seize and arrest the white
assailant. In Cincinnati the same year, Louis Donnelly, a cook at a local
saloon, spent the Fourth idly shooting a pistol at cats in a deserted alley.
Unfortunately for Donnelly, a white man wandered into the alley. Donnelly shot the young man but protested his innocence, claiming that it

was an accident even as the police hauled him to jail. The *Cincinnati Enquirer* protested as well, but not in favor of Donnelly. Instead, they argued simply that "the Fourth of July need not be a day of human butchery in Cincinnati," especially when perpetuated by African-Americans.[48]

African-Americans found themselves in a very precarious position in postbellum July Fourth commemorations in the urban Midwest. They were eager to participate in Independence Day celebrations and seemed to consider it an important part of what it meant to be an American. As Brian Page, in his work on postbellum Memphis, argues, "celebrating the Fourth of July became a rite of identity, history and memory for African Americans, who made the day their own unique event." But African-American midwesterners also hesitated to parade their new enfranchisement around the drunken white racists that seemed especially vicious (and numerous) on July 4. Instead, African-American revelers often escaped to nearby parks or groves to celebrate American independence without fear of racial retribution.[49]

In the postbellum era, midwesterners celebrated the Fourth of July nearly universally, if in a dramatically different manner than their antebellum predecessors. Some businesses remained open, families gathered together to relax and enjoy one another's company, boys shot off fireworks and attended circuses, and young men played baseball, bet on horse races, or went on relaxing picnics with loved ones. The meaning of the holiday and its association with American patriotism also evolved. With the exception of African-Americans, still in the early stages of determining the boundaries of their new political citizenship, Independence Day no longer served as a dividing ground, ostracizing outsiders and defining the limits of American cultural identity. Instead, the holiday became a commodity, reinforcing rampant commercialism and leisure time, and signifying a transformation in the nation's political, social, economic, and cultural arenas. As the *Chicago Tribune* reported in 1869, the Fourth of July had become "a day of enthusiasm, of hilarity, and festivity" rather than one of solemnity and remembrance. As 1876, the year of the American Centennial, approached, civic boosters forced urban midwesterners to face their past—balancing veneration of the founders with a future promising commercial enterprise, technological progress, and a new generation of national heroes.[50]

5 / "The End of a Century": Celebrating the Centennial, 1876

"When at this distance of time we look back through the vista of a hundred revolving years, and see the whole train of events which followed the declaration of independence as effects follow a cause, and when we observe the glorious results . . . it is easy in our enthusiasm to see the path of duty and of honor which lay before our ancestors."[1]

—GEORGE L. CONVERSE

Henry C. Noble, a Columbus attorney, addressed a large crowd on July 3, 1876, in commemoration of the national centennial. Noble devoted much of his Independence Day oration to brief anecdotes about the region's early history, reminding listeners that, just one hundred years earlier, the Midwest existed only "in a state of nature; its forests unbroken by the labors of civilized man." After detailing the progress in the intervening years, Noble finally reached his central argument. "We have come together to-night to commemorate the end of the first century of our National existence," Noble proclaimed to the enthusiastic crowd, adding that "To-morrow the new century begins." Many midwesterners agreed with Noble's assertion, marking 1876 both as the end of one era, rich with history, and the beginning of another, full of promise.[2]

The Importance of 1876

As the one-hundredth anniversary of American independence, the centennial celebration of July Fourth, 1876 provides closure to the larger story of developing regional conceptions of American patriotism, nationalism, and the mode of commemorating Independence Day in the mid-nineteenth-century urban Midwest. Celebrations in 1876 differed imperceptibly from those in the preceding decade, and many of the prevalent issues of the era remained pertinent in the year of the American centennial, as leisure, recreation, and commercialization dominated the day's informal events. But 1876 was remarkable in an important way, as celebrations of the national birthday stimulated renewed debate about the past and present. On the Centennial Fourth of July, many urban mid-westerners (particularly civic boosters) took an opportunity to step back and take stock of the United States, reconsidering their shared past and discussing the relationship between the nation's birth and what it meant to be an American. Boosters insisted that citizens commemorate the day in the style of their forefathers: listening to patriotic oratory and read-ings of the Declaration of Independence, marching in processions, and solemnly recalling the sacrifices made by the founding generation. Some midwesterners acted accordingly, allowing civic-sponsored celebrations to once again play an important role in commemorations of the holiday. But many midwesterners continued their preference for commercialism, recreation, and leisure. The struggle for civic boosters in 1876, perhaps even more so than in years previous, was convincing midwesterners to recall the glories of America's past while celebrating the vitality of its present and future.

PAST AND PRESENT CLASH IN THE NEW YEAR

Discussions about the role of historical memory and how commemo-rating the national centennial helped define what it meant to be an American began as early as January 1876. Next to the Fourth of July, January 1st was the most celebrated date in 1876, and orators and revel-ers used the opportunity to promote the nation's glorious past. In India-napolis, fire alarm bells rang in the year; a few minutes before midnight, the bells "were made to strike 1776, and at precisely 12 o'clock 1876 was struck." In the Queen City, the *Cincinnati Daily Times* reminded readers that, in 1776, Americans were not yet independent on the first of January (it wasn't, of course, until June 11 that Jefferson composed his famous rebuke of British tyranny), stating that "it would be well to remember that no hundredth anniversary of anything looking toward National Independence had yet arrived." In Chicago, the *Inter-Ocean* welcomed the New Year with an extensive article surveying American history, enti-tled "Progress of the Republic—Chronology of the Principal Events from 1776 to 1876." This editorial included details about the presidential elec-tions, wars, technological innovations, and significant acts of Congress that had defined, at least in the mind of the editor of the *Inter-Ocean*, the first century of the nation.[3]

Despite incessant reminders about the past while greeting the New Year, revelers also acted to promote the present status of the nation and the progress of the United States as it looked forward, rather than backward, to its July national centennial. In Chicago, "the shooting of Chinese crackers and cannon reminded the spectator more of the 4th of July than mid-winter" as people thronged the city streets to welcome 1876, while in Cincinnati, the "Centennial Jamboree," kicking off the New Year, became "a day of social enjoyment." Also on that day, Reverend S. A. W. Jewett of Chicago preached a sermon entitled "Forgetting the Past" in which he quoted a particularly pertinent piece of scripture. "But this one thing I do," Jewett recited from the third chapter of Philippians, "forgetting those things which are behind and reaching forth unto those things which are before." The *Inter-Ocean* echoed this sentiment, albeit in less religious language, reminding citizens that "but while the Declaration of Independence, the organization of the government, and the war of the first Revolution constitute the striking features of remembrance," the "growth of the country in a hundred years, in population, territory, wealth and influence among the nations of the earth, cannot fail to inspire feelings of the liveliest satisfaction."[4]

Celebrations of New Year's Day throughout the urban Midwest merely previewed the coming Independence Day. One Indianapolis newspaper reported of the city's New Year's celebration that "the echoes of the guns fired last night and to-day will gather strength as they roll along the months to the culminating day of the year—the Fourth of July." Similarly, a Cincinnati broadsheet reminded readers that "the beginning of the true centennial year—the Fourth of July" remained a few months away, urging "our intensely patriotic people" to "restrain the further ebullition of their joy" until midsummer. Editorials and sermons delivered early in 1876 merely provided a prelude to the coming Independence Day but already included midwesterners wrestling with issues of historical memory. Soon after greeting the first day of 1876, residents of midwestern cities began planning for the Centennial Fourth. By late June, every midwestern urban center featured extensive arrangements for celebrating the coming anniversary.[5]

URBAN MIDWESTERNERS AND THE CENTENNIAL FOURTH

Each midwestern city had a different mode of celebrating the Fourth of July in 1876. Sampling the individual celebrations (first the official, civic-sponsored fetes and then the unofficial celebrations inaugurated by the patriotic masses) in these five urban centers demonstrates the ways in which midwesterners compartmentalized the past and present, trying both to honor historical memory and celebrate what the nation had become. Most of the various commemorations resembled earlier festivities, but in 1876, every event and decision seemed magnified in light of the national centennial.

As the Fourth of July approached, Cleveland's civic boosters ramped up preparations for celebrations planned and paid for by their municipal government. For decades, civic boosters implored local leaders to sponsor official community-wide remembrances of the Fourth of July. It took a national centennial for their pleas to be heard, as Cleveland's city council budgeted more than $1,500 for an extensive fireworks show, a naval regatta (in honor of Commodore Perry's heroic actions in the Battle of Lake Erie during the War of 1812), and a military procession featuring twelve bands, three thousand singing schoolchildren, and numerous war veterans. One newspaper editor promised "the greatest Fourth ever celebrated in Cleveland." In fact, some Clevelanders so eagerly anticipated the Fourth of July that they began celebrating on June 28, as veterans of Cleveland's leading militia company—the Grays—clustered in a nearby military encampment constructed especially for the centennial. Planners set up the camp "in true military style," complete with tents, temporary barracks, a mess hall, drill, and guard duty. The militiamen, mostly Civil War veterans, spent their days telling and retelling war stories and reliving past martial glories. At sunrise on July 4, several of these veterans loaded and fired cannons. Their artillery salute broke the sleepy quietude of Cleveland, but church and fire bells soon joined the cacophony in a sound recalled by one bystander as "noise enough for a hundred years to come." The clamor did not cease after the artillery revelry as thousands of strangers poured into the city from excursion trains, bringing with them noisy children and the incessant sounds of a pleasure-seeking horde. Crowds thronged the city streets on Independence Day, drawn by the street parade (stretching out over two miles and lasting for several hours) and the aforementioned military encampment. Looking back on the centennial Fourth of July, the *Plain Dealer* proclaimed that only three events in the city's past compared with the celebration of that day: Abraham Lincoln's funeral procession, the unveiling of the monument to Oliver Hazard Perry, and the city's first balloon ascension.[6]

In Columbus, civic preparations began on June 21 when the city council appointed a special committee charged with planting a tree in Capitol Square in honor of the centennial. By the 28th, the city council had received, by private subscription, more than two thousand dollars for a citywide, civic commemoration of the holiday. The council distributed the funds among numerous endeavors, allocating eight hundred dollars for an extensive fireworks display, four hundred dollars to pay for instrumental music, and two hundred dollars for the "committee on Fun" to properly inaugurate the Fourth of July through exuberant festivity. Unlike their Cleveland counterparts, citizens of Ohio's capital city did not wait until sunrise to welcome the centennial. Instead, at precisely midnight a local scientist named Professor Mendenhall opened up rows of calcium lights, pointed at and illuminating the dome of the capitol building. The brilliant luminosity signaled area residents that the Centennial Fourth had arrived at last. Columbus citizens responded by ringing bells, blowing train steam whistles, and firing cannonade. As in Cleveland, the din was deafening but impressive. In fact, the editor of the *Ohio State Journal* only lamented that the "noise cannot be printed, photographed or engraved," as 50,000 people joined in a spontaneous, cacophonous revelry in the middle of the night. Although Columbus's mayor had earlier proclaimed a ban on fireworks (insistent that his town should not burn down on the Centennial Fourth), hundreds of boys spent the hours before dawn shooting off crackers, further illuminating the night sky and, in the poetic words of one local editor, "flinging explosives in the face of the infant Second Century."[7]

The rest of the day in Columbus was tame by comparison, although thousands of men, women, and children poured into Ohio's capital city to commemorate the occasion. A procession, representing the different trades and manufacturers of the city, marked the prominent event of the daytime celebration, paid for and sponsored by the city council's subscription efforts. Numerous commercial floats participated in the parade. Manufacturers bore the Goddess of Liberty clutching a 25- foot-tall staff carrying the American flag. Blesch & Kile, a local plumbing firm, constructed a float complete with "workmen busily engaged in putting up work," and the Singer Sewing Machine company sent ten wagons, one including young ladies demonstrating the company's newest needlework technology. The editor of the *Ohio State Journal* summed up the day in Columbus with a final closing line. "Taken altogether," he concluded, "the one hundredth anniversary of American independence was a day that will long be remembered by the citizens of Columbus and all those who participated in the celebration on that day."[8]

Indianapolis's centennial commemoration mirrored Columbus's festivities. Anticipating large crowds, railroad companies commissioned special trains to bring residents of Indiana's vast rural hinterland to the Circle City. An estimated 25,000 men, women, and children poured into town on these excursion cars, flooding the capital with strangers. An extensive parade organized and funded by the Indianapolis city council attracted many of these visitors. Hundreds of participants, including members of voluntary organizations, manufacturers, and trade associations, marched in a long procession, cheered on by thousands of spectators. Summing up the day's efforts in the midst of a devastating economic depression, the *Indiana State Sentinel* proclaimed that, "It was hard times yesterday, and will be to-morrow, but to-day is the Centennial Fourth of July" and should be celebrated accordingly. In spite of conditions crippling the present, many revelers in Indianapolis determined to commemorate the nation's past and anticipate a better future.[9]

The Fourth of July in Cincinnati revolved around two main spectacles, both governmentally sponsored: an all-day festivity at the Exposition Hall and an extensive military procession. The city of Cincinnati had acquired the Exposition Hall in 1870, purchasing the edifice (which once housed German singing societies) for a citywide industrial exposition. In 1876, civic leaders approved the demolition of the hall, but not before it held the city's official celebration of the national centennial. The thousands assembling at the Hall on July Fourth listened intently to both an oration lauding the city's past and the "children of the Public Schools" serenading the crowd with patriotic tunes. "The audience was almost entirely composed of country people," the *Cincinnati Enquirer* reported, noting that they represented "the great, strong, conservative middle class of the country," particularly "farmers and mechanics." In addition, there was a strong native-born character at the Exposition Hall with just "a sprinkling of Young Africa," as the city's vast German population held their own festivities concurrently. The German commemoration received little notice in the local newspapers other than to account for the lack of foreign-born Cincinnatians at the Exposition Hall. Military parading marked the other prominent Fourth of July celebration in the Queen City. The procession, praised as "the feature of the day" by one newspaper editor, included local ward militias, Mexican and Civil War veterans, and, perhaps most interestingly, a conscription of young men outfitted with Revolutionary War–style garb and weapons. The latter consisted of 3,200 men attired from head to toe in replica Continental uniforms and carrying facsimile muskets. One company in this group dressed as "Lexington farmers armed with pitchforks after the manner of their grandfathers," while another appeared "in squirrel caps and hunting shirts to represent Colonel Dan Morgan's scouts." In total, 12,000 men marched in the Cincinnati Independence Day procession, constituting an "immense" and "prodigious" spectacle in the words of one local citizen. Newspapers praised the extensive parade as even more imposing and impressive than its counterparts in other midwestern cities, reporting that it took the marchers a full 90 minutes to pass a given point along the winding route.[10]

Celebrations in Chicago differed markedly from those found in other midwestern cities. On July 2, the *Chicago Times* published an article rebuking citizens for not properly celebrating July Fourth in the past. "Theoretically, we have a nation holiday," the editorial began, "but practically we have not. The Fourth of July is a holiday by law and by tradition, but its observance is by no means general." The *Times* lamented the lack of past *civic* commemoration as city council and other boosters repeatedly failed to organize a citywide commemoration of the day. Due to civic booster negligence or oversight (there are no extant reports of why Chicago lacked an official procession or orator), Chicago's foreign-born population dominated centennial commemorations. Chicago Germans, led by the local *Turngemeinde* gymnastic organization, kicked off their planned three-day festivities on July 2 at Wright's Grove. The *Chicago Times* weighed in on the planned three-day gala. "Upon a centennial insurrection like that now about to break out," one article began, "all the enthusiasm, drunkenness, and explosiveness of the common Fourth is not only intensified, but prolonged over a period of time thrice the common length." Between six and seven hundred people attended the opening festivities on the second while, at night, the number "swelled to nearly 1,000." Recreational and commercial interests drew the most interest and acclaim as Wright's Grove featured shooting galleries, concerts, dancing, "the wheel of fortune . . . and a dozen more devices for the encouragement of enjoyment."[11]

The next night, on the eve of the Centennial Fourth, socialists congregating in Ogden Grove dominated festivities in Chicago. One local newspaper denigrated this political assembly, noting that, by celebrating on the third, the socialists not only promoted subversiveness and divisiveness, but also "entirely ignored the existence of the Fourth of July and all that name implies." The socialists adopted an alternative declaration of independence during their celebration, proclaiming freedom from capitalist domination and promoting the inalienable rights of workers. Just ten years later, the infamous Haymarket Square bombings drew international attention to Chicago's socialist community. But on July 4, 1876, theirs was a peaceful demonstration, marred only by jeering spectators reminding socialists that the Fourth should be "a day for solemn reflection" rather than an opportunity to demean capitalism.[12]

NATIONAL EVENTS IN 1876 AND THE CENTENNIAL EXPOSITION

A number of remarkable national events also marked the one hundredth year of American independence. A little-known author with the pen name Mark Twain published a book entitled *Tom Sawyer*, soon one of the definitive novels of the late nineteenth century. Baseball owners, seeking to increase their power over players and to dictate the terms and direction of America's new leading pastime, organized the National League with eight clubs stretching from Boston to St. Louis and including the A. G. Spalding–led Chicago White Stockings and a new iteration of the Cincinnati Reds. Scandals rocked the presidency of Ulysses S. Grant, with charges of political corruption tainting the name of the erstwhile Civil War general. As the national government forcibly removed Native Americans onto marginal land set aside for reservations, the United States Army sent General George Custer to round up indolent and resistant tribes. In June, Custer led his infamous attack on the Sioux, only to be massacred, along with hundreds of his men, by Chief Sitting Bull and his warriors. And finally, the 1876 presidential election pitting Democrat contender Samuel Tilden against Republican candidate Rutherford B. Hayes ended in controversy. The Electoral College faced deadlock, resulting in a political compromise giving the Republicans the White House and Democrats promises to cease Reconstruction efforts.

America's Centennial Exposition, held in Philadelphia, drew the greatest national attention in 1876. Long before the centennial, Americans began discussing how to best celebrate their one hundredth anniversary of independence from Great Britain. John L. Campbell, a professor at Indiana's Wabash College, proposed a national commemoration of the centennial. In 1866, Campbell penned a letter to Philadelphia's mayor Morton McMichael imploring him to approve and coordinate a large celebration in recognition of Independence Day. Recognizing the potential profitability and international exposure such an event would generate for his city, McMichael readily agreed. Civic boosters in Philadelphia immediately began planning for the Centennial Exposition, although Congress did not approve funding until five years later.[13]

On March 3, 1871, Congress passed legislation enabling the formation of a Centennial Commission charged with organizing and setting up the national celebration in Philadelphia—much to the chagrin of boosters promoting Chicago, New York City, Cincinnati, or Boston. The commissioners, appointed by President Grant, consisted of one representative from each state and territory in the United States. Over the course of nine meetings, the commission hammered out provisions for the celebration. In particular, Congress charged the commission to absolve the national government of any costs associated with building the Exposition. Instead, funds were to be raised by selling bonds and through donations from the city of Philadelphia and the state of Pennsylvania, both of which would undoubtedly benefit from the commerce and visibility afforded them by the Exposition. Following the final meeting of the commissioners, in early 1872 workers descended on Philadelphia and began the monumental building task.[14]

Although commissioners and workers on site remained optimistic, detractors constantly reminded boosters of the inherent difficulties facing the ambitious project. In the early 1870s, the United States still reeled from the aftereffects of the Civil War and struggled with tenuous Reconstruction efforts, attempting to restore order and prosperity to the South while realigning race relations in both the North and in the former Confederacy. In addition, shortly after construction of the Exposition began, a crippling financial panic threatened not only the future of the national celebration but also the solvency of the American economy.

Despite remarkable odds, the Centennial Exposition opened in May 1876, just two months behind schedule, enclosing more than two hundred buildings within its perimeter. On opening day, nearly 200,000 spectators poured into the three-mile radius containing the exhibits and buildings, eagerly drinking in the sights and sounds of the imposing and impressive Exposition. After this auspicious opening, attendance dropped precipitously and some observers feared that the Exposition would prove to be a financial disaster and embarrassment to both the Centennial Commission and the United States. But as the Fourth of July approached in Philadelphia, attendance at the Centennial Exposition climbed in anticipation of the great event.[15]

While the Centennial Exposition became an unparalleled commercial, technological, and financial success, it masked the still-virulent racism and sexism of the era. As historian Matthew Dennis notes, "while working to reconcile regions, the exposition did little to include women, immigrants, labor, or African-Americans and other nonwhites." Dennis concludes that, in fact, "the Centennial Exposition often proved actively hostile" to minorities and women. To white, male Americans, the Centennial Exposition would embody the virtues of America's early past and demonstrate the nation's progress. Issues like slavery, the Civil War, and women's rights threatened the peacefulness of the day. Although there was a Women's Pavilion meant to venerate the work of women in the formation and development of America, there was no similar edifice in honor of black sacrifices. And even women found little to celebrate on the centennial Fourth, still lacking suffrage or many other basic rights of citizenship. In fact, a group of radical feminists, led by Susan B. Anthony, interrupted the reading of the Declaration of Independence in Independence Square, meant to be one of the high points of the day, to protest stagnant women's rights legislation.[16]

Despite this racial and gendered tension, enormous crowds flocked to the Philadelphia Centennial Exposition on July Fourth. The city's festivities centered on two locations: the Exposition grounds and Independence Square, the site of the signing of the Declaration of Independence. As the sun rose on the Fourth, nearly half a million people greeted the holiday in Philadelphia, spilling out into the surrounding avenues.[17]

Independence Day revelers in Philadelphia also witnessed perhaps the most important result of the centennial celebration (both in that city and throughout the nation): heated debate comparing progress and the past, evaluating historical remembrance and the promising present. The Centennial Exposition in Philadelphia epitomized this discussion as its intended goals included promoting sectional and international goodwill and demonstrating the achievements made by the American people since declaring their independence in 1776. Visitors marveled at the Corliss Steam Engine (powering most of the machinery housed at the Exposition), Alexander Graham Bell's telephone prototype, an early version of a typewriter, an electric dynamo that promised to harness electricity, Horticultural and Agricultural Halls, and a variety of eating establishments, including "The Great American restaurant, two French restaurants, the German Restaurant, the Restaurant of the South . . . the Vienna Bakery and Coffee House; and the New England Log House and Modern Kitchen." But spectators also toured Philadelphia to visit sites of historic importance. The *Chicago Inter-Ocean* reported that "of the myriad of visitors to the Centennial few will go away without seeing or desiring to see the many objects of historical interest to be found in and about Philadelphia" like Independence Hall, the Liberty Bell, and Independence Square. As historian William Pierce Randel argues, "the Exhibition fully confirmed the sense, newly born in 1876, that the American nation had a past—a glorious past, one to be proud of and to commemorate." The group of national heroes commemorated in Philadelphia included luminaries like Washington, Jefferson, Lincoln, and Grant. Exhibitions reminded Americans that they had twice defeated Great Britain, one of the great nineteenth-century world powers, and had repeatedly repelled Mexican designs on the American Southwest. In addition, arches spanned the avenues of the city, bearing signs like "1776–1876" and "welcome to all nations." The Centennial Exposition vividly exhibited this shared American past, transmitted through newspaper coverage to rapt audiences throughout the nation.[18]

National Symbols and Historical Memory in the Midwest

Urban midwesterners also vibrantly displayed America's glorious history through emotive patriotic symbolism. In Chicago, an arch formed out of leaves spanned one of the main concourses, decorated with a centerpiece marked by the dual portraits of Washington and Lincoln and bearing the slogan "1776–1876," reminding passers-by of the true purpose for celebrating the centennial. In fact, the *Chicago Tribune* reported, "there was scarcely a foot of ground" in the city "that did not bear some reminder of the day" as residents papered the Windy City in red, white, and blue. Perhaps the most visible display of historical patriotism, however, occurred in Cincinnati's military parade. Thousands of men dressed in the uniforms of the Continental Army and marching with "Revolutionary muskets" joined a company portraying "Lexington farmers armed with pitchforks after the manner of their grandfathers" and men "dressed in squirrel caps and hunting shirts to represent Colonel Dan Morgan's scouts." This powerful imagery clearly demonstrates the historical influence of the founders in the mode of celebrating Independence Day. The founding generation was to be glorified and emulated. Dressing in the manner of their forefathers, particularly on Independence Day, visibly reminded spectators of how historical memory shaped commemorations of the Fourth of July.[19]

Historical memory also found an outlet through the written and spoken word. Columbus's keynote speaker, Henry C. Noble, included a lavish description of the benefits of living in the United States, but reminded listeners that in order "to appreciate these blessings, it is fit for us to spend a short time together in a review of our history." Noble continued his talk by reciting memorable events from America's past, including wars with Britain and notable technological achievements marking the preceding hundred years. Likewise, the *Indiana State Sentinel* lamented that the Fourth of July, "like Washington and his compatriots has been almost forgotten." To combat this forgetfulness, which the editor claimed threatened the very moral fiber of the nation, the newspaperman urged readers to "revive the memory of their deeds and sacrifices," in order to

FIGURE 9. "July 4th Greetings," date unknown.

"bring the great national holiday into deserved prominence." In Chicago, the *Inter-Ocean* published an article entitled "The End of a Century." In this piece, the author encouraged readers to "rejoice . . . this is a day to be reverenced and remembered." In addition, as reports of centennial celebrations reverberated through the nation, the *Inter-Ocean* reminded readers that centennial commemorations auspiciously signified that "the sentiment born at Lexington and Concord is still abroad in the land." These were idealized versions of the past presented to listeners and readers. Just as costumed celebrants in Cincinnati played the roles of white, male troops defending the nation from the oppressive British, orators and editors often left out women, labor struggles, ethnic animosity, and racial turmoil in their lily-white visions of the nation's history. Orations and editorials pertaining to the Fourth explicitly tied the founding era to romanticized visions of the centennial year, encouraging listeners and readers alike to remember (parts of) the past and to take to heart the sacrifices of the (idealized version of the) founding generation, embracing the good and conveniently forgetting the troublesome.[20]

July Fourth also marked an opportune time for religious leaders to reaffirm the place of organized religion in the history of the United States. In Indianapolis, no less than five churches held special Independence Day gatherings on the Sunday before the holiday. At one Presbyterian Church, the minister simply recited a verse from the book of Deuteronomy that read, "Remember the days of old." At the Mayflower Congregational Church, Reverend Hyde reminded parishioners that, emboldened by Christianity, "the immortal Washington led the infant nation through the struggle of the Revolution," and that "belief in God and trust in his overruling power was the very essence of the character of those who secured our heritage of liberty." Reverend Bradley of Christ Church was even more insistent, urging listeners to turn away from the sin and vice prevalent in national politics, recalling that "the founders of our Nation never disgraced the names signed on the Declaration of Independence." Bradley's solution was to "remember to-day their voices and denounce our extravagance and sin." And finally, at the Fletcher Place Church, congregants framed the pulpit with a large shield bearing the motto, "God and country, inseparable," providing an apt backdrop for Reverend Curtiss's speech in which he argued that "the world never saw greater heroes than made this nation."[21]

These civic boosters, while praising the nation's history and urging citizens to recall the glories of the United States, reminded readers and listeners of their duty as patriotic Americans to pass their historical knowledge and pride to subsequent generations, a task long promoted by midwestern boosters. An article in the Inter-Ocean argued that the Fourth of July provided an apt opportunity to discuss "how the heritage can be best transmitted to those who come after us," imploring Chicagoans to talk to their children about the meaning of Independence

Day and what it meant to be an American. Similarly, the editor of the *Chicago Times* offered that "every man who rises from his warm bed this morning carries on his shoulders the responsibility of a hundred years ago," urging that "he is supposed to work for the perpetuity of those principles that his forefathers instituted." "He ought to know, and probably does," the editor continued, "that he is expected to hand down [these principles] as intact, as stainless as they were bequeathed to him." Not only was historical knowledge important, but boosters deemed imparting it to future generations equally vital to the continued success of the nation.[22]

Columbus's *Ohio State Journal* on July 5, 1876, published the most extensive reminder of America's hundred-year history found in reports from the urban Midwest. The newspaper that day included an entire section on notable local events in the city's history, including tales of the original settlers, the decision to make Columbus the state capital, and the construction of the elaborate capitol building. After this lengthy background, the newspaper provided "the history of early celebration of the Fourth of July in this city," although the editor reminded readers that many of these early occasions were "greatly shrouded in obscurity." Despite being "a howling wilderness," Columbus's first settlers still held celebrations in which "the immortal Declaration of Independence was no doubt read with as much, or more, veneration then as now." To educate readers about the exact nature of early celebrations of the Fourth of July in Columbus, the *Journal* published brief remarks about each Independence Day commemoration between 1826 and 1876. For instance, the paper remarked that in 1826, 24 Revolutionary soldiers graced the day's procession, which concluded with 13 toasts and boisterous revelry. The newspaper blithely remarked that in 1855, the year of the Bloody Fourth, "a man named Foster was killed," and that "many had narrow escapes," while in 1875, there was simply "no celebration of the day." Again, midwesterners whitewashed the past, leaving out the troublesome events of 1855 and romanticizing the celebrations of the early pioneers for their simplicity, unanimity, and golden age quality.[23]

PROGRESS AND THE PRESENT

In spite of the success of civic boosters encouraging midwesterners to use the Fourth of July to recall their shared history, raucous commercial festivities and calls from patriotic citizens to hail American progress dominated celebrations of the American centennial. The editorial printed in the *Ohio State Journal* in 1876 included a lengthy and exhaustive expository of local events leading up to the American centennial, but it was not as grand as the editors had hoped. In fact, the editors had originally planned a seven-column editorial including elements of national progress as well as local anecdotes, complete with allusions to the Northwest Ordinance, the Virginia and Kentucky Resolutions, the Burr conspiracy, and the events leading up to the Civil War. But once word of this ambitious project reached the ears of local citizens, the response was decidedly negative. The newspaper reported that one Columbus citizen remarked, "Oh, shoot that! That's the same thing as This Centennial Year [an editorial published earlier in the year]—you can't fool us!" In response to criticism, the newspaper gave up its proposed seven-column editorial, lamenting that "people would rather go and see a naughty little boy tie a package of fire-crackers to a confiding dog's tail than to read an editorial seven miles long on The Centennial Year." In this instance, spectacle and the present clearly won out over somber historical reminiscences about the past.[24]

The Columbus editor's disgust centered on a perceived lack of historical consciousness by many local citizens and issues of memory confronted in the centennial year. Civic boosters saw 1876 as a time to remember and publicly praise the efforts of the Founding Fathers and recall the sacrifices made by colonists declaring their independence from Britain. But instead, it seemed as though very few people (civic boosters aside) cared much about America's past. Although posters and banners venerated the heroes of 1776 and numerous editorials and speeches recounted their deeds, there was an underlying fear that the past was slipping further and further away from the public consciousness. The editor of the *Cincinnati Enquirer* recommended that his readers peruse the Declaration of Independence "before you start out to 'celebrate' today." In particular, the editor remarked that "we have printed it for the convenience of people who are not familiar with its provisions. You will be surprised when you read it to discover what a clear, logical, enthusiastic document it is." After public readings of the Declaration of Independence ceased to be a central aspect of the commemoration of Independence Day in the late antebellum era, few midwesterners marked its recitation as a necessary part of their day's festivities. Perhaps in response, the *Chicago Times* reprinted the entire saga of how the Founding Fathers declared independence, attesting that "not one out of one hundred knows anything about the origin of national independence." On July 5, the *Chicago Tribune* included an editorial noting that the centennial celebration "like the hundred Fourths which preceded it" was simply over. "Nothing of it remains to-day," the paper concluded, except hangovers and boys a few dollars poorer from having exploded their supplies of firecrackers and Roman Candles. Looking solely at historical consciousness, it would seem as though midwesterners cared little for the nation, the Fourth of July, or the centennial anniversary of American independence. This was not entirely the case. Instead, understandings of what it meant to be a patriotic, loyal American had evolved to the point that most midwest-erners recognized the patriotism in spectacle, the liberty in recreation, and the freedom in leisure.[25]

While civic boosters lamented a lack of historical interest among the citizenry of the urban Midwest, some midwesterners actively shied away from the legacy of the past. Rather than confront race, gender, or class (issues with roots in America's past), citizens chose blissfully uncontro-versial spectacle. Outside of the "sprinkling of Young Africa" mentioned just briefly in reports from Cincinnati's centennial commemoration, African-Americans remained invisible in 1876 midwestern celebrations, despite their important presence in earlier postbellum years and during the Civil War. Instead, as was the case in the antebellum urban Midwest, African-Americans remained wary of a drunken, nationalistic white American populace bent on venerating the positive attributes of their ancestors and unwilling to confront the racist legacy of America's past.

The nationally circulating *Harper's Weekly* perhaps best formulated the sentiments of its midwestern readers, proclaiming that "we are not a people fond of official pageants nor of government celebrations. The Fourth of July, 1776, was emphatically the People's day, and the festival of its centennial anniversary should be a popular, not an official, festival." Emphasizing that Independence Day served as the "People's day" would provide the holiday with a common man sensibility, a day on which work-ers and bosses, men and women, and rich and poor could all be equally loyal Americans, participating in the rites of American nationalism, wav-ing flags and spending the day as they best saw fit. A class component was clearly present as well and, indeed, throughout postbellum Independence Day celebrations. Civic boosters, primarily upper- and middle-class rep-resentatives, promoted official commemorations reminding midwestern-ers of their (gilded vision of the) past while other midwesterners often chose less contentious unofficial commemorations.[26]

LEISURE, RECREATION, AND COMMERCIALISM

Instead of following the lead of civic boosters focusing on the role of the past in centennial celebrations, many urban midwesterners continued to celebrate the holiday through leisure, recreation, and commercialism. Fireworks vendors did brisk business around the centennial Fourth of July, reaffirming the holiday's connections to both Young America and rampant commercialism. Chicago's Schweitzer & Beer claimed to have the "Largest Assortment in the West," while Cleveland's J. Featherstone recommended any of his 100 varieties of Chinese lanterns to illuminate city streets on the Fourth of July. Many firms explicitly tied Independence Day celebrations to commercialism. The American Fire-Works Company, headquartered in Chicago, recommended that parties intending to celebrate Independence Day (adding the caveat that "everybody ought to celebrate this Centennial year") should "remember the location of this Company" when it came time to buy provisions for the annual commemoration of the holiday. In perhaps the ultimate example of progress meeting the past, in Chicago, "huge sentinels painted on canvas and dressed in the Continental costume of 1776" decorated one grove visited by thousands of the city's German citizens exuberantly celebrating the Fourth of July. Yet these painted sentinels did not serve to remind Chicagoans of their shared cultural heritage, but instead to symbolically protect "the beer stands scattered through the woods."[27]

Instead of forgoing commercial interests to bond together in a good old-fashioned Fourth, the centennial year drew even more attention to the marketable aspects of the holiday emerging in the previous decade. The *Indiana State Sentinel* remarked that "as a people, we Americans are not much addicted to holidays, being generally too close on the heels of the almighty dollar to stop for side-shows." Past Independence Day celebrations, the newspaper argued, had been halfhearted attempts at properly commemorating the nation's birth. But on the Centennial Fourth, a special day both on the year's calendar and in the continuing march of America's progress, "we are apt to encompass the entire swine when we do set out to amuse or be amused." In Columbus, committees formed expressly by the city council handed down this dictum to encourage exuberant celebrations on the centennial: the city's Committee on Decoration requested that all houses and businesses decorate their establishments in red, white, and blue, while the aptly named Committee on Fun rallied support for recreational endeavors on the nation's hundredth anniversary. In response, residents flooded the city in patriotic colors:

the streets and buildings bore flags and banners proclaiming America's birth, including a display on High Street in which large flags fluttered in the breeze, each bearing the name of one of the original 13 states. The editor of one Columbus paper reminded readers that "it is only once in a hundred years that we have a chance to indulge in a liberal display of the National colors," and encouraged Columbus's citizens to go all-out in decorating their homes and businesses.[28]

Leisure remained an important aspect of the Centennial Fourth, as it had been for more than a decade. The average Chicagoan, the *Tribune* reported, "went out on the lake, either with his wife or sweetheart." He then "borrowed a fishing-rod, bought a dime's worth of minnows, and sat on the breakwater or one of the piers all day." If fishing was not his game, the Chicagoan "perambulated around town, and at occasional intervals drank to the health of the American Eagle; he rolled a string of ten-pins; he punched the ivories to the extent of three or four games sandwiched with the seductive and yet hugely intoxicating rum-punch." "But he did not march in procession," the newspaper charged, "he positively refused to keep step to the tapping of the spirit-stirring drum." Instead, "he would be blessed first before he would stand in a crowd, and listen to the reading of the Declaration of Independence, or Washington's Farewell Address." Again, there seemed to be a class component evident in this celebration as civic boosters promoted solemn remembrance while the editor's symbolic common man chose to drink liquor, play games, and relax. In Cleveland, citizens acted like this Chicago commoner, escaping to Monumental Park for picnics and relaxation. Their numbers were uncountable, according to local newspapers, as men and women of all ages mixed with children drawn to "peddlers around with peanuts and lemonade," and 3,000 young people singing the patriotic hymn "America."[29]

As was the case in earlier Independence Day celebrations, recreation and amusements provided an additional allure for pleasure seekers on the Centennial holiday. In Cincinnati, city-goers could choose from several plays, an orchestra performing patriotic songs, and extensive fireworks. Clevelanders witnessed a naval regatta with a first prize consisting of both a championship pennant and $75. In Chicago, horse racing took preeminence as Dexter Park drew over five thousand citizens to gamble and watch the day's races. Many celebrants attended baseball games. In Chicago, a contest between the local White Stockings and visiting Philadelphia Athletics in the newly constituted National League drew thousands of spectators to watch the home team pummel the visiting squad. The White Stockings, under Spalding, were exceedingly popular in the Windy City, having joined the fledgling National League earlier in the year. On the Fourth of July, with two of the best professional baseball teams in the nation playing in Chicago, "the largest crowd which has witnessed a ball contest since 1870" packed the grounds. The stadium filled to overflowing as two strong clubs, along with "the additional inducement of the holiday," necessitated the hasty construction of several rows of temporary bleachers to sate avid Chicago baseball fans.[30]

In other midwestern cities, less formal recreational pursuits took preeminence. Columbus's Fair Grounds housed numerous events. Some men and women danced at the Fine Art Hall, reconfigured especially for the holiday, while the Fair Grounds track drew others to watch a velocipede race, a half-mile foot race, a sack race, a blindfold race, and a jumping match. Still more Columbus spectators congregated at a greased pole, 20 feet in height with a ham and five silver dollars perched precariously at its summit. A barker urged passers-by to try to climb the post to claim the prizes—provided, of course, contestants paid a small fee. Similarly, in Indianapolis, the city's Exposition grounds housed numerous recreational diversions. Among the more notable events were sack races and both "a hog race and a race for a hog," as well as "foot-races, slow-mule races, blindfold wheelbarrow-races, the trick shower bell, the Russian bath, the slippery pole," and "the celebrated English jingling match." The latter was a game in which 25 to 30 participants consented to be blindfolded and then ran aimlessly around into one another's arms, drawing mirthful laughter from contestants and spectators alike.[31]

INTERNAL TURMOIL

Joyous celebrations marked America's one hundredth birthday celebration. Urban midwesterners vacillated between reveling in the progress and potential for the American nation and paying homage to turmoil about commemorating America's contentious past. Civic boosters constantly reminded local citizens of their shared national heritage by reprinting the Declaration of Independence, and alluding to the sacrifices of the Founding Fathers and nationally significant events binding America's diverse citizenry together. But many men and women still chose to celebrate the holiday with leisurely picnics, baseball games, and enticing amusements. As historian Richard Gowers notes, "Americans on the Fourth were not meant to forget the past as much as they were meant to engage in recreation so that they would not confront the legacy of the past." Confronting American history meant not only recalling its heroes, the glories of 1776, and America's victorious wars, but also facing reminders about difficult issues like slavery, the Civil War, and failing Reconstruction efforts. Many midwesterners, in turn, celebrated the centennial Fourth as they had in the previous decade—by congratulating themselves on America's amazing progress and engaging in diverting games and amusements. The front page of the *Chicago Times* on July 4, 1876, included perhaps the most telling sign that commemorations of the centennial pitted the past against the present. While other newspapers provided readers with reprintings of the Declaration of Independence, the words to patriotic hymns, or reports of the Centennial Exposition in Philadelphia, the *Times* opened with a giant map bearing the legend "American Railroads in 1876." Taglines for the article read "Telling of the Wonderful Part the Railway Has Played in America's Mighty Progress," "The United States in 1776 and 1876—An Amazing Contrast," "Railroads—the Sinews of the Nation," and, most tellingly, "Railroad Builders the True Fathers of the Nation."After such a laudatory introduction, the article continued by detailing the efforts of railroad magnates in developing the nation's interior, and transforming the midwestern urban centers—particularly Chicago—into regional (and even national) economic, manufacturing, and transportation hubs. In fact, the article argued incontrovertibility that "the history of transportation in the United States from 1776 to 1876, forms the brightest page of our centennial record."[32]

In 1876, midwestern civic boosters provided constant reminders about the past, insisting that citizens remember the hundredth anniversary of the nation and the role of history in regional understandings of American cultural citizenship. Public discourse and the modes of celebrating the Fourth of July saw civic boosters—adherents of America's glorious (but perhaps dangerous) past—and the majority of other citizens—aspirants lauding the nation's present (and less controversial) state—view the day quite differently. In 1876, more than in any previous year, midwesterners came together to celebrate the nation's past through universally commemorating the Fourth of July. But in so doing, citizens purposefully ignored much of America's history, preferring the pomp and showiness of postbellum commemorations and the whitewashed history reprinted in local newspapers to the somber recollections of the antebellum Midwest. As the United States began its second century, most midwesterners waved a hasty good-bye to the past and embraced the nation's glorious present.

Epilogue

Americans celebrated the Fourth of July in 1876 with great enthusiasm. The Centennial Exposition in Philadelphia was an unarguable success, drawing millions of visitors to the City of Brotherly Love while thousands of midwesterners attended festivities held throughout the region, celebrating the pomp and circumstance of the hundredth anniversary commemoration. But midwesterners remained conflicted about how to balance remembering the past, celebrating the present, and promoting the future. Orators and newspaper editors used the occasion to remind readers of their patriotic obligations to carry the torch of the founding generation while most revelers preferred to watch baseball games, bet on horse races, picnic with family and friends, shoot off fireworks, or publicly praise American progress. Debates about the past helped define what it meant to be an American citizen, as discussions about the historical integrity of the Fourth of July pervaded Independence Day celebrations in 1876.

The national centennial also proved to be a pivotal year in American history. It spelled the formal end of the Reconstruction era as Republicans agreed to remove federal troops from the South in return for Democratic recognition of Ohioan Rutherford B. Hayes's victory over Samuel J. Tilden in the fall presidential race. Eighteen seventy-six also marked an important turning point in American culture: one historian characterized the year as standing on the "cusp between America's Century of Work and its Century of Play." Indeed, the next 50 years witnessed a remarkable increase in the popularity of baseball, boxing, and football as well as the invention and popularization of the sport of basketball.[1]

While 1876 marked the end of an era in American history, the importance of the Independence Day holiday persisted. Americans continued to position and plan celebrations of the Fourth of July as a means to define what it meant to be an American citizen, closely tying patriotic loyalty and conceptions of nationalism to commemorations of the holiday. Three events, in particular, highlight this continued centrality of Independence Day to definitions and developments of American nationalism. The first was a boxing match between African-American pugilist Jack Johnson and his opponent, the "Great White Hope" James J. Jefferies, on July 4, 1910, reflecting ongoing issues of race and racism in America. The second involved the movement to ban fireworks on Independence Day, demonstrating not only the Progressive agenda of activist government but also well-defined class conceptions about the proper mode of celebrating the Fourth of July. The final event revolved around a hot dog eating contest that swelled into an international event, showcasing both ethnic American identification and a nationalist ethos celebrating consumption.

Race in Twentieth-century Independence Day Celebrations

In 1908, African-American boxer Jack Johnson won the world heavyweight championship, crushing the overmatched Tommy Burns for the title. The white media lampooned Johnson as possessing ape-like, subhuman qualities and terrified readers by divulging Johnson's renowned love of white women, exacerbating existing racial stereotypes and making Johnson a target of white racial hostility. Almost immediately, the search began for a white challenger who could reclaim the heavyweight title from Johnson. In 1910, they found their "Great White Hope"—retired boxer James J. Jeffries. Jeffries, who had left the ring as the undefeated heavyweight champion, agreed to fight Johnson (in his words) "for the sole purpose of proving that a white man is better than a Negro." Promoters scheduled the bout for the Fourth of July, 1910, to decide, once and for all, who was the superior fighter and, by extension, the superior race. It wasn't even close. Johnson pummeled the overmatched Jeffries in front of 22,000 spectators in Reno, Nevada as the partisan crowd unmercifully booed the champion. In the fifteenth round, Jeffries's corner men threw in the towel to prevent Johnson from knocking out their fighter. Elated African-Americans throughout the nation raucously celebrated

Johnson's victory. Their white neighbors, infuriated at the embarrassing defeat of their "Great White Hope" and this newly created link between African-Americans and the Fourth of July, reacted violently, inciting race riots throughout the nation. As historian Leonard Sweet argues, "no other July 4 in the nation's history had generated such widespread attention and interest." Jack Johnson's victory in 1910 was more than just another boxing match and would have been important had it been fought on any other day in the year. But because it took place on the Fourth of July, it had added meaning (and far-reaching consequences) for African-Americans and white Americans alike.[2]

Social Class in Twentieth-century Independence Day Celebrations

Another important development in post-1876 Fourth of July celebrations was the evolving class element associated with commemorations of the holiday. In the antebellum era, upper- and middle-class civic boosters dominated formal commemorations of the Fourth of July. After the war, Independence Day became increasingly appropriated by lower classes as a day of relaxation, leisure, and exuberance. As historian Matthew Dennis notes, "the holiday came to signify everything and nothing." Progressive Era reformers focused not on the empty rhetoric of the holiday, but instead on the issue of its suitability and safety, particularly the role played by fireworks in celebrating the Fourth of July. Banning fireworks was certainly not a new initiative. In the early 1870s, many midwestern cities outlawed the use of incendiaries—although both children and law enforcement officials regularly ignored these ordinances—in light of the terrible conflagration in Portland, Maine, in 1866. But in the early 1900s, Progressives attacked Fourth of July fireworks with renewed vigor. In 1903, the *Journal of the American Medical Association* began compiling statistics regarding injuries on the Fourth of July. Their results were astounding. In 1909, the journal reported that fireworks on the previous Fourth of July killed more Americans than had perished while fighting the British at Bunker Hill. In response to the *Journal*'s findings, the Playground Association of America, at its annual meeting in Pittsburgh in 1909, began a campaign for a "Safe and Sane Fourth," imploring Independence Day celebrants to enjoy the holiday in a quiet and reflective fashion rather than in raucous revelry. This effort was more than just part of a Progressive agenda aimed at protecting children. A class aspect was also undeniable, as advocates of the Safe and Sane Fourth took direct aim at rowdy working-class commemorations of the holiday.

In a way, the movement continued the agenda of civic boosters from the pre-1876 era, promoting civic processions, temperate picnics, and non-threatening oratory over loud fireworks, drunken parties, and slurred partisan speeches—advocating that Independence Day be used as a "tool of civic education and social transformation." Thus, class, through the Safe and Sane Movement, also became an important cultural marker in post-1876 commemorations of the Fourth.[3]

Ethnicity in Twentieth-century Independence Day Celebrations

Race—epitomized by Jack Johnson—and class—as embodied by the Safe and Sane Movement—marked two important aspects of American culture and society (and commemorations of the Fourth of July) in the late nineteenth and early twentieth centuries. But another, and perhaps more important, marker of cultural citizenship in this era became ethnicity. Ethnocentric nativism returned with a vengeance during the First World War. Instead of targeting Catholics or political radicals, this movement demanded "100% Americanism" from all citizens, particularly those of Germanic heritage. On July 4, 1916, four immigrants met outside a small hot dog stand on Coney Island to resolve an argument, typical in this hypersensitively nationalistic era, about who was the most patriotic or "the most American." To settle their dispute, the men agreed to a hot dog eating contest, deeming it a true test of American patriotism. James Mullen downed 13 hot dogs in 12 minutes, earning the victory and ostensibly the title of most American. Immigrants did not always resort to hot dog eating to demonstrate their patriotic loyalty, but they did often use the Fourth of July as an opportunity to display their loyalty and understandings of American nationalism—just as they had for generations. Ethnic Americans on Independence Day during the interwar era used the holiday, as had their predecessors in the mid-nineteenth century, to promulgate their understandings of what it meant to be a patriotic American citizen. These developments concerned many middle-class reformers attempting to exert control over the method of Americanization. Reformers responded by creating celebrations to "script the holiday" and tie the Fourth to the "100% American" movement. Clevelanders created "Americanization Day" in 1915 to define and educate various ethnic groups about their roles in the American polity on the Fourth. In Indianapolis in 1918, Progressive reformers organized an Americanization Day parade in the midst of the First World War to overtly remind citizens of their obligations to be "100% American." One historian neatly summarizes the intentions of twentieth-century reformers as follows: "when reform leaders spoke of 'Americanizing the Fourth' what they really meant was Americanizing the immigrant."[4]

Clearly the Fourth of July remained an important event in developing notions about what it meant to be a patriotic American. While concluding this study in 1876 neatly breaks *Parading Patriotism* into a 50-year span, bookended by the semicentennial and centennial celebrations, many of the important issues debated on Independence Day between 1826 and 1876 remained contentious decades later. Conceptions of Americanization and the proper mode of celebrating the holiday—both of which changed drastically over time—as well as tension between civic leaders (middle- and upper-class white men and women) and the most exuberant celebrants (primarily young people, ethnic Americans, and working-class citizens) remained central to the commemoration of the Fourth of July. In 1976, in honor of the national bicentennial, Chicago historian Frank Jewell reminisced about Independence Day festivities in the city's storied past. Jewell concluded his discussion with a telling observation of the festivities planned for 1920: "the Fourth of July was now celebrated in the same manner as we do today. Small fireworks were exploded by children, but larger ones were limited to safe displays. Most Chicagoans took to their cars in search of a good time and celebrated to suit themselves." For over two hundred years, the Fourth of July has been a vitally important aspect of American culture and has helped construct how citizens define what it means to be an American. Between 1826 and 1876, this development transformed life in the urban Midwest, as a growing and evolving region sought to define itself and its relationship to American national identity through patriotic posturing and celebrating the Fourth of July.[5]

NOTES

Preface

1. Gerald Stanley Lee, *Crowds: A Moving-Picture of Democracy*. Book Five, Part Three (New York: Doubleday, Page, & Co., 1913).

2. *Cleveland Plain Dealer*, July 5–7, 1845.

3. Ibid.; Jakob Mueller, *Memoirs of a Forty-eighter: Sketches from the German-American Period of Storm and Stress of the 1850s*, trans. Steven Rowan (Cleveland: Rudolf Schmidt Printing Company, 1896), 34.

4. On the inherent problems of naming the region, see especially James Shortridge, *The Middle West: Its Meaning in American Culture* (Lawrence: University Press of Kansas, 1989); for Census Bureau definitions, see the "Census Regions and Divisions Map," <http://www.census.gov/geo/www/us_regdiv.pdf≥ (accessed November 4, 2011); on the region's role as a migratory crossroads facilitating trade and cultural exchange, see Lucy Eldersveld Murphy and Wendy Hamand Venet, eds., *Midwestern Women: Work, Community, and Leadership at the Crossroads* (Bloomington: Indiana University Press, 1997).

5. Jon Teaford, *Cities of the Heartland: The Rise and Fall of the Industrial Midwest* (Bloomington: Indiana University Press, 1993), vii; Andrew Cayton, Richard Sisson, and Christian Zacher, eds., "Genuine America," in *The American Midwest: An Interpretive Encyclopedia*, (Bloomington: Indiana University Press, 2007), 69. Ohio's growth, in particular, played a central role in these larger developments. Of the five cities studied in this work, three are located in the state: Cleveland, Cincinnati, and Columbus. The importance of nineteenth-century Ohio relied partially on geography; in an east-to-west pattern of migration, settlers naturally populated Ohio before the territories of Indiana, Illinois, Michigan, and Wisconsin. Similarly, the westerly flowing Ohio River brought travelers to Marietta, Portsmouth, and Cincinnati before Vincennes, Madison, New Albany, or Cairo, allowing Ohio port cities to grow at a much faster rate than their Indiana or Illinois counterparts, particularly before steamboats made upriver travel viable. Indeed, in the 1830 census, only five towns from states carved out of the Old Northwest Territory—Cincinnati, Zanesville, Dayton,

Steubenville, and Chillicothe—ranked in the top ninety nationally in population. All were located in Ohio. By 1860, Chicago, Milwaukee, and Detroit joined Cincinnati among the top twenty population centers in the nation, but Ohio included four in the top fifty while no other midwestern state could claim even two. In 1880, five Ohio cities figured in the top fifty nationally while each of the other states from the Old Northwest had just one apiece. So while the other states created from the Northwest Territory, and the cities of Chicago and Indianapolis in particular, certainly provide important insight into the growth and maturation of the urban Midwest, Ohio led the way in many regards in the mid-nineteenth century. Campbell Gibson, *Population of the 100 Largest Cities and Other Urban Places in the United States: 1790 to 1990* (Washington, DC: U.S. Census Bureau), <http://www.census.gov/population/www/documentation/twps0027.html≥ (accessed September 16, 2010).

6. Michel-Guillaume Jean de Crèvecoeur, *Letters from an American Farmer* (Belfast: James Magee, 1783), 34; David M. Potter, "The Historian's Use of Nationalism and Vice Versa," *The American Historical Review* 67 (4) (July 1962): 924–50; Ernest Gellner, *Thought and Change* (London: Weidenfield & Nicholson, 1964), 168; Benedict Anderson, *Imagined Communities* (London: Verso, 1983). On other constructions of nineteenth-century American nationalism, see Richard R. Beeman, *The Varieties of Political Experience in Eighteenth-Century America* (Philadelphia: University of Pennsylvania Press, 2004); Beeman, "Deference, Republicanism, and the Emergence of Popular Politics in Eighteenth-Century America," *William and Mary Quarterly* 49 (July 1992): 401–30; Sacvan Bercovitch, *The Rites of Assent: Transformations in the Symbolic Construction of America* (New York: Routledge, 1993); John Bodnar, *Remaking America: Public Memory, Commemoration, and Patriotism in the Twentieth Century* (Princeton: Princeton University Press, 1992); Mike Cronin and David Mayall, eds., *Sporting Nationalisms: Identity, Ethnicity, Immigration, and Assimilation* (London: Frank Cass, 1998); George Dangerfield, *The Awakening of American Nationalism, 1815–1828* (New York: Harper & Row, 1965); Gerhard K. Friesen and Walter Schatzberg, eds., *The German Contribution to the Building of the Americas* (Worcester, MA: Clark University Press, 1977); John R. Gillis, ed., *Commemorations: The Politics of National Identity* (Princeton: Princeton University Press, 1994); Jon Gjerde, *The Minds of the West: Ethnocultural Evolution in the Rural Middle West, 1830–1917* (Chapel Hill: University of North Carolina Press, 1997); Oscar Handlin, *The Uprooted: The Epic Story of the Great Migrations That Made the American People* (New York: Grosset & Dunlap, 1951); John Higham, *Strangers in the Land: Patterns of American Nativism, 1860–1925* (New Brunswick, NJ: Rutgers University Press, 1955); Andrew Holman, "Something to Admire: Cultural Nationalism, Symbolic Dissonance, and the Fourth of July in New England's Canadian Borderlands, 1840–1870," *Dublin Seminar for New England Folklife. Annual Proceedings* 25 (2000): 137–48; Michael Kammen, *Mystic Chords of Memory: The Transformation of Tradition in American Culture* (New York: Alfred A. Knopf, 1991); Kammen, "Commemoration and Contestation in American Culture: Historical Perspectives," *Amerikastudien* 48 (2) (2003): 185–205; Cecilia Elizabeth O'Leary, *To Die For: The Paradox of American Patriotism* (Princeton: Princeton University Press, 1999); Roy Rosenzweig and David Thelen, *The Presence of the Past: Popular Uses of History in American Life* (New York: Columbia University Press, 1998); Robert E. Shalhope, "Republicanism and Early American Historiography," *The William and Mary Quarterly*, 3rd Ser., Vol. 39, No. 2 (April 1982): 334–56; Shalhope,

"Toward a Republican Synthesis: The Emergence of an Understanding of Republicanism in American Historiography," *The William and Mary Quarterly*, 3rd Ser., Vol. 29, No. 1. (Jan. 1972), 49–80; Lyn Spillman, *Nation and Commemoration: Creating National Identities in the United States and Australia* (Cambridge: Cambridge University Press, 1997); John L. Thomas, "Nationalizing the Republic, 1877–1920," in *The Great Republic: A History of the American People*, ed. Bernard Bailyn et al. (Lexington, MA: Heath and Company, 1977); and Ernest Lee Tuveson, *Redeemer Nation: The Idea of America's Millennial Role* (Chicago: University of Chicago Press, 1980).

7. For an excellent discussion of this approach, see Kathleen Conzen and David Gerber, "The Invention of Ethnicity: A Perspective from the U.S.A.," *Journal of American Ethnic History* 12 (1) (Fall 1992): 3–42. See also David A. Gerber, "'The Germans Take Care of Our Celebrations': Middle-Class Americans Appropriate German Ethnic Culture in Buffalo in the 1850s," in *Hard at Play: Leisure in America, 1840–1940*, ed. Kathryn Grover (Amherst: The University of Massachusetts Press, 1992), 39–60; Donna R. Gabaccia, "Liberty, Coercion, and the Making of Immigration Historians," *The Journal of American History* 84 (2) (Sept. 1997): 570. For an extensive historiography of topics associated with assimilation, see Russel Kazal, "Revisiting Assimilation: The Rise, Fall, and Reappraisal of a Concept in American Ethnic History," *The American Historical Review* 100 (2) (April 1995): 437–71.

8. Juan Delgado-Moreira, "Cultural Citizenship and the Creation of European Identity," *Electronic Journal of Sociology* 2 (1997), 3.

9. John Bodnar argues that patriotism "embodies both official and vernacular interests." See John Bodnar, *Remaking America: Public Memory, Commemoration, and Patriotism in the Twentieth Century* (Princeton: Princeton University Press, 1992). Another classic Bodnar work is *The Transplanted* (Bloomington: Indiana University Press, 1987), which serves to counteract Handlin's assimilationist arguments in *The Uprooted*.

10. Matthew Dennis, *Red, White and Blue Letter Days: An American Calendar* (Ithaca, NY: Cornell University Press, 2002), 2, 4. On early celebrations, see Diana Karter Appelbaum, *The Glorious Fourth: An American Holiday, An American History* (New York: Facts on File, 1989); William Cohn, "A National Celebration: The Fourth of July in American History," *Cultures* 3 (1) (1976): 141–56; Robert Pettus Hay, "Freedom's Jubilee: One Hundred Years of the Fourth of July, 1776–1876" (PhD diss., University of Kentucky, 1967); Hay, "Frontier Patriotism on Parade: Westward the Glorious Fourth of July," *Journal of the West* 5 (3) (July 1966): 309–20; Len Travers, *Celebrating the Fourth: Independence Day and the Rites of Nationalism in the Early Republic* (Amherst: University of Massachusetts Press, 1997); Charles Warren, "Fourth of July Myths," *The William and Mary Quarterly* 2 (3) (July 1945): 237–72; and David Waldstreicher, *In the Midst of Perpetual Fetes* (Chapel Hill: University of North Carolina Press, 1997). For twentieth-century celebrations, see Dennis, *Red, White and Blue Letter Days*; John Gillis, ed., *Commemorations: The Politics of National Identity* (Princeton: Princeton University Press, 1994); Mitch Kachun, *Festivals of Freedom: Memory and Meaning in African American Emancipation Celebrations, 1808–1915* (Amherst: University of Massachusetts Press, 2003); and Ellen M. Litwicki, *America's Public Holidays, 1865–1920* (Washington: Smithsonian Institution Press, 2000). Other historians have certainly studied Independence Day as a cultural marker, but most of their works are either sweeping syntheses or focused local studies. For an example of

the former see William Cohn, "A National Celebration: The Fourth of July in American History," *Cultures* 3 (1) (1976): 141–56; for the latter, Cora Dolbee, "The Fourth of July in Early Kansas 1854–1857," *Kansas Historical Quarterly* 10 (1) (Feb. 1941): 34–78.

11. See, for example, Appelbaum, *The Glorious Fourth*; Hay, "Frontier Patriotism on Parade"; and Travers, *Celebrating the Fourth*.

12. Richard Gowers, "Contested Celebrations: The Fourth of July and Changing National Identity in the United States, 1865–1918" (PhD diss., University of New South Wales, 2004), 4; Ellen M. Litwicki, "'Our Hearts Burn with Ardent Love for Two Countries': Ethnicity and Assimilation," in Amitai Etzioni and Jared Bloom, eds., *We Are What We Celebrate: Understanding Holidays and Rituals* (New York: New York University Press, 2004), 213–45; Litwicki, "Visions of America: Public Holidays and American Cultures, 1776–1900" (PhD diss., University of Virginia, 1992); Litwicki, *America's Public Holidays*; Scott C. Martin, *Killing Time: Leisure and Culture in Southwestern Pennsylvania, 1800–1850* (Pittsburgh: University of Pittsburgh Press, 1995); Martin, "The Fourth of July in Southwestern Pennsylvania, 1800–1850," *Pittsburgh History* 75 (2) (1992): 58–71. For more on Gilded Age celebrations of the Fourth of July, see Roy Rosenzweig, *Eight Hours For What We Will: Workers and Leisure in an Industrial City, 1870–1920* (Cambridge: Cambridge University Press, 1983), 66.

Introduction

1. *Cincinnati Gazette*, July 11, 1826.

2. Ibid.

3. Andrew R. L. Cayton and Susan E. Gray, eds., *The American Midwest: Essays on Regional History* (Bloomington: Indiana University Press, 2001); R. Douglas Hurt, *The Ohio Frontier: Crucible of the Old Northwest, 1720–1830* (Bloomington: Indiana University Press, 1996); Harry N. Scheiber, *The Old Northwest: Studies in Regional History, 1787–1910* (Lincoln: University of Nebraska Press, 1969).

4. John Melish, *Travels in the United States of America in the Years 1806 and 1807, and 1809, 1810 & 1811*, vol. 2 (Cincinnati, 1827), 64–66; Clara Longworth de Chambrun, *Cincinnati: Story of the Queen City* (New York: Charles Scribner's Sons, 1939); Steven J. Ross, *Workers on the Edge: Work, Leisure, and Politics in Industrializing Cincinnati, 1788–1890* (New York: Columbia University Press, 1985), 6; Timothy Flint, *Recollections of the Last Ten Years: passed in occasional residences and journeyings in the valley of the Mississippi, from Pittsburg and the Missouri to the Gulf of Mexico, and from Florida to the Spanish frontier: in a series of letters to the Rev. James Flint, of Salem, Massachusetts* (Boston: Cummings, Hilliard, and Co., 1826), 37; "The Commercial Growth and Greatness of the West: As Illustrating the Dignity and Usefulness of Commerce," *The Merchants Magazine* 17 (Nov. 1847): 503, cited in Teaford, *Cities of the Heartland*; Benjamin Drake, *Cincinnati in 1826* (Cincinnati: Morgan, Lodge, and Fisher, 1827), 57.

5. Carol Poh Miller and Robert Wheeler, *Cleveland: A Concise History, 1796–1990* (Bloomington: Indiana University Press, 1990), 15, 17, 24–25, 33; Campbell Gibson, *Population of the 100 Largest Cities and Other Urban Places in the United States: 1790 to 1990* (Washington, D.C.: U.S. Census Bureau), <http://www.census.gov/population/www/documentation/twps0027.html> (accessed September 16, 2010).

6. Betsy Green Deshler in John Green Deshler, "Early history of Columbus, by John

G. Deshler. Talk given before Columbus Real Estate Board, Tuesday, Nov. 18, 1919," Ohio Historical Society. For population figures, see Osman Castle Hooper, *History of the City of Columbus Ohio: From the Founding of Franklinton in 1797 Through the World War Period to the Year 1920* (Columbus: The Memorial Publishing Company, 1920), 33. For more about the early growth of Columbus, see Charles C. Cole Jr., *A Fragile Capital: Identity and the Early Years of Columbus, Ohio* (Columbus: The Ohio State University Press, 2001); and Fay Maxwell, *Early German Village History, South Columbus, Ohio* (Columbus: Elic Press, 1971).

7. Edward A. Leary, *Indianapolis: The Story of a City* (Indianapolis: The Bobbs-Merrill Company, Inc., 1971), 18, 21; William Robeson Holloway, *Indianapolis: A Historical and Statistical Sketch of the Railroad City, a Chronicle of its Social, Municipal, Commercial, and Manufacturing Progress, with full statistical tables* (Indianapolis: Indianapolis Journal Print, 1870), 31.

8. Milo Quaife, *Checagou: From Indian Wigwam to Modern City, 1673–1835* (Chicago: University of Chicago Press, 1933).

9. On the rising middle class and their efforts to control American social, cultural, and political life, see especially Stuart Blumin, *The Emergence of the Middle Class: Social Experience in the American City, 1760–1900* (Cambridge: Cambridge University Press, 1989); and Mary Ryan, *Cradle of the Middle Class: The Family in Oneida County, New York, 1790–1865* (Cambridge: Cambridge University Press, 1981).

10. Carl Abbott, *Boosters and Businessmen: Popular Economic Thought and Urban Growth in the Antebellum Middle West* (Westport, CT: Greenwood Press, 1981).

11. Clergy regularly gave patriotic sermons on and around the Fourth while Independence Day orations were typically reserved for local attorneys.

12. Robert Pettus Hay, "Freedom's Jubilee: One Hundred Years of the Fourth of July, 1776–1876" (PhD diss., University of Kentucky, 1967).

13. For an extensive discussion of these early divisive political celebrations, see Hay, "Freedom's Jubilee."

14. *Albany Daily Advertiser*, July 10, 1788.

15. Simon P. Newman, *Parades and the Politics of the Street: Festive Culture in the Early American Republic* (Philadelphia: University of Pennsylvania Press, 1997), 83, 102.

16. Charles Cist, *Cincinnati in 1841: Its Early Annals and Future Prospects* (Cincinnati: J. A. James, E. Morgan & Co., 1841), 159–60; Ross, *Workers on the Edge*, 23.

17. "Moses Cleaveland Papers, 1754–1806," container 1, folder 5, MS 3233, Western Reserve Historical Society (hereafter WRHS), Cleveland; Miller and Wheeler, *Cleveland*, 23; "The Journal of Emily (Nash) Patchin Halkins Pike from Plainfield, Massachusetts in 1812/3 to Troy Township, Geauga County, Ohio, in 1812–1888," Chardon Library, cited in Robert A. Wheeler, ed., *Visions of the Western Reserve: Public and Private Documents of Northeastern Ohio, 1750–1860* (Columbus: Ohio State University Press, 2000), 267–68.

18. Hooper, *History of the City of Columbus*, 33; Cole, *A Fragile Capital*, 20.

19. Holloway, *Indianapolis*, 20; *Indianapolis Gazette*, June 29, 1822; Leary, *Indianapolis*; *Indianapolis Gazette*, July 6, 1822.

20. Bernard J. Cigrand, "Chicago's Historic Fourths of July," *Fort Dearborn Magazine* (July 1920): 26.

21. Andrew Burstein, *America's Jubilee* (New York: Alfred A. Knopf, 2001).

22. "Jubilee of Independence," *Christian Watchman* (Boston), July 7, 1826; American Periodicals Series Online, p. 127; Paul Leicester Ford, *The Writings of Thomas Jefferson*, vol. 12 (New York: G. P. Putnam's Sons, 1892–99), 311.

23. *Columbus Ohio State Journal*, July 6, 1826; *Liberty Hall and Cincinnati Gazette*, June 30, 1826; *Cleveland Herald*, July 14, 1826; Newman, *Parades and the Politics of the Street*; David Waldstreicher, *In the Midst of Perpetual Fetes* (Chapel Hill: University of North Carolina Press, 1997). See also, for example, *Indianapolis Gazette*, July 6, 1824; David Hudson Jr., Journal, July 4, 1825; David Hudson Family Papers, 1799–1836, container 1, folder 3, MS 3893, WRHS.

24. *Columbus Ohio State Journal*, June 15, 1826. For a similar refrain, see *Wooster Ohio Oracle*, July 21, 1826; DeWitt Clinton, "Address delivered by Governor DeWitt Clinton of New York at ceremonies breaking ground on the Ohio Canal . . ., " in Hawken, ed., *Trumpets of Glory*, 120.

25. *Liberty Hall and Cincinnati Gazette*, July 7, 11, 1826.

26. *Indianapolis Gazette*, July 25, 1826.

27. James R. Heintze, *The Fourth of July Encyclopedia* (Jefferson, NC: McFarland & Company, Inc. Publishers, 2007), 5; Nathaniel S. Prime, *The Year of Jubilee, but not to Africans: A Discourse, delivered July 4th, 1825, being the 49th Anniversary of American Independence* (Salem, NY: Dodd and Stevenson, 1825), 7.

28. *Cleveland Herald*, June 23, July 7, 1826.

29. Richard J. Hooker, "The American Revolution Seen through a Wine Glass," *William and Mary Quarterly* 11 (1) (Jan. 1954): 52–77; *Baltimore Weekly Register* 25 (1823), 276.

30. The toasts given in Cleveland in 1826 were typical of those throughout the nation in the 1820s. See *Cleveland Herald*, July 7, 1826. See also Burstein, *America's Jubilee*, especially pp. 252–54 for other toasts; *Columbus Ohio State Journal*, July 6, 1826. In fact, toasting was an English tradition formerly celebrated in the colonies on the King's and Queen's birthdays. Americans appropriated the tradition, replacing the King and Queen with George Washington and the president of the United States. Hooker, "The American Revolution Seen through a Wine Glass."

31. *Columbus Ohio State Journal*, July 6, 1826; *Cleveland Herald*, July 7, 1826.

32. *Cleveland Herald*, July 7, 1826; *Columbus Ohio State Journal*, July 6, 1826; Harry F. Lupold and Gladys Haddad, *Ohio's Western Reserve: A Regional Reader* (Kent, OH: The Kent State University Press, 1988).

33. Burstein, *America's Jubilee*, 266.

34. *Cleveland Herald*, July 21, 1826.

35. *Liberty Hall and Cincinnati Gazette*, July 11, 1826.

36. *Columbus Ohio State Journal*, July 20, 1826.

1 / "The Sabbath of Liberty"

1. *Columbus Ohio State Journal*, July 12, 1848.

2. Jed Dannenbaum, *Drink and Disorder: Temperance Reform in Cincinnati from the Washingtonian Revival to the WCTU* (Urbana: University of Illinois Press, 1984), 47; Thomas Low Nichols, *Forty Years of American Life*, vol. 1 (London: J. Maxwell and Co., 1864), 152. On Midwest uniqueness, see Andrew R. L. Cayton and Susan E. Gray, *The American Midwest: Essays on Regional History* (Bloomington: Indiana University Press, 2001).

3. *Cleveland Herald*, July 6, 1827; Carol Poh Miller and Robert Wheeler, *Cleveland: A Concise History, 1796-1990* (Bloomington: Indiana University Press, 1990), 38.

4. Charles C. Cole Jr., *A Fragile Capital: Identity and the Early Years of Columbus, Ohio* (Columbus: The Ohio State University Press, 2001); Jonathan Forman, "The First Year of the Second Epidemic of Asiatic Cholera in Columbus, Ohio—1849," *Ohio Archaeological and Historical Quarterly* 53 (4) (Oct.-Dec. 1944): 303-12. Cholera also ravaged Cincinnati, as it did many midwestern urban areas in the first half of the nineteenth century. On cholera in the Queen City, see Theodore W. Eversole, "The Cincinnati Cholera Epidemic of 1849," *Queen City Heritage* 41 (Fall 1983): 21-30; Ruth C. Carter, "Cincinnatians and Cholera: Attitudes Toward the Epidemics of 1832 and 1849," *Queen City Heritage* 50 (3) (1992): 32-48. On the influence of the cholera epidemic as a stimulus for Christian politics, see Adam Jortner, "Cholera, Christ, and Jackson: The Epidemic of 1832 and the Origins of Christian Politics in Antebellum America," *Journal of the Early Republic* 27 (2) (Summer 2007): 233-64.

5. Edward A. Leary, *Indianapolis: The Story of a City* (Indianapolis: The Bobbs-Merrill Company, Inc., 1970), 45, 49, 69.

6. Charles Joseph Latrobe, *The Rambler in North America*: MDCCCXXXII-MDCCCXXXIII, vol. 2 (London: R. B. Seeley and W. Burnside, 1835), 202; Perry Duis, *Challenging Chicago: Coping with Everyday Life, 1837-1920* (Urbana: University of Illinois Press, 1998); Milo Quaife, *Checagou: From Indian Wigwam to Modern City, 1673-1835* (Chicago: University of Chicago Press, 1933); Henry Justin Smith, *Chicago's Great Century: 1833-1933* (Chicago: Consolidated Publishers, Inc., 1933), 32.

7. *Indianapolis Indiana Democrat*, July 4, 1849; *Columbus Ohio State Journal*, June 26, July 10, 1839; *Cleveland Herald*, June 22, 1842.

8. Mary Ryan, *Civic Wars: Democracy and Public Life in the American City During the Nineteenth Century* (Berkeley: University of California Press, 1997), 15; Len Travers, *Celebrating the Fourth: Independence Day and the Rites of Nationalism in the Early Republic* (Amherst: University of Massachusetts Press, 1997). Other monographs making similar arguments include Diana Karter Appelbaum, *The Glorious Fourth: An American Holiday, An American History* (New York: Facts on File, 1989); and Robert Pettus Hay, "Freedom's Jubilee: One Hundred Years of the Fourth of July, 1776-1876" (PhD diss., University of Kentucky, 1967). On empty rhetoric, see Joel Buttles Diaries, July 4, 1842, Ohio Historical Society (hereafter OHS), Columbus; *Cincinnati Enquirer*, June 25, 1839; *Columbus Ohio State Journal*, July 13, 1833; and *Indianapolis Indiana Democrat*, July 4, 1849. Sometimes, newspapers created their own flawed memories of past Independence Days, praising old-fashioned Fourths for their unity and conviviality. See Ellen M. Litwicki, "Visions of America: Public Holidays and American Cultures, 1776-1900" (PhD diss., University of Virginia, 1992).

9. *Cleveland Plain Dealer*, July 7, 1845; *Cleveland Herald*, July 6, 1846; *Columbus Ohio State Journal*, June 30, 1841.

10. For an excellent debate on the rise of political interest in this era, see Glenn Altschuler and Stuart Blumin, "Political Engagement and Disengagement in Antebellum America: A Roundtable," *Journal of American History* 84 (1997): 855-909. On Jacksonian America, the standard texts include Harry L. Watson, *Liberty and Power: The Politics of Jacksonian America* (New York: Hill and Wang, 1990); and Arthur M. Schlesinger, *The Age of Jackson* (Boston: Little, Brown & Co., 1945).

11. *Columbus Ohio State Journal*, July 7, 1837; July 1, 1840; and Charles C. Cole Jr.,

A Fragile Capital: Identity and the Early Years of Columbus, Ohio (Columbus: Ohio State University Press, 2001).

12. Len Travers does an exceptional job of deconstructing this transformation. See Len Travers, *Celebrating the Fourth: Independence Day and the Rites of Nationalism in the Early Republic* (Amherst: University of Massachusetts Press, 1997); Buttles Diaries, July 4, 1845; *Indianapolis Indiana State Sentinel*, July 11, 1843; *Cleveland Plain Dealer*, July 3, 1848.

13. *Indiana State Sentinel* (Indianapolis), July 5, 1845; Jane Shaffer Elsmere, *Henry Ward Beecher: The Indiana Years, 1837–1847* (Indianapolis: Indiana Historical Society, 1973), 231–32. A similar occurrence, though not resulting in loss of life, occurred in Cincinnati in 1849 when "a loafer" amused himself by randomly attacking members of the city's African-American population. His reign of terror ended when one of his victims fought back, attacking his assailant with the backend of a revolver. See *Cincinnati Enquirer*, June 24, 1849.

14. W. J. Rorabaugh, *The Alcoholic Republic: An American Tradition* (New York: Oxford University Press, 1979), 152; Frederick Marryat, *A Diary in America: With Remarks on Its Institutions*, ed. Sydney Jackman (New York: Alfred A. Knopf, 1962), 389.

15. W. J. Rorabaugh marks this transition in the late 1820s. However, in the Midwest, this was a later phenomenon, as the growth of temperance institutions peaked after those in the eastern cities that are included in Rorabaugh's study. Rorabaugh, *Alcoholic Republic*; Ian R. Tyrrell, *Sobering Up: From Temperance to Prohibition in Antebellum America, 1800–1860* (Westport, CT: Greenwood Press, 1979); *Columbus Ohio State Journal*, July 7, 1846.

16. Hay, "Freedom's Jubilee"; *Columbus Ohio State Journal*, July 15, 1830; Robert Lowery 1836 Aug 9 Letter from Elyria Ohio, OHS, VFM 1790.

17. Ronald G. Walters, *American Reformers, 1815–1860* (New York: Hill and Wang, 1997); Joseph R. Gusfield, *Symbolic Crusade: Status Politics and the American Temperance Movement* (Urbana: University of Illinois Press, 1963); Ian Tyrrell, *Sobering Up*; Abner Crosby Diary, 1817–1874, Western Reserve Historical Society, MS 1157; *Cleveland Western Courier*, January 26, 1838; Leary, *Indianapolis*; Smith, *Chicago's Great Century*; Dannenbaum, *Drink and Disorder*.

18. *Cincinnati Enquirer*, June 30, 1842; *Indianapolis Indiana Journal*, July 4, 1842; *Cincinnati Enquirer*, July 8, 1844.

19. Tyrrell, *Sobering Up*; *Cleveland Plain Dealer*, July 8, 1845; *Columbus Ohio State Journal*, July 7, 1846; Dannenbaum, *Drink and Disorder*. The Sons of Temperance did have some influence in Columbus, where, in 1846 and 1848, the organization sponsored Fourth of July celebrations with respectable results. But as in the other cities, their success in Columbus was temporary.

20. *Cincinnati Advertiser and Journal*, July 8, 1839; *Cincinnati Enquirer*, July 7, 1846. Newspaper accounts around the Fourth are littered with stories detailing these occurrences. See, for example, *Cincinnati Enquirer*, July 7, 1847; *Cleveland Herald*, July 5, 1849; and *Columbus Ohio State Journal*, July 7, 1849. There is a dearth of information explicitly connecting the Fourth of July to notions of masculinity and violence. On individual examples of July 4 violence, see James R. Heintze, *The Fourth of July Encyclopedia* (Jefferson, NC: McFarland & Company, Inc. Publishers, 2007), 12, 17, 50, 205. For other studies of midwestern masculinity and its ties to violent culture, see

Nicole Etcheson, "Manliness and the Political Culture of the Old Northwest, 1790–1860," *Journal of the Early Republic* 15 (1) (Spring 1995): 59–77; and Ryan L. Dearinger, "Violence, Masculinity, Image, and Reality on the Antebellum Frontier," *Indiana Magazine of History* 100 (1) (March 2004): 26–55.

21. William Robeson Holloway, *Indianapolis: A Historical and Statistical Sketch of the Railroad City, a Chronicle of its Social, Municipal, Commercial, and Manufacturing Progress, with full statistical tables* (Indianapolis: Indianapolis Journal Print, 1870), 41; *Chicago Democrat*, July 6, 1836. Fireworks were also a problematic issue. They were praised as visible and audible signs of patriotic celebration, but derided for safety reasons. In fact, many cities banned fireworks on the Fourth, though their efforts usually proved unsuccessful. See, for example, *Columbus Ohio State Journal*, July 19, 1834.

22. On African-American celebrations, see Stephen Elliot James, "The Other Fourth of July: The Meanings of Black Identity at American Celebrations of Independence, 1770–1863" (PhD diss., Harvard University, 1997).

23. *Cleveland Herald*, July 11, 1828; *Columbus Ohio State Journal*, July 2, 1839; *Indianapolis Indiana Democrat* (Indianapolis), June 22, July 20, 1831; Leonard I. Sweet, "The Fourth of July and Black Americans in the Nineteenth Century: Northern Leadership Opinion Within the Context of the Black Experience," *The Journal of Negro History* 61 (3) (July 1976): 260. On midwestern abolitionists, see Andrew R. L. Cayton and Peter S. Onuf, *The Midwest and the Nation: Rethinking the History of an American Region* (Bloomington: Indiana University Press, 1990).

24. Caleb W. McDaniel, "The Fourth and the First: Abolitionist Holidays, Respectability, and Radical Interracial Reform," *American Quarterly* 57 (1) (2005): 138. For example, by 1845, of the 12,000 residents of Cleveland, just 56 were African-American. Miller and Wheeler, *Cleveland*, 40; *Cincinnati Enquirer*, June 25, 1848; *Columbus Ohio State Journal*, July 2, 1829; July 10, 1844; *Indianapolis Indiana Democrat*, July 1, 1840.

25. Caleb W. McDaniel, "The Fourth and the First," 137. In addition, some African-Americans celebrated Pinkster, a holiday of inversion, though no record exists of its celebration in the Midwest. See, for example, Bradford Verter, "Interracial Festivity and Power in Antebellum New York: The Case of Pinkster," *Journal of Urban History* 28 (2002): 398–427. For an excellent discussion of African-American celebrations throughout the nation, see Mitch Kachun, *Festivals of Freedom: Memory and Meaning in African American Emancipation Celebrations, 1808–1915* (Amherst: University of Massachusetts Press, 2003).

26. Dannenbaum, *Drink and Disorder*.

27. *Cleveland Herald*, August 6, 1827; *Indianapolis Indiana Democrat*, July 10, 1839; *Cleveland Herald*, July 15, 1830; Frances Milton Trollope, *Domestic Manners of the Americans*, vol. 1 (New York: Dodd, Mead, 1901), 120; Linda K. Kerber, "The Republican Mother: Women and the Enlightenment—An American Perspective," in *Toward an Intellectual History of Women: Essays by Linda K. Kerber* (Chapel Hill: University of North Carolina Press, 1997), 43; Litwicki, "Visions of America," 29.

28. *Indianapolis Indiana Democrat*, July 17, 1839; *Cleveland Plain Dealer*, July 1, 1846; *Indianapolis Indiana State Sentinel*, July 11, 1843.

29. Robert Neelly Bellah, "Civil Religion in America," *Journal of the American Academy of Arts and Sciences* 96 (1) (Winter 1967): 1–21; *Columbus Ohio State Journal*, July 13, 1833. My understanding of this era has been particularly enriched by Paul Johnson's monograph on Rochester, New York. See Paul E. Johnson, *A Shopkeeper's*

Millennium: Society and Revivals in Rochester, New York, 1815–1837 (New York: Hill and Wang, 1978).

30. *Indianapolis Democrat*, July 9, 1831; July 12, 1849; Buttles Diaries, July 4, 1844; *Cincinnati Advertiser and Journal*, July 11, 1840. Organizers did not invite Catholics to these fetes, but with minuscule populations of Irish in the Midwest in the 1840s—which would not be the case in the 1850s—their exclusion was seldom discussed.

31. *Indianapolis Indiana Journal*, July 5, 1842; *Indianapolis Indiana State Sentinel*, July 10, 1847; Buttles Diaries, July 4, 1845.

32. *Chicago Democrat*, June 25, 1845; *Indianapolis Indiana Democrat*, July 6, 1836.

33. Abner Crosby Diary, July 4, 1830, and July 4, 1841, WRHS; *Cincinnati Enquirer*, June 26, July 5, 1847; *Columbus Ohio State Journal*, July 7, 1847; Mr. Klots to Carl Mayer, July 18, 1858, Charles Mayer Papers, 1838–1895, Indiana Historical Society.

34. *National Anniversary: A Copy of the Remarks Introductory to the Reading of the Declaration of Independence by Samuel R. Miller, and a copy of the Oration delivered by Bellamy Storer . . .* (Cincinnati, 1829); Rev. Charles B. Boynton, *Oration, Delivered on the Fifth of July, 1847, Before the Native Americans of Cincinnati* (Cincinnati: Tagart & Gardner, 1847); Jon Gjerde, *The Minds of the West: Ethnocultural Evolution in the Rural Middle West, 1830–1917* (Chapel Hill: University of North Carolina Press, 1997).

35. *Celebration of the Fourth of July, 1834, By the Fraternity of Victuallers of Cincinnati: Containing the Proceedings of the Day, the Patriotic Address Delivered on the Occasion, and the Toasts* (Cincinnati: F. S. Benton, 1834); *Indiana State Sentinel* (Indianapolis), July 11, 1843; *Ohio State Journal* (Columbus), July 13, 1833; *Cleveland Plain Dealer*, July 3, 1847; Appelbaum, *The Glorious Fourth*.

36. The classic study of American civil religion is Robert N. Bellah, "Civil Religion in America," *Journal of the American Academy of Arts and Sciences* 96 (1) (1967): 1–21. Ernest Lee Tuveson, *Redeemer Nation: The Idea of America's Millennial Role* (Chicago: University of Chicago Press, 1980), 186; Bercovitch, *The Rites of Assent*, 39. On this shift and the importance of religion in antebellum America, see also Mark Y. Hanley, *Beyond a Christian Commonwealth: The Protestant Quarrel with the American Republic, 1830–1860* (Chapel Hill: The University of North Carolina Press, 1994); Nathan O. Hatch, *The Democratization of American Christianity* (New Haven: Yale University Press, 1989); and James H. Moorhead, *American Apocalypse: Yankee Protestants and the Civil War, 1860–1869* (New Haven: Yale University Press, 1978).

37. Joyce Appleby, *Inheriting the Revolution: The First Generation of Americans* (Cambridge, MA: The Belknap Press, 2000); *Liberty Hall and Cincinnati Gazette*, July 7, 1826; July 11, 1826; *Indianapolis Gazette*, July 25, 1826.

38. *Columbus Ohio State Journal*, July 13, 1833; *Indianapolis Democrat*, July 4, 1834; Buttles Diaries, July 4, 1842; July 4, 1845; *Indianapolis Indiana State Sentinel*, July 11, 1843; *Cleveland Plain Dealer*, July 3, 1848.

39. Bercovitch, *Rites of Assent*; Appleby, *Inheriting the Revolution*. An example was Jesse Hopkins, who noted that celebrations in 1826 were transformative as "heaven itself mingled visibly in the celebration, and hallowed the day anew by a double apotheosis." Jesse Hopkins, *The Patriot's Manual: Comprising Various Standard and Miscellaneous Subjects, Interesting to Every American Citizen* (Utica, NY: William Williams, 1828), 182. See also John Bodnar, *Remaking America: Public Memory, Commemoration, and Patriotism in the Twentieth Century* (Princeton: Princeton University Press, 1992) for more on the role of 1826 as a turning point.

40. *Columbus Ohio State Journal*, June 15, 1826.

2 / "Americans Ruling America"

1. *Cincinnati Daily Enquirer*, July 7, 1855.

2. The summary of these events is culled from three newspaper accounts—*Columbus Der Wesbote*, July 7, 1855; *Columbus Ohio State Journal*, July 5, 1855; and *Columbus Ohio Statesman*, July 6, 1855.

3. Jon Teaford, *Cities of the Heartland: The Rise and Fall of the Industrial Midwest* (Bloomington: Indiana University Press, 1993), 34.

4. On Chicago, see Perry Duis, *Challenging Chicago: Coping with Everyday Life, 1837–1920* (Urbana: University of Illinois Press, 1998); Henry Justin Smith, *Chicago's Great Century* (Chicago: Consolidated Publishers, Inc., 1933); Duis, *The Saloon: Public Drinking in Chicago and Boston, 1880–1920* (Urbana: University of Illinois Press, 1983); James Merriner, *Grafters and Goo Goos: Corruption and Reform in Chicago, 1833–2003* (Carbondale: Southern Illinois University Press, 2004). On Cincinnati, see Carl Wittke, "Ohio's Germans, 1840–1875," *The Ohio Historical Quarterly* 66 (4) (Oct. 1957): 339–54; Jed Dannenbaum, *Drink and Disorder: Temperance Reform in Cincinnati from the Washingtonian Revival to the WCTU* (Urbana: University of Illinois Press, 1984). On Cleveland, see Werner D. Mueller, "Cleveland's 19th century German Community and its 'Forty-Eighters,'" an overview and interpretation; for Cleveland in the 1800s, see ibid., "ecclesiastical despots" vs. "the immigrant Teuton" (August 1995), Cincinnati Historical Society; Carol Poh Miller and Robert Wheeler, *Cleveland: A Concise History, 1796–1990* (Bloomington: Indiana University Press, 1990). On Columbus, see Charles C. Cole Jr., *A Fragile Capital: Identity and the Early Years of Columbus, Ohio* (Columbus: Ohio State University Press, 2001); Margaret Sittler, "The German Element in Columbus Before the Civil War," Master's thesis, Ohio State University, 1932, quoted in Osman Castle Hooper, *History of the City of Columbus Ohio: From the Founding of Franklinton in 1797 Through the World War Period to the Year 1920* (Columbus: The Memorial Publishing Company, 1920), 39. On Indianapolis, see Edward A. Leary, *Indianapolis: The Story of a City* (Indianapolis: The Bobbs-Merrill Company, Inc., 1971); Census of Population and Housing, 1860, <http://www.census.gov/prod/www/abs/decennial/1860.htm≥ (accessed May 25, 2010).

5. On antebellum drinking culture and temperance efforts, see W. J. Rorabaugh, *The Alcoholic Republic: An American Tradition* (New York: Oxford University Press, 1979); Dannenbaum, *Drink and Disorder*; Joseph R. Gusfield, *Symbolic Crusade: Status Politics and the American Temperance Movement* (Urbana: University of Illinois Press, 1963); Ian R. Tyrrell, *Sobering Up: From Temperance to Prohibition in Antebellum America, 1800–1860* (Westport, CT: Greenwood Press, 1979); *Cleveland Plain Dealer*, July 1, 1854. On abolitionist sentiment and the Fourth of July in this period, see *Cleveland Plain Dealer*, July 6, 1854; *Columbus Ohio Statesman*, July 3, 1855; *Columbus Ohio State Journal*, July 6, 1854; July 5, 1853; *Indianapolis Indiana State Sentinel*, June 27, 1850; June 30, 1853.

6. Tyler Anbinder, *Five Points: The Nineteenth-Century New York City Neighborhood that Invented Tap Dance, Stole Elections, and Became the World's Most Notorious Slum* (New York: The Free Press, 2001); Noel Ignatiev, *How the Irish Became White* (New York: Routledge, 1995); Dale T. Knobel, *Paddy and the Republic: Ethnicity and Nationality in Antebellum America* (Middletown, CT: Wesleyan University Press,

1986); Matthew Frye Jacobson, *Whiteness of a Different Color: European Immigrants and the Alchemy of Race* (Cambridge: Harvard University Press, 1998); *Chicago Tribune*, February 26, March 2, 1855.

7. *Cleveland Plain Dealer*, July 5, 1854; Cincinnati *Enquirer*, July 6, 1854.

8. Although Germany did not unify until 1871, for ease of use the term "German" will be used to refer to immigrants of Teutonic ancestry. Cole, *A Fragile Capital*; James Bergquist, "German Communities in American Cities: An Interpretation of the Nineteenth-Century Experience," *Journal of American Ethnic History* 4 (1) (1984): 9–30; Wili Paul Adams, *The German-Americans: An Ethnic Experience*, trans. LaVern J. Rippley and Eberhard Reichmann (Indianapolis: Max Kade German-American Center, 1993); La Vern J. Rippley, *The German-Americans* (Boston; Twayne Publishers, 1976); Don Heinrich Tolzmann, *The German-American Experience* (Amherst, NY: Humanity Books, 2000).

9. W. D. Howells, "In an Old-Time State Capital, First Paper," *Harper's Monthly Magazine* 129 (Sept. 1914): 596; Gotthilft Willig Letter, March 30, 1852, Chicago Historical Society.

10. Wittke, "Ohio's Germans"; *Cleveland Plain Dealer*, July 2, 1856.

11. La Vern J. Rippley, *The German-Americans*; Adams, *German-Americans*. On German celebratory culture, see especially Kathleen Neils Conzen, *Immigrant Milwaukee 1836–1860: Accommodation and Community in a Frontier City* (Cambridge: Harvard University Press, 1976).

12. Assimilationist arguments include Adams, *The German-Americans*; Oscar Handlin, *The Uprooted: The Epic Story of the Great Migrations That Made the American People* (New York: Grosset & Dunlap, 1951); and John Higham, *Strangers in the Land: Patterns of American Nativism, 1860–1925* (New Brunswick, NJ: Rutgers University Press, 1955). On cultural retention, see especially Donna R. Gabaccia, "Liberty, Coercion, and the Making of Immigration Historians," *The Journal of American History* 84 (2) (Sept. 1997): 570–75; and Roger Daniels, *Coming to America: A History of Immigration and Ethnicity in American Life* (New York: HarperCollins, 1990). On invented ethnicity, see Kathleen Conzen and David Gerber, "The Invention of Ethnicity: A Perspective from the U.S.A.," *Journal of American Ethnic History* 12 (1) (Fall 1992): 3–42; and Werner Sollors, ed., *The Invention of Ethnicity* (New York: Oxford University Press, 1989). For an extensive historiographical treatment of this issue, see Russell Kazal, "Revisiting Assimilation: The Rise, Fall, and Reappraisal of a Concept in American Ethnic History," *The American Historical Review* 100 (2) (April 1995): 437–71.

13. *Cincinnati Volksfreund*, November 13, 1848, quoted in Adams, *German-Americans*, 33. See also Anonymous letter to *Atlantis*, January 1857, quoted in Adams, *The German-Americans*, 4–6; and Bergquist, "German Communities in American Cities"; John Peck, *A New Guide for Emigrants to the West: Containing Sketches of Michigan, Ohio, Indiana, Illinois, Missouri, Arkansas, with the Territory of Wisconsin, and the Adjacent Parts* (Boston: Gould, Kendall & Lincoln, 1843), 107.

14. On this layering process, see especially Frank Trommler and Elliott Shore, *The German-American Encounter: Conflict and Cooperation Between Two Cultures 1800–2000* (New York: Berghahn Books, 2001).

15. Frances Trollope, *Domestic Manners of the Americans*, vol. 1 (New York: Dodd, Mead, 1901), 8. On this phenomenon in eastern cities, see Matthew Dennis, *Red, White*

and Blue Letter Days: An American Calendar (Ithaca, NY: Cornell University Press, 2002); David A. Gerber, "'The Germans Take Care of Our Celebrations': Middle-Class Americans Appropriate German Ethnic Culture in Buffalo in the 1850s," in *Hard at Play: Leisure in America, 1840–1940*, ed. Kathryn Grover (Amherst: University of Massachusetts Press, 1992), 39–60; and Tolzmann, *German-American Experience.*

16. *Columbus Ohio State Journal*, July 12, 1853; *Cleveland Plain Dealer*, July 5, 1856; James Heintze, *The Fourth of July in Sound, Spectacle and Symbol* (Washington, DC: The Author, 1999). This was also the case in Milwaukee, where Germans had "virtually monopolized the city's Fourth of July parade." Kathleen Neils Conzen, "Ethnicity as Festive Culture: Nineteenth-Century German America on Parade," in Sollors, *Invention of Ethnicity*, 45; Jakob Mueller, *Memoirs of a Forty-eighter: Sketches from the German-American Period of Storm and Stress of the 1850s*, trans. Steven Rowan (Cleveland: Rudolf Schmidt Printing Company, 1896), 34; Sittler, "German Element in Columbus."

17. A wealth of secondary literature explores the roots of nativism and its early agenda. Some of the most influential includes Tyler Anbinder, *Nativism and Slavery: The Northern Know-Nothings and the Politics of the 1850s* (New York: Oxford University Press, 1992); Ray Allen Billington, *The Origins of Nativism in the United States, 1800–1844* (New York: Arno Press, 1974); Roger Daniels, *Coming to America: A History of Immigration and Ethnicity in American Life* (New York: HarperCollins, 1990); Dale T. Knobel, *"America for the Americans": The Nativist Movement in the United States* (New York: Twayne Publishers, 1996); Elliot Gorn, "'Good-Bye Boys, I Die a True American': Homicide, Nativism, and Working-Class Culture in Antebellum New York City," *The Journal of American History* 74 (2) (Sept. 1987): 388–410.

18. Quoted in Philip Gleason, "Trouble in the Colonial Melting Pot," *Journal of American Ethnic History* 20 (1) (2000): 3; Gorn, "'Good-Bye Boys,'" 394; *Cincinnati Enquirer*, July 8, 1854. Some historians have argued that the Alien and Sedition Acts marked the beginnings of anti-immigrant sentiment in the Americas. However, these acts protected against internal rather than external threats—a much different agenda than the nativism of the 1840s and later. See Knobel, *"America for the Americans."*

19. *Transactions of the Fifth Annual Meeting of the Western Literary Historical Society and the College of Professional Teachers, October 1835* (Cincinnati, 1836), 82; *Columbus Ohio State Journal*, July 10, 1839; July 3, 1844.

20. *Indianapolis Indiana State Sentinel*, July 11, 1844; *Cleveland Plain Dealer*, July 7, 1845; Boynton, *Oration.*

21. Higham, *Strangers in the Land*; John B. Weaver, "Ohio Republican Attitudes Towards Nativism, 1854–1855," *Old Northwest* 9 (4) (1983–1984): 289–305; Knobel, *"America for the Americans"*; La Vern Rippley, "The Columbus Germans." *Report— Society for the History of the Germans in Maryland* 33 (1968): 1–46; *Chicago Daily Democratic Press*, April 24, 1855; *Chicago Literary Budget*, December 23, 1854; Bruce McKittrick Cole, "The Chicago Press and the Know-Nothings, 1850–1856" (Master's thesis, University of Chicago, 1948).

22. These are based on Tyler Anbinder's definitions as outlined in *Nativism and Slavery.*

23. Michael Feldberg, *The Philadelphia Riots of 1844: A Study of Ethnic Conflict* (Westport, CT: Greenwood Press, 1975); Paul A. Gilje, *Rioting in America* (Bloomington: Indiana University Press, 1996).

24. Although no large-scale conflicts marred Indianapolis or Cleveland, these cities also encountered heated conversations about the place of ethnicity on the Fourth. See, for example, *Cleveland Plain Dealer*, July 3, 1852; *Indianapolis Indiana State Sentinel*, July 8, 1852.

25. On the Lager Beer Riots, see Adam Criblez, "'A Motley Array': Changing Perceptions of Chicago Taverns, 1833–1871," *The Journal of Illinois History* (Winter 2005): 262–80; and R. W. Renner, "In a Perfect Ferment: Chicago, the Know-Nothings, and the Riot for Lager Beer," *Chicago History* 5 (1976): 161–70; *Chicago Tribune*, March 5, 1855; Mabel McIlvaine, *Reminiscences of Chicago during the Forties and Fifties* (Chicago: Lakeside Press, 1913). On similar events in Indianapolis, see Leary, *Indianapolis*, 75; William Robeson Holloway, *Indianapolis: A Historical and Statistical Sketch of the Railroad City, a Chronicle of its Social, Municipal, Commercial, and Manufacturing Progress, with full statistical tables* (Indianapolis: Indianapolis Journal Print, 1870).

26. Wittke, "Ohio's Germans"; Dannenbaum, *Drink and Disorder*; William Baughin, "'Ballots and Bullets': The Election Day Riots of 1855," *Historical and Philosophical Society of Ohio Bulletin* 21 (1963): 267–72; *Cincinnati Enquirer*, June 19–28, July 4–6, 1855.

27. *Columbus Ohio State Journal*, May 29–31, July 8–11, 1855; Ripley, "The Columbus Germans."

28. *Columbus Ohio State Journal*, July 7, 1855.

29. *Columbus Der Wesbote*, July 7, 1855; *Columbus Ohio State Journal*, July 12, 1853; June 23, 1854.

30. *Cincinnati Daily Enquirer*, July 7, 1855. It is interesting to note that, outside of Cincinnati, other midwestern urban centers paid little heed to the events in Columbus. The *Milwaukee Sentinel*, for instance, blamed the Turners for inciting the riot, claiming that "there was no excuse for their conduct." *Milwaukee Daily Sentinel*, July 6, 1855.

31. Renner, "In a Perfect Ferment."

32. *Chicago Tribune*, June 28, 1855; *Columbus Ohio State Journal*, July 3–5, 1856; *Cincinnati Enquirer*, July 4–6, 1856. In Indianapolis, for example, in 1856, area newspapers warned against "Black Republicans" and their factionalism that threatened to tear the nation apart. See *Indianapolis Indiana State Sentinel*, July 3, 1856.

3 / "We shall still celebrate, but not as of old"

1. *Chicago Tribune*, July 4, 1864.

2. Peter J. Parish, *The North and the Nation in the Era of the Civil War*, ed. Adam I. P. Smith and Susan-Mary Grant (New York: Fordham University Press, 2003), 164.

3. Parish, *North and the Nation*, 114–15; George B. Forgie, *Patricide in the House Divided: A Psychological Interpretation of Lincoln and His Age* (New York: W. W. Norton & Co., 1979), 3–8, 12. There is a wealth of literature about late antebellum nationalism and sectionalism. See, for instance, Carl N. Degler, "One Among Many: The Civil War in Comparative Perspective," Twenty-ninth Annual Robert Fortenbaugh Memorial Lecture, Gettysburg College, 1990; Earl J. Hess, *Liberty, Virtue, and Progress: Northerners and their War for the Union* (New York: New York University Press, 1988); Melinda Lawson, *Patriot Fires: Forging a New American Nationalism in the Civil War North* (Lawrence: University Press of Kansas, 2002); James H. Moorhead, *American Apocalypse: Yankee Protestants and the Civil War, 1860–1869* (New Haven: Yale

University Press, 1978); John R. Neff, *Honoring the Civil War Dead: Commemoration and the Problem of Reconciliation* (Lawrence: University Press of Kansas, 2005); and Peter J. Parish, *The North and the Nation in the Era of the Civil War*, ed. Adam I. P. Smith and Susan-Mary Grant (New York: Fordham University Press, 2003).

4. *Cincinnati Enquirer*, June 24, July 5, 1857; *Columbus Ohio State Journal*, July 3, 1857; *Cleveland Plain Dealer*, July 3–6, 1858.

5. *Indianapolis Indiana State Sentinel*, July 6, June 23, June 27, 1859.

6. Ibid., July 4, 1859.

7. Ibid., July 4, 1860; *Cincinnati Enquirer*, July 4, 1860.

8. Of course, an abundant historiography exists on the causes of the American Civil War. Some of the more recent additions include Edward L. Ayers, *What Caused the Civil War? Reflections on the South and Southern History* (New York: Norton, 2005); *Why The Civil War Came*, ed. Gabor S. Boritt (New York: Oxford University Press, 1996); William W. Freehling, *The Road to Disunion* (New York: Oxford University Press, 1990); Michael F. Holt, *The Fate of Their Country: Politicians, Slavery Extension, and the Coming of the Civil War* (New York: Hill and Wang, 2005); Gary J. Kornblith, "Rethinking the Coming of the Civil War: A Counterfactual Exercise," *Journal of American History* 90 (1) (June 2003): 76–105; Bruce Levine, *Half Slave and Half Free: The Roots of Civil War* (New York: Hill and Wang, 2005); Chandra Manning, *What this Cruel War was Over: Soldiers, Slavery, and the Civil War* (New York: Vintage Books, 2007); Michael A. Morrison, *Slavery and the American West: The Eclipse of Manifest Destiny and the Coming of the Civil War* (Chapel Hill: University of North Carolina Press, 1997); Parish, *North and the Nation*, 130; Moorhead, *American Apocalypse*.

9. *Indianapolis Indiana State Sentinel*, April 15, 1861; Emma Lou Thornbrough, *Indiana in the Civil War Era, 1850–1880* (Indianapolis: Indiana Historical Bureau and Indiana Historical Society, 1965). Opposition both to Lincoln and to the war effort were high in parts of Indiana, despite the fact that the state sent tens of thousands of young men to fight for the Union cause. In fact, Sugar Creek Township, in Shelby County, seceded from the United States, although its secession was more symbolic than effective in drumming up support for the Confederacy; Matt Martin to S. S. Cox, Dec. 3, 1861, Samuel Sullivan Cox Papers, Brown University Library, quoted in Frank L. Klement, *The Copperheads in the Middle West* (Chicago: University of Chicago Press, 1960).

10. Klement, *Copperheads in the Middle West*, 139; Brayton Harris, *Blue & Gray in Black & White: Newspapers in the Civil War* (Washington: Brassey's, 1999), 100; Thornbrough, *Indiana in the Civil War Era*; Lloyd Wendt, *Chicago Tribune: The Rise of a Great American Newspaper* (Chicago: Rand McNally & Company, 1931). On the rise of the partisan press in the early nineteenth century, see Jeffrey L. Pasley, "*The Tyranny of Printers*": *Newspaper Politics in the Early American Republic* (Charlottesville: University of Virginia Press, 2003).

11. *Indiana State Sentinel* (Indianapolis), July 10, 1861. On America's puritanical heritage, see chapter 2.

12. Hess, *Liberty, Virtue, and Progress*, quoted in James M. McPherson, *For Cause and Comrades: Why Men Fought in the Civil War* (New York: Oxford University Press, 1997), 16.

13. "The Lounger. A Short Fourth of July Oration," *Harper's Weekly*, July 13, 1861.

14. On the importance of the Western Theater in the Civil War and the role of midwesterners, see James H. Bissland, *Blood, Tears, and Glory: How Ohioans Won the Civil War* (Wilmington, OH: Orange Frazer Press, 2007), and Richard Brady Williams, *Chicago's Battery Boys: The Chicago Mercantile Battery in the Civil War's Western Theater* (El Dorado Hills, CA: Savas Beatie, 2008). The most famous group of Civil War soldiers from the Midwest was the Iron Brigade. On their experiences, see Alan T. Nolan, *The Iron Brigade: A Military History* (New York: The Macmillan Company, 1961). Of the 750,000 troops, roughly 300,000 were from Ohio, 190,000 from Indiana, and 250,000 from Illinois. Bissland, *Blood, Tears, and Glory*, 5, 61.

15. *Cincinnati Enquirer*, July 5, 1861; *Indianapolis Indiana State Sentinel*, July 10, 1861; *Columbus Ohio State Journal*, July 3, 1861; *Chicago Tribune*, July 6, 1861.

16. *Chicago Tribune*, July 1–6, 1861.

17. Parish, *North and the Nation*, 66; Cecilia Elizabeth O'Leary, *To Die For: The Paradox of American Patriotism* (Princeton: Princeton University Press, 1999).

18. *Cleveland Plain Dealer*, July 1, 1861; *Cincinnati Enquirer*, July 5, 1861; *Columbus Ohio State Journal*, July 3–5, 1861; Silas William Blizard, July 4, 1861, Diaries and Records, Indiana Historical Society; *Chicago Tribune*, July 4, 1861. This was an outgrowth of a phenomenon of noontime prayer meetings, first held by a YMCA in New York City in 1857, which spread throughout the nation. Moorhead, *American Apocalypse*.

19. *Chicago Tribune*, June 25, 1861; *Cincinnati Enquirer*, July 5, 1861.

20. Bissland, *Blood, Tears, and Glory*, 149, 151, 167.

21. *Cincinnati Enquirer*, July 4, 1862; *Cleveland Plain Dealer*, July 3, 1862.

22. *Chicago Tribune*, June 28, July 4, 1862; Ellen M. Litwicki, "Visions of America: Public Holidays and American Cultures, 1776–1900" (PhD diss., University of Virginia, 1992); *Columbus Ohio State Journal*, July 3, 1862. On the development of wartime benevolent societies, see Parish, *North and the Nation*.

23. *Cincinnati Enquirer*, July 2, 5, 1862.

24. Blizard Diaries, July 4, 1862; *Cincinnati Enquirer*, July 5, 1862.

25. *Cleveland Plain Dealer*, June 20, 25, July 3–5, 1862.

26. *Cleveland Plain Dealer*, July 5, 1862. Neither man's name was provided in the newspaper report of the incident. Instead, they were referred to as a "somewhat aged gentleman of the colored persuasion" and "a somewhat inebriated Gentleman of the English persuasion."

27. On Morgan's Raid in Ohio, see Bissland, *Blood, Tears, and Glory*.

28. *Indiana State Sentinel* (Indianapolis), January 15, 1863; Frank L. Klement, *The Copperheads in the Middle West* (Chicago: University of Chicago Press, 1960). Chandra Manning offers that the Emancipation Proclamation changed "a war to preserve the Union into a war to reform it," arguing that it forced northern soldiers to confront the reality that slavery was a national, rather than sectional, concern. See Chandra Manning, *What this Cruel War was Over: Soldiers, Slavery, and the Civil War* (New York: Vintage Books, 2007). In the urban Midwest, far from the lines of battle, there was certainly less unanimity regarding this controversial document.

29. Leonard I. Sweet, "The Fourth of July and Black Americans in the Nineteenth Century: Northern Leadership Opinion Within the Context of the Black Experience," *The Journal of Negro History* 61 (3) (July 1976): 260; *Cincinnati Enquirer*, June 23, 1863; Census of Population and Housing, 1860 Census, <http://www.census.gov/

prod/www/abs/decennial/1860.htm≥ (accessed April 25, 2008). By comparison, Cook County, Illinois (Chicago), was 0.7% African-American (1,007 African-Americans and 143,947 white Americans); Cuyahoga County, Ohio (Cleveland), was 1.1% (894 and 77,130); Franklin County, Ohio (Columbus), was 3.1% (1,578 and 48,783); Marion County, Indiana (Indianapolis), was 2.1% (825 and 39,030). *Cleveland Plain Dealer*, June 15, July 6, 1863. Unfortunately, no record exists of the number of recruits added in Cleveland that day. On previous African-American celebrations in the Midwest, see chapter 2.

30. *Chicago Tribune*, July 4, 1863; *Columbus Ohio State Journal*, July 4, 6, 1863. On the role of death and the war, see Drew Gilpin Faust, *This Republic of Suffering: Death and the American Civil War* (New York: Alfred A. Knopf, 2008). Faust argues that "death created the modern American union" as soldiers and loved ones were forced to reevaluate society, culture, and politics through the experiences of dying and killing. On the celebration in Chicago, see James B. Stovey to May, August 4, 1863, Chicago Area Topical Collection on Chicago Description, 1835–[ongoing], Chicago Historical Society. Perhaps the day's celebration was enlivened because, according to Stovey, "getting drunk was the order of the day."

31. *Columbus Ohio State Journal*, July 7, 1863; *Cleveland Plain Dealer*, July 7–8, 1863; *Chicago Tribune*, June 26, 1864. Chandra Manning, in particular, discusses the divine providence of Union victories at Gettysburg and Vicksburg, in Manning, *What this Cruel War was Over*. The victory at Vicksburg resulted in far more adulation than Lee's defeat at Gettysburg. James Bissland persuasively explains this discontent by relating that a much smaller percentage of Union soldiers hailed from the Midwest at Gettysburg than on the Western Theater. See Bissland, *Blood, Tears, and Glory*. For more on Vicksburg, see Christopher Waldrep, *Vicksburg's Long Shadow: The Civil War Legacy of Race and Remembrance*. American Crisis Series (Lanham, MD: Rowman and Littlefield Publishers, Inc., 2005).

32. *Chicago Tribune*, June 26, July 8, 1864; *Columbus Ohio State Journal*, June 28, July 1, 1864. For more on African-American celebrations of the Fourth, and the role of black benevolent aid societies, see Brian D. Page, "'Stand By the Flag': Nationalism and African-American Celebrations of the Fourth of July in Memphis, 1866–1887," *Tennessee Historical Quarterly* 58 (Winter 1999): 284–301.

33. *Chicago Tribune*, July 3, 6, 1864.

34. *Cleveland Plain Dealer*, June 30, July 5, 1864.

35. *Chicago Tribune*, July 6, 1864; Elisabeth A. Gookin Diary, July 4, 1864, Gookin Family Papers, Newberry Library, Chicago; *Columbus Ohio State Journal*, July 6, 1864; *Cleveland Plain Dealer*, July 5, 1864.

36. This was most prevalent in Chicago and Columbus, each of which housed Civil War prisons. See George Levy, *To Die in Chicago: Confederate Prisoners at Camp Douglas, 1862–1865* (Gretna, LA: Pelican Publishing Company, 1999), and Roger Pickenpaugh, *Camp Chase and the Evolution of Union Prison Policy* (Tuscaloosa: University of Alabama Press, 2007).

37. Cornelius Madden Papers, Letter to Father and Mother, April 10, 1865, Ohio Historical Society, Columbus, quoted in Christine Dee, ed., *Ohio's War: The Civil War in Documents* (Athens: Ohio University Press, 2006), 193–94.

38. Gookin Diary, April 15, 1865; Parish, *North and the Nation*.

39. *Chicago Tribune*, June 24, July 4, 1865; *Cincinnati Gazette*, June 26, 28, 1865;

Cleveland Plain Dealer, June 19, 27, 1865; *Columbus Ohio State Journal*, July 1, 1865; *Indianapolis Indiana State Sentinel*, June 30, 1865.

40. *Chicago Tribune*, June 30, July 4, 1865; *Cincinnati Gazette*, July 4, 1865. On connections between 1776 and 1865, see Sacvan Bercovitch, *The Rites of Assent: Transformation in the Symbolic Construction of America* (New York: Routledge, 1993); Parish, *North and the Nation*; and Ernest Lee Tuveson, *Redeemer Nation: The Idea of America's Millennial Role* (Chicago: University of Chicago Press, 1980).

41. *Chicago Tribune*, June 30, July 6, 1865; *Cleveland Plain Dealer*, July 3–5, 1865; *Columbus Ohio State Journal*, July 4, 1865; Blizard Diaries, July 4, 1865.

42. Susan Mary Grant, *North over South: Northern Nationalism and American Identity in the Antebellum Era* (Lawrence: University Press of Kansas, 2000); *Chicago Tribune*, June 26, 1865; Lawson, *Patriot Fires*, 3. One outlet was the formation of Memorial Day, discussed in the succeeding chapter, in which Americans from the North and South could come together to mourn lost loved ones in a more politically neutral environment.

43. Henry Winter Davis, "Oration of Hon. Henry Winter Davis, of Maryland, delivered at the Great Sanitary Hall, July 4th, 1865," Chicago Historical Society. On this transition in Reconstruction efforts, see especially Heather Cox Richardson, *The Death of Reconstruction: Race, Labor, and Politics in the Post–Civil War North, 1865–1901* (Cambridge: Harvard University Press, 2001). Chandra Manning argues from an opposite perspective, that by war's end Union troops were consciously fighting against slavery and to reform the Union. Manning, *What this Cruel War was Over*.

44. *Chicago Tribune*, July 3, 1870; *Cincinnati Enquirer*, July 3, 1871; Margarethe Winkelmeiner to parents, brother, and sister-in-law, 8/21/1868, quoted in *News from the Land of Freedom: German Immigrants Write Home*, ed. Walter Kamphoefner, Wolfgang Helbich, and Ulrike Sommer, trans. Susan Carter Vogel (Ithaca, NY: Cornell University Press, 1991), 581–82.

45. *Chicago Tribune*, July 3, 1864.

4 / "The Fourth Celebrates Itself"

1. *Chicago Tribune*, July 6, 1875.

2. *Chicago Tribune*, July 4, 6, 1866.

3. "Fourth of July, 1876," *Harper's Weekly*, March 14, 1874.

4. *Chicago Tribune*, July 5, 1869; July 4–5, 1871; July 6, 1875.

5. *Cincinnati Enquirer*, July 3, 1868; July 2, 4, 1870; July 4, 6, 1871; July 4, 1875.

6. *Cleveland Plain Dealer*, July 5, 1866; July 2, 1869; July 5, 1872.

7. *Indianapolis Journal*, July 3, 1866, June 28, 1867; *Indianapolis Indiana State Sentinel*, July 6, 1869; July 5, 1869; July 6, 1870.

8. *Columbus Ohio State Journal*, July 4, 6, 1868; June 24, July 4, 1871; July 4, 1872.

9. William Cronon, *Nature's Metropolis: Chicago and the Great West* (New York: W. W. Norton & Co., 1991); the United States Census Bureau, <http://www.census.gov/population/www/documentation/twps0027.html≥ (accessed June 23, 2008); Steven J. Ross, *Workers on the Edge: Work, Leisure, and Politics in Industrializing Cincinnati, 1788–1890* (New York: Columbia University Press, 1985); Henry Justin Smith, *Chicago's Great Century 1833–1933* (Chicago: Consolidated Publishers, Inc., 1933); Carol Poh Miller and Robert Wheeler, *Cleveland: A Concise History, 1796–1990* (Bloomington: Indiana University Press, 1990), 72; Michael Sheppard Speer, "Urbanization and

Reform: Columbus, Ohio, 1870–1900" (PhD diss., The Ohio State University, 1972); Edward A. Leary, *Indianapolis: The Story of a City* (Indianapolis: The Bobbs-Merrill Company, Inc., 1971), 117.

10. On Midwest regionality, see Andrew R. L. Cayton and Susan E. Gray, *The American Midwest: Essays on Regional History* (Bloomington: Indiana University Press, 2001).

11. See especially Michael McGerr, *The Decline of Popular Politics: The American North, 1865–1928* (New York: Oxford University Press, 1986); and Mark Summers, *Party Games: Getting, Keeping, and Using Power in Gilded Age Politics* (Chapel Hill: The University of North Carolina Press, 2004).

12. Matthew Dennis, *Red, White and Blue Letter Days: An American Calendar* (Ithaca, NY: Cornell University Press, 2002), 15. Scott Martin has also written several pieces about the commercialization of the Fourth in Pennsylvania. See Scott C. Martin, *Killing Time: Leisure and Culture in Southwestern Pennsylvania, 1800–1850* (Pittsburgh: University of Pittsburgh Press, 1995), and Martin, "The Fourth of July in Southwestern Pennsylvania, 1800–1850," *Pittsburgh History* 75 (2) (1992): 58–71. On the relationship between work and play, see especially Roy Rosenzweig, *Eight Hours For What We Will: Workers and Leisure in an Industrial City, 1870–1920* (Cambridge: Cambridge University Press, 1983).

13. William Andrew Manning Papers, July 4, 1867, Western Reserve Historical Society; ibid., July 4, 1869; July 4, 1870; July 4, 1872.

14. *Cleveland Plain Dealer*, June 28, 1871; June 17, 21; July 1, 5, 1872.

15. *Cincinnati Enquirer*, June 28, 1873; Davis L. James Diaries, Cincinnati Historical Society, July 3, 1869; July 4, 1870. On the rise of fireworks, see Richard Gowers, "Contested Celebrations: The Fourth of July and Changing National Identity in the United States, 1865–1918" (PhD diss., University of New South Wales, 2004), 361.

16. *Chicago Tribune*, July 3, 1867, July 4, 1872; Dennis, *Red, White and Blue Letter Days*.

17. *Indianapolis Indiana State Sentinel*, July 1, 1868; *Indianapolis Journal*, July 6, 1866; *Cleveland Plain Dealer*, July 5, 1873.

18. *Cleveland Plain Dealer*, June 29, July 3, 1868; *Indianapolis Indiana State Sentinel*, July 1, 1868.

19. Scott C. Martin, *Killing Time: Leisure and Culture in Southwestern Pennsylvania, 1800–1850* (Pittsburgh: University of Pittsburgh Press, 1995), 71.

20. *Columbus Ohio State Journal*, July 6, 1871; *Chicago Tribune*, July 5, 1868. Much of the production remained local in the 1860s and 1870s, but the beginnings of mass culture certainly existed. On the postbellum economy, see Alfred Chandler, *The Visible Hand: The Managerial Revolution in American Business* (Cambridge: Harvard University Press, 1977); Heather Cox Richardson, *The Greatest Nation of the Earth: Republican Economic Policies during the Civil War* (Cambridge: Harvard University Press, 1997); and Alan Trachtenberg, *The Incorporation of America: Culture and Society in the Gilded Age* (New York: Hill and Wang, 1982).

21. *Cleveland Plain Dealer*, July 5, 1872, July 5, 1873; *Columbus Ohio State Journal*, July 4, 1872; *Columbus Morning Journal*, July 2, 1867; *Columbus Ohio State Journal*, June 30, 1874.

22. *Cincinnati Enquirer*, July 4, 1875; *Columbus Morning Journal*, June 28, 1868; *Cleveland Plain Dealer*, June 30, 1874; *Chicago Tribune*, June 24, 1872.

23. *Columbus Ohio State Journal*, June 24, July 1, 1871. On P. T. Barnum, see especially Bluford Adams, *E Pluribus Barnum: The Great Showman and the Making of U.S. Popular Culture* (Minneapolis: University of Minnesota Press, 1997); and Neil Harris, *Humbug: The Art of P.T. Barnum* (Chicago: University of Chicago Press, 1973).

24. *Chicago Tribune*, July 4, 1866, July 3, 1868; *Cleveland Plain Dealer*, July 4, 1868.

25. Several monographs deal with changing labor patterns in the postbellum era. Among the most influential is Amy Dru Stanley's *From Bondage to Contract*. Stanley argues that the Civil War altered conceptions of wage labor, revolving around issues of dependence and freedom. For many workers, therefore, holidays marked rare escapes from the workplace and, by extension, from the tedium of wage labor. Amy Dru Stanley, *From Bondage to Contract: Wage Labor, Marriage, and the Market in the Age of Slave Emancipation* (New York: Cambridge University Press, 1998).

26. *Cincinnati Enquirer*, July 4, 1875; *Columbus Morning Journal*, July 5, 1869; *Columbus Ohio State Journal*, July 4, 1870. On work and leisure, see especially Stephen Ross, *Workers on the Edge: Work, Leisure, and Politics in Industrializing Cincinnati, 1788–1890* (New York: Columbia University Press, 1985); and Rosenzweig, *Eight Hours For What We Will*. On the middle class and leisure, see especially Cindy Aron, *Working At Play: A History of Vacations in the United States* (New York: Oxford University Press, 2001).

27. Elvira Sheridan Badger Papers, July 4, 1866, Newberry Library; ibid., July 4, 1873; July 4, 1874; Gookin Diary, July 4, 1869; July 4, 1870; July 4, 1871; July 4, 1875. *Chicago Tribune*, June 28, 1867; *Columbus Ohio State Journal*, July 2, 1872. By comparison, before the war, the Badgers were much more likely to go into town to celebrate the day. In 1859, for example, Badger reported that "Mr. Badger has taken the children down town and bought them a lot of candy . . . amusement this morning the glorious fourth—innumerable." The Gookin family, during the war, generally spent the day in Chicago, traipsing about town watching parades and listening to orations. Gookin Diary, July 4, 1864; ibid., July 4, 1865. On family life, see Susan Kellogg and Steven Mintz, *Domestic Revolutions: A Social History of American Family Life* (New York: The Free Press, 1988); Steven Mintz, *Huck's Raft: A History of American Childhood* (Cambridge, MA: The Belknap Press of Harvard University Press, 2004); and Viviana A. Zelizer, *Pricing the Priceless Child: The Changing Social Value of Children* (New York: Basic Books, Inc., 1981).

28. *Chicago Tribune*, July 2, 1871; *Columbus Morning Journal*, July 7, 1868.

29. Mike Cronin and David Mayall, eds., *Sporting Nationalisms: Identity, Ethnicity, Immigration, and Assimilation* (Londong: Frank Cass, 1998); S. W. Pope, *Patriotic Games: Sporting Traditions in the American Imagination, 1876–1926* (New York: Oxford University Press, 1997), 5.

30. *Chicago Tribune*, July 6, 1866; July 3, 1867; July 3, 1868; July 4, 1871; *Cincinnati Enquirer*, July 6, 1872; *Cleveland Plain Dealer*, July 3, 1866; July 1, 1867; *Columbus Ohio State Journal*, July 6, 1874. On the development of horse racing, see Curtis Miner, "And They're Off! Pennsylvania's Horse Racing Tradition," *Pennsylvania Heritage* 31 (2) (2005): 26–35. Horse racing was also popular in the South before the Civil War. See Ted Ownby, *Subduing Satan: Religion, Recreation, and Manhood in the Rural South, 1865–1920* (Chapel Hill: The University of North Carolina Press, 1993).

31. Peter Levine, *A. G. Spalding and the Rise of Baseball: The Promise of American Sport* (New York: Oxford University Press, 1985). Spalding was a very successful

Chicago businessman, building the nation's leading sporting-goods store in the late nineteenth century. Pope, *Patriotic Games*, 72. On the origins of baseball, see George B. Kirsch, *Baseball in Blue and Gray: The National Pastime During the Civil War* (Princeton: Princeton University Press, 2003).

32. Kirsch, *Baseball in Blue and Gray*, 24; Harvey Frommer, *Old Time Baseball: America's Pastime in the Gilded Age* (Lanham, MD: Taylor Trade Publishing, 2006). Frommer's work also provides a useful chart delineating the various recorded Civil War baseball games. Levine, *A. G. Spalding*; Pope, *Patriotic Games*, 4, 63.

33. Marshall D. Wright, *The National Association of Base Ball Players, 1851–1870* (Jefferson, NC: McFarland & Co., 2000); Larry Bowman, "Soldiers at Play: Baseball on the American Frontier," *Nine: A Journal of Baseball History & Culture* 9 (1–2) (2000–2001): 35–49; James Tootle, *Baseball in Columbus* (Chicago: Arcadia Publishing, 2003); *Chicago Tribune*, July 6, 1867; July 2, 1871; Warren N. Wilbert, *Opening Pitch: Professional Baseball's Inaugural Season, 1871* (Lanham, MD: The Scarecrow Press, Inc., 2008); *Cleveland Plain Dealer*, July 5, 1866; July 1, 1868; *Indianapolis Indiana State Sentinel*, July 6, 1870. Among Cartwright's rules were decisions about fair and foul balls, three strikes, punctuality, and batting order. See Frommer, *Old Time Baseball*.

34. Greg Rhodes and John Snyder, *Redleg Journal: Year by Year and Day by Day with the Cincinnati Reds since 1866* (Cincinnati: Road West, 2000); *The Field* (London), July 11, 1874, quoted in Dean A. Sullivan, ed., *Early Innings: A Documentary History of Baseball, 1825–1908* (Lincoln: University of Nebraska Press, 1997), 89; Lawrence Baldassaro and Richard A. Johnson, eds., *The American Game: Baseball and Ethnicity* (Carbondale: Southern Illinois University Press, 2002). On the Red Stockings' western trip, see Robert Knight Barney, "Of Rails and Red Stockings: Episodes in the Expansion of the 'National Pastime' in the American West," *Journal of the West* 17 (3) (1978): 61–70.

35. *Indianapolis Journal*, June 29, 1867; *Chicago Tribune*, July 4, 1870; July 2, 1871; *Columbus Morning Journal*, July 4, 1868; *Columbus Ohio State Journal*, July 4, 1871; *Indianapolis Indiana State Sentinel*, July 6, 1870; *Cleveland Plain Dealer*, July 1, 3, 1867; *Chicago Tribune*, July 2, 1871; *Cincinnati Enquirer*, July 3, 1868. On the Kekionga and Cleveland teams, see Warren N. Wilbert, *Opening Pitch: Professional Baseball's Inaugural Season, 1871* (Lanham, MD: The Scarecrow Press, Inc., 2008).

36. Pope, *Patriotic Games*, 107. See also Edward J. Rielly, ed., *Baseball and American Culture: Across the Diamond* (New York: The Haworth Press, 2003).

37. *Cincinnati Enquirer*, July 4, 1872; *Chicago Tribune*, July 5, 1872; July 4, 1873. There are many examples of newspapers claiming that the old-fashioned celebrations of the Fourth were dead. See, for example, *Chicago Tribune*, July 4, 1868; July 4, 1874; July 5, 1875; and *Cleveland Plain Dealer*, July 3, 1869.

38. *Chicago Tribune*, June 27, 1869. On Memorial Day, see Dennis, *Red, White and Blue Letter Days*; Caroline E. Janney, *Burying the Dead but Not the Past: Ladies' Memorial Associations and the Lost Cause* (Chapel Hill: University of North Carolina Press, 2007); Michael Kammen, "Commemoration and Contestation in American Culture: Historical Perspectives," *Amerikastudien* 48 (2) (2003): 185–205; and Ellen M. Litwicki, *America's Public Holidays, 1865–1920* (Washington: Smithsonian Institution Press, 2000).

39. *Chicago Tribune*, July 4, 1867; *Cincinnati Enquirer*, July 4, 1870; *Chicago Tribune*, July 4, 5, 1874. The rebirth of the Grand Army of the Republic (founded in 1861

in Illinois) and the formation of the Daughters of the American Revolution in the 1890s revived patriotic memory in celebrations of the Fourth of July, but did not affect these postbellum commemorations. See Ann Arnold Hunter, *A Century of Service: The Story of the DAR* (Washington, DC: National Society Daughters of the American Revolution, 1991) and Stuart McConnell, *Glorious Contentment: The Grand Army of the Republic, 1865–1900* (Chapel Hill: University of North Carolina Press, 1992).

40. *Columbus Morning Journal*, June 26, 1866; Margarethe Winkelmeiner to parents, brother, and sister-in-law, 8/21/1868, quoted in *News from the Land of Freedom: German Immigrants Write Home*, ed. Walter Kamphoefner, Wolfgang Helbich, and Ulrike Sommer, trans. Susan Carter Vogel (Ithaca, NY: Cornell University Press, 1991), 581–82.

41. David Blight, *Race and Reunion: The Civil War in American Memory* (Cambridge, MA: The Belknap Press, 2001). For an alternative view, downplaying reconciliation efforts, see John R. Neff, *Honoring the Civil War Dead: Commemoration and the Problem of Reconciliation* (Lawrence: University Press of Kansas, 2005).

42. *Chicago Tribune*, July 6, 1866; July 4, 1867; July 4, 1868; June 27, 1869.

43. *Cincinnati Enquirer*, June 28, 1866; *Cleveland Plain Dealer*, July 3, 1866.

44. Jack S. Blocker, *A Little More Freedom: African Americans Enter the Urban Midwest, 1860–1930* (Columbus: Ohio State University Press, 2008).

45. Jon Teaford, *Cities of the Heartland: The Rise and Fall of the Industrial Midwest* (Bloomington: Indiana University Press, 1993), 64.

46. *Columbus Morning Journal*, July 6, 1867; *Cleveland Plain Dealer*, July 3–5, 1873.

47. *Cincinnati Enquirer*, July 2, 1870; July 6, 1872.

48. *Indianapolis Indiana State Sentinel*, July 6, 1868; *Columbus Ohio State Journal*, July 5, 1875; *Cincinnati Enquirer*, July 4, 1875.

49. Brian D. Page, "'Stand By the Flag': Nationalism and African-American Celebrations of the Fourth of July in Memphis, 1866–1887," *Tennessee Historical Quarterly* 58 (Winter 1999): 284–301. Another important work on African-American celebrations of the Fourth in the postbellum South is Mitch Kachun, *Festivals of Freedom: Memory and Meaning in African American Emancipation Celebrations, 1808–1915* (Amherst: University of Massachusetts Press, 2003). Kachun argues that emancipation festivals gave African-Americans the opportunity to congregate, educate, and agitate. Unlike Page, Kachon seems to place greater animus on white Republican troops imposing July Fourth celebrations than on spontaneous African-American commemorations of the holiday.

50. *Chicago Tribune*, June 24, 1869.

5 / "The End of a Century"

1. *Columbus Ohio State Journal*, July 5, 1876.

2. Henry C. Noble, *Centennial Historical Address* (Columbus: Ohio State Journal Book and Job Rooms, 1876). In fact, Walter Nugent refers to 1876 as "Act I, Scene I" of modern America. See Lillian B. Miller, Walter T. K. Nugent, and H. Wayne Morgan, *1876: The Centennial Year* (Indianapolis: Indiana Historical Society, 1973), 31.

3. *Indianapolis Journal*, January 1, 1876; *Cincinnati Daily Times*, January 4, 1876; *Chicago Inter-Ocean*, January 1, 1876.

4. *Cincinnati Daily Times*, January 3, 1876; *Chicago Inter-Ocean*, January 1–3, 1876. The scripture reference is from Philippians 3:13–14.

5. *Indianapolis Journal*, January 1, 1876; *Cincinnati Daily Times*, January 4, 1876.

In some places, the planning actually began years earlier. See, for example, *Cleveland Plain Dealer*, July 3, 1867; and *Cincinnati Enquirer*, July 3, 1871.

6. *Cleveland Plain Dealer*, June 28, July 1, July 5, 1876; Emma Betts Sterling Diaries, July 4, 1876, Western Reserve Historical Society.

7. *Columbus Ohio State Journal*, June 28, July 4, 1876.

8. *Columbus Ohio State Journal*, July 5, 1876.

9. *Indianapolis Indiana State Sentinel*, July 4, 1876.

10. *Cincinnati Enquirer*, June 25, July 2, 5, 1876; Davis L. James Diaries, July 4, 1876, Cincinnati Historical Society.

11. *Chicago Times*, July 2, 3, 1876.

12. *Chicago Tribune*, July 4, 1876; Ellen M. Litwicki, "Visions of America: Public Holidays and American Cultures, 1776–1900" (PhD diss., University of Virginia, 1992).

13. William Pierce Randel, *Centennial: American Life in 1876* (Philadelphia: Chilton Book Co., 1969), 283.

14. Ibid.; Linda P. Gross and Theresa R. Snyder, *Images of America: Philadelphia's 1876 Centennial Exhibition* (Charleston, SC: Arcadia, 2005); "Fourth of July, 1876," *Harper's Weekly*, March 14, 1874.

15. Randel, *Centennial*; Gross and Snyder, *Images of America*; Litwicki, "Visions of America"; Miller, Nugent, and Morgan, *1876*.

16. Matthew Dennis, *Red, White and Blue Letter Days: An American Calendar* (Ithaca, NY: Cornell University Press, 2002); Michael Kammen, "Commemoration and Contestation in American Culture: Historical Perspectives," *Amerikastudien* 48 (2) (2003): 185–205.

17. *Columbus Ohio State Journal*, July 4, 1876.

18. *Chicago Inter-Ocean*, April 27, May 12, 1876; Randel, *Centennial*, 304; *Chicago Inter-Ocean*, July 5, 1876. Numerous midwesterners travelled to the Exposition. So many headed east that summer that the *Columbus Ohio State Journal* offered subscribers the opportunity to receive copies of the paper while vacationing near Philadelphia so that they could keep up with local news even while abroad. *Columbus Ohio State Journal*, June 20, 1876. Those who did travel to Philadelphia usually discussed both the Exposition's technological marvels and the historicity associated with the event. See, for example, Emma Betts Sterling Diaries, July 6, 1876; and Davis L. James Diaries, July 1, 1876.

19. *Chicago Tribune*, July 5, 1876; *Cincinnati Enquirer*, July 2, 1876.

20. Noble, *Centennial Historical Address*; *Indiana State Sentinel*, June 28, 1876; *Chicago Inter-Ocean*, July 4, 1876.

21. This quote is taken from Deuteronomy 32:7. *Indianapolis Journal*, July 3, 1876.

22. *Chicago Inter-Ocean*, July 4, 1876; *Chicago Times*, July 4, 1876.

23. *Columbus Ohio State Journal*, July 5, 1876.

24. *Columbus Ohio State Journal*, July 5, 1876.

25. *Cincinnati Enquirer*, July 4, 1876; *Chicago Times*, July 4, 1876; *Chicago Tribune*, July 5, 1876.

26. "Fourth of July, 1876," *Harper's Weekly*, March 14, 1874.

27. *Chicago Tribune*, June 25, July 1, 3, 1876; *Cleveland Plain Dealer*, June 23, 1876.

28. *Indianapolis Indiana State Sentinel*, June 28, 1876; *Columbus Ohio State Journal*, June 29, 1876.

29. *Chicago Tribune*, July 5, 1876; *Cleveland Plain Dealer*, July 5, 1876.

30. *Cincinnati Enquirer,* July 1, 1876; *Cleveland Plain Dealer,* July 6, 1876; *Chicago Tribune,* July 5, 1876.

31. *Columbus Ohio State Journal,* July 5, 1876; *Indianapolis State Sentinel,* June 28, 1876; *Indianapolis Journal,* July 1, 1876.

32. Richard Gowers, "Contested Celebrations: The Fourth of July and Changing National Identity in the United States, 1865–1918" (PhD diss., University of New South Wales, 2004), 51; *Chicago Times,* July 4, 1876.

Epilogue

1. Michael Oriard, *Sporting with the Gods: The Rhetoric of Play and Game in American Culture* (New York: Cambridge University Press, 1991), 11.

2. <http://observer.guardian.co.uk/osm/story/0,,1072750,00.html≥ (accessed June 13, 2010); Leonard I. Sweet, "The Fourth of July and Black Americans in the Nineteenth Century: Northern Leadership Opinion Within the Context of the Black Experience," *The Journal of Negro History* 61 (3) (July 1976): 274; Randy Roberts, *Papa Jack: Jack Johnson and the Era of White Hopes* (New York: Free Press, 1983).

3. Matthew Dennis, *Red, White and Blue Letter Days: An American Calendar* (Ithaca, NY: Cornell University Press, 2002), 69, 71.

4. Roger Daniels, *Coming to America: A History of Immigration and Ethnicity in American Life* (New York: HarperCollins, 1990); Dale T. Knobel, *"America for the Americans": The Nativist Movement in the United States* (New York: Twayne Publishers, 1996); *New York Times,* August 31, 2003; Sean Mehegan, *Restaurant Business* 104 (13) (September 15, 2005), 46–47. Ninety-one years later, and still on the Fourth of July, American professional eater Joey "Jaws" Chestnut ended the six-year reign of Japan's Takeru Kobayashi, returning the coveted Mustard Belt to the United States, after consuming an astounding 66 hot dogs in 12 minutes. <http://www.nathansfamous.com/PageFetch/getpage.php?pgid=26≥ (accessed August 26, 2008); Ellen M. Litwicki, *America's Public Holidays, 1865–1920* (Washington: Smithsonian Institution Press, 2000), 152; William Cohn, "A National Celebration: The Fourth of July in American History," *Cultures* 3 (1) (1976): 153; Dennis, *Red, White and Blue Letter Days.*

5. Frank Jewell, "Looking Backward, Celebrating the Fourth of July," *Chicago History* 7 (2) (Summer 1978): 120–22.

Bibliography

Primary Sources

UNPUBLISHED ARCHIVAL MATERIAL

Elvira Sheridan Badger Papers, Newberry Library, Chicago.
Silas William Blizard, Diaries and Records, Indiana Historical Society, Indianapolis.
Joel Buttles Diaries, Ohio Historical Society, Columbus.
Chicago Area Topical Collection on Chicago Description, Chicago Historical Society.
Moses Cleaveland Papers, Western Reserve Historical Society, Cleveland.
Abner Crosby Diary, Western Reserve Historical Society, Cleveland.
Henry Winter Davis, "Oration of Hon. Henry Winter Davis, of Maryland, delivered at the Great Sanitary Hall, July 4th, 1865," Chicago Historical Society.
Gookin Family Papers, Newberry Library, Chicago.
David Hudson Family Papers, Western Reserve Historical Society, Cleveland.
Davis L. James Diaries, Cincinnati Historical Society.
Robert Lowery Papers, Ohio Historical Society, Columbus.
William Andrew Manning Papers, Western Reserve Historical Society, Cleveland.
Charles Mayer Papers, Indiana Historical Society, Indianapolis.
Emma Betts Sterling Diaries, Western Reserve Historical Society, Cleveland.
Gotthilft Willig Letter, Chicago Historical Society.

NEWSPAPERS

Baltimore Weekly Register

Chicago Daily Democratic Press
Chicago Democrat
Chicago Inter-Ocean
Chicago Literary Budget
Chicago Times
Chicago Tribune
Christian Watchman (Boston)
Cincinnati Advertiser and Journal
Cincinnati Daily Times
Cincinnati Enquirer
Cincinnati Gazette
Cleveland Herald
Cleveland Plain Dealer
Cleveland Western Courier
Columbus Morning Journal
Daily Advertiser (Albany)
Der Wesbote (Columbus)
Harper's Weekly
Indiana Democrat (Indianapolis)
Indiana State Sentinel (Indianapolis)
Indianapolis Gazette
Indianapolis Journal
Liberty Hall and Cincinnati Gazette
Massachusetts Spy (Worcester)
Milwaukee Daily Sentinel
New York Times
Ohio Oracle (Wooster)
Ohio State Journal (Columbus)
Ohio Statesman (Columbus)

PUBLISHED

Boynton, Rev. Charles B. *Oration, Delivered on the Fifth of July, 1847, Before the Native Americans of Cincinnati*. Cincinnati: Tagart & Gardner, 1847.

Celebration of the Fourth of July, 1834, By the Fraternity of Victuallers of Cincinnati: Containing the Proceedings of the Day, the Patriotic Address Delivered on the Occasion, and the Toasts. Cincinnati: F. S. Benton, 1834.

Cist, Charles. *Cincinnati in 1841: Its Early Annals and Future Prospects*. Cincinnati: J. A. James, E. Morgan & Co., 1841.

Crèvecoeur, J. Hector St. John de. *Letters from an American Farmer*. Belfast: James Magee, 1783.

Drake, Benjamin. *Cincinnati in 1826*. Cincinnati: Morgan, Lodge, and Fisher, 1827.

Flint, Timothy. *Recollections of the Last Ten Years, passed in occasional residences and journeyings in the valley of the Mississippi, from Pittsburg and the Missouri to the Gulf of Mexico, and from Florida to the Spanish frontier: in a series of letters to the Rev. James Flint, of Salem, Massachusetts.* Boston: Cummings, Hilliard, and Co., 1826.

Ford, Paul Leicester, ed. *The Writings of Thomas Jefferson.* New York: G. P. Putnam's Sons, 1892–99.

Hopkins, Jesse. *The Patriot's Manual: Comprising Various Standard and Miscellaneous Subjects, Interesting to Every American Citizen.* Utica, NY: William Williams, 1828.

Latrobe, Charles Joseph. *The Rambler in North America,* vol. 2. London: R. B. Seeley and W. Burnside, 1835.

Marryat, Frederick. *A Diary in America: With Remarks on Its Institutions,* ed. Sydney Jackman. New York: Alfred A. Knopf, 1962.

McIlvaine, Mabel. *Reminiscences of Chicago during the Forties and Fifties.* Chicago: Lakeside Press, 1913.

Melish, John. *Travels in the United States of America in the Years 1806 & 1807, and 1809, 1810 & 1811,* vol. 2. Cincinnati, 1827.

Merrill, Walter M., and Louis Ruchames, eds. *Letters of William Lloyd Garrison,* vol. 1. Cambridge, MA: The Belknap Press, 1971–1981.

Mueller, Jakob. *Memoirs of a Forty-eighter: Sketches from the German-American Period of Storm and Stress of the 1850s,* trans. Steven Rowan. Cleveland: Rudolf Schmidt Printing Company, 1896.

Mueller, Werner D. "Cleveland's 19th century German Community and its 'Forty-Eighters': an overview and interpretation, or Cleveland in the 1800s: 'ecclesiastical despots' vs. 'the immigrant Teuton,'" August 1995, Cincinnati Historical Society.

National Anniversary: A Copy of the Remarks Introductory to the Reading of the Declaration of Independence by Samuel R. Miller, and a copy of the Oration delivered by Bellamy Storer . . . Cincinnati, 1829.

Nichols, Thomas Low. *Forty Years of American Life,* vol. 1. London: J. Maxwell and Co., 1864.

Noble, Henry C. *Centennial Historical Address.* Columbus: Ohio State Journal Book and Job Rooms, 1876.

Peck, John. *A New Guide for Emigrants to the West: Containing Sketches of Michigan, Ohio, Indiana, Illinois, Missouri, Arkansas, with the Territory of Wisconsin, and the Adjacent Parts.* Boston: Gould, Kendall & Lincoln, 1843.

Prime, Nathaniel S. *The Year of Jubilee, but not to Africans: A Discourse, delivered July 4th, 1825, being the 49th Anniversary of American Independence.* Salem, NY: Dodd and Stevenson, 1825.

Transactions of the Fifth Annual Meeting of the Western Literary Historical Society and the College of Professional Teachers, October 1835. Cincinnati, 1836.

Trollope, Frances Milton. *Domestic Manners of the Americans*, vol. 1. New York: Dodd, Mead, 1901.

Secondary Sources

Abbott, Carl. *Boosters and Businessmen: Popular Economic Thought and Urban Growth in the Antebellum Middle West*. Westport, CT: Greenwood Press, 1981.

Adams, Bluford. *E Pluribus Barnum: The Great Showman and the Making of U.S. Popular Culture*. Minneapolis: University of Minnesota Press, 1997.

Adams, Willi Paul. *The German-Americans: An Ethnic Experience*. Trans. LaVern J. Rippley and Eberhard Reichmann. Indianapolis: Max Kade German-American Center, 1993.

Altschuler, Glenn, and Stuart Blumin. "Political Engagement and Disengagement in Antebellum America: A Roundtable." *Journal of American History* 84 (1997): 855–909.

Anbinder, Tyler. *Five Points: The 19th-Century New York City Neighborhood that Invented Tap Dance, Stole Elections, and Became the World's Most Notorious Slum*. New York: The Free Press, 2001.

———. *Nativism and Slavery: The Northern Know Nothings and the Politics of the 1850s*. New York: Oxford University Press, 1992.

Anderson, Benedict. *Imagined Communities*. London: Verso, 1983.

Appelbaum, Diana Karter. *The Glorious Fourth: An American Holiday, An American History*. New York: Facts on File, 1989.

Appleby, Joyce. *Inheriting the Revolution: The First Generation of Americans*. Cambridge, MA: The Belknap Press, 2000.

Aron, Cindy. *Working At Play: A History of Vacations in the United States*. New York: Oxford University Press, 2001.

Ayers, Edward L. *What Caused the Civil War? Reflections on the South and Southern History*. New York: Norton, 2005.

Baldassaro, Lawrence, and Richard A. Johnson, eds. *The American Game: Baseball and Ethnicity*. Carbondale: Southern Illinois University Press, 2002.

Barney, Robert Knight. "Of Rails and Red Stockings: Episodes in the Expansion of the 'National Pastime' in the American West." *Journal of the West* 17 (1978): 61–70.

Baughin, William. "'Ballots and Bullets': The Election Day Riots of 1855." *Historical and Philosophical Society of Ohio Bulletin* 21 (1963): 267–72.

Beeman, Richard R. "Deference, Republicanism, and the Emergence of Popular Politics in Eighteenth-Century America." *William and Mary Quarterly* 49 (July 1992): 401–30.

———. *The Varieties of Political Experience in Eighteenth-Century America*. Philadelphia: University of Pennsylvania Press, 2004.

Bellah, Robert Neelly. "Civil Religion in America." *Journal of the American Academy of Arts and Sciences* 96 (Winter 1967): 1–21.

Bercovitch, Sacvan. *The Rites of Assent: Transformations in the Symbolic Construction of America*. New York: Routledge, 1993.

Bergquist, James. "German Communities in American Cities: An Interpretation of the Nineteenth-Century Experience." *Journal of American Ethnic History* 4 (1984): 9–30.

Billington, Ray Allen. *The Origins of Nativism in the United States, 1800-1844*. New York: Arno Press, 1974.

Bissland, James H. *Blood, Tears, and Glory: How Ohioans Won the Civil War*. Wilmington, OH: Orange Frazer Press, 2007.

Blight, David. *Race and Reunion: The Civil War in American Memory*. Cambridge, MA: The Belknap Press, 2001.

Blocker, Jack S. *A Little More Freedom: African Americans Enter the Urban Midwest, 1860-1930*. Columbus: Ohio State University Press, 2008.

Blumin, Stuart. *The Emergence of the Middle Class: Social Experience in the American City, 1760-1900*. Cambridge, UK: Cambridge University Press, 1989.

Bodnar, John. *Remaking America: Public Memory, Commemoration, and Patriotism in the Twentieth Century*. Princeton: Princeton University Press, 1992.

Boritt, Gabor S., ed. *Why The Civil War Came*. New York: Oxford University Press, 1996.

Bowman, Larry. "Soldiers at Play: Baseball on the American Frontier." *Nine: A Journal of Baseball History & Culture* 9 (2000-2001): 35–49.

Burstein, Andrew. *America's Jubilee*. New York: Alfred A. Knopf, 2001.

Carter, Ruth C. "Cincinnatians and Cholera: Attitudes Toward the Epidemics of 1832 and 1849." *Queen City Heritage* 50 (1992): 32–48.

Cayton, Andrew R. L., and Susan E. Gray, eds. *The American Midwest: Essays on Regional History*. Bloomington: Indiana University Press, 2001.

Cayton, Andrew R. L., and Peter S. Onuf. *The Midwest and the Nation: Rethinking the History of an American Region*. Bloomington: Indiana University Press, 1990.

Cayton, Andrew R. L., Richard Sisson, and Christian Zacher, eds. *The American Midwest: An Interpretive Encyclopedia*. Bloomington: Indiana University Press, 2007.

Chambrun, Clara Longworth de. *Cincinnati: Story of the Queen City*. New York: Charles Scribner's Sons, 1939.

Chandler, Alfred Jr. *The Visible Hand: The Managerial Revolution in American Business*. Cambridge, MA: The Belknap Press, 1977.

Cigrand, Bernard J. "Chicago's Historic Fourths of July." *Fort Dearborn Magazine* (July 1920): 26.

Cohn, William. "A National Celebration: The Fourth of July in American History." *Cultures* 3 (1976): 141–56.

Cole, Bruce McKittrick. "The Chicago Press and the Know-Nothings, 1850–1856." Master's thesis, University of Chicago, 1948.

Cole, Charles Jr. *A Fragile Capital: Identity and the Early Years of Columbus, Ohio.* Columbus: Ohio State University Press, 2001.

Conzen, Kathleen. *Immigrant Milwaukee 1836–1860: Accommodation and Community in a Frontier City.* Cambridge: Harvard University Press, 1976.

———, and David Gerber. "The Invention of Ethnicity: A Perspective from the U.S.A." *Journal of American Ethnic History* 12 (Fall 1992): 3–42.

Criblez, Adam. "'A Motley Array': Changing Perceptions of Chicago Taverns, 1833–1871." *The Journal of Illinois History* (Winter 2005): 262–80.

Cronin, Mike, and David Mayall, eds. *Sporting Nationalisms: Identity, Ethnicity, Immigration, and Assimilation.* London: Frank Cass, 1998.

Cronon, William. *Nature's Metropolis: Chicago and the Great West.* New York: W.W. Norton & Co., 1991.

Dangerfield, George. *The Awakening of American Nationalism, 1815–1828.* New York: Harper & Row, 1965.

Daniels, Roger. *Coming to America: A History of Immigration and Ethnicity in American Life.* New York: HarperCollins, 1990.

Dannenbaum, Jed. *Drink and Disorder: Temperance Reform in Cincinnati from the Washingtonian Revival to the WCTU.* Urbana: University of Illinois Press, 1984.

Dearinger, Ryan L. "Violence, Masculinity, Image, and Reality on the Antebellum Frontier." *Indiana Magazine of History* 100 (March 2004): 26–55.

Dee, Christine, ed. *Ohio's War: The Civil War in Documents.* Athens: Ohio University Press, 2006.

Degler, Carl N. "One Among Many: The Civil War in Comparative Perspective." *Twenty-ninth Annual Robert Fortenbaugh Memorial Lecture.* Gettysburg College, 1990.

Delgado-Moreira, Juan. "Cultural Citizenship and the Creation of European Identity." *Electronic Journal of Sociology* 2 (1997). <www.sociology.org>.

Dennis, Matthew. *Red, White and Blue Letter Days: An American Calendar.* Ithaca, NY: Cornell University Press, 2002.

Duis, Perry. *Challenging Chicago: Coping with Everyday Life, 1837–1920.* Urbana: University of Illinois Press, 1998.

———. *The Saloon: Public Drinking in Chicago and Boston, 1880–1920.* Urbana: University of Illinois Press, 1983.

Elsmere, Jane Shaffer. *Henry Ward Beecher: The Indiana Years, 1837–1847.* Indianapolis: Indiana Historical Society, 1973.

Etcheson, Nicole. "Manliness and the Political Culture of the Old Northwest, 1790–1860." *Journal of the Early Republic* 15 (Spring 1995): 59–77.

Etzioni, Amitai, and Jared Bloom, eds. *We Are What We Celebrate: Understanding Holidays and Rituals.* New York: New York University Press, 2004.

Eversole, Theodore W. "The Cincinnati Cholera Epidemic of 1849." *Queen City Heritage* 41 (Fall 1983): 21–30.

Faust, Drew Gilpin. *This Republic of Suffering: Death and the American Civil War*. New York: Alfred A. Knopf, 2008.

Feldberg, Michael. *The Philadelphia Riots of 1844: A Study of Ethnic Conflict*. Westport, CT: Greenwood Press, 1975.

Forgie, George B. *Patricide in the House Divided: A Psychological Interpretation of Lincoln and His Age*. New York: W.W. Norton & Co., 1979.

Forman, Jonathan. "The First Year of the Second Epidemic of Asiatic Cholera in Columbus, Ohio—1849." *Ohio Archaeological and Historical Quarterly* 52 (October–December 1944): 303–12.

Freehling, William W. *The Road to Disunion*. New York: Oxford University Press, 1990.

Frommer, Harvey. *Old Time Baseball: America's Pastime in the Gilded Age*. Lanham, MD: Taylor Trade Publishing, 2006.

Gabaccia, Donna R. "Liberty, Coercion, and the Making of Immigration Historians." *The Journal of American History* 84 (September 1997): 570–75.

Gellner, Ernest. *Thought and Change*. London: Weidenfeld & Nicholson, 1964.

Gerber, David A. "'The Germans Take Care of Our Celebrations': Middle-Class Americans Appropriate German Ethnic Culture in Buffalo in the 1850s." In *Hard at Play: Leisure in America, 1840–1940*, edited by Kathryn Grover. Amherst: The University of Massachusetts Press, 1992.

Gibson, Campbell. *Population of the 100 Largest Cities and Other Urban Places in the United States: 1790 to 1990*. Washington, DC: U.S. Census Bureau. <http://www.census.gov/population/www/documentation/twps0027. html>.

Gilje, Paul A. *Rioting in America*. Bloomington: Indiana University Press, 1996.

Gillis, John, ed. *Commemorations: The Politics of National Identity*, pp. 74–89. Princeton: Princeton University Press, 1994.

Gjerde, Jon. *The Minds of the West: Ethnocultural Evolution in the Rural Middle West, 1830–1917*. Chapel Hill: University of North Carolina Press, 1997.

Gleason, Philip. "Trouble in the Colonial Melting Pot." *Journal of American Ethnic History* 20 (2000): 3–17.

Gorn, Elliot. "'Good-Bye Boys, I Die a True American': Homicide, Nativism, and Working-Class Culture in Antebellum New York City." *The Journal of American History* 74 (Sept. 1987): 388–410.

Grant, Susan-Mary. *North over South: Northern Nationalism and American Identity in the Antebellum Era*. Lawrence: University Press of Kansas, 2000.

Gross, Linda P., and Theresa R. Snyder. *Images of America: Philadelphia's 1876 Centennial Exhibition*. Charleston, SC: Arcadia, 2005.

Gusfield, Joseph R. *Symbolic Crusade: Status Politics and the American Temperance Movement*. Urbana: University of Illinois Press, 1963.

Handlin, Oscar. *The Uprooted: The Epic Story of the Great Migrations That Made the American People*. New York: Grosset & Dunlap, 1951.

Hanley, Mark Y. *Beyond a Christian Commonwealth: The Protestant Quarrel with the American Republic, 1830-1860.* Chapel Hill: University of North Carolina Press, 1994.

Harris, Brayton. *Blue & Gray in Black & White: Newspapers in the Civil War.* Washington: Brassey's, 1999.

Harris, Neil. *Humbug: The Art of P.T. Barnum.* Chicago: University of Chicago Press, 1973.

Hatch, Nathan O. *The Democratization of American Christianity.* New Haven: Yale University Press, 1989.

Hawken, Henry A., ed. *Trumpets of Glory: Fourth of July Orations, 1786-1861.* Granby, CT: The Salmon Brook Historical Society, 1976.

Hay, Robert Pettus. "Freedom's Jubilee: One Hundred Years of the Fourth of July, 1776-1876." PhD diss., University of Kentucky, 1967.

———. "Frontier Patriotism on Parade: Westward the Glorious Fourth of July." *Journal of the West* 5 (July 1966): 309-20.

Heintze, James R. *The Fourth of July Encyclopedia.* Jefferson, NC: McFarland & Company, Inc. Publishers, 2007.

———. *The Fourth of July in Sound, Spectacle and Symbol.* Washington, DC: The Author, 1999.

Higham, John. *Strangers in the Land: Patterns of American Nativism, 1860-1925.* New Brunswick, NJ: Rutgers University Press, 1955.

Holloway, William Robeson. *Indianapolis: A Historical and Statistical Sketch of the Railroad City, a Chronicle of its Social, Municipal, Commercial, and Manufacturing Progress, with full statistical tables.* Indianapolis: Indianapolis Journal Print, 1870.

Holman, Andrew. "Something to Admire: Cultural Nationalism, Symbolic Dissonance, and the Fourth of July in New England's Canadian Borderlands, 1840-1870." *Dublin Seminar for New England Folklife. Annual Proceedings* 25 (2000): 137-48.

Holt, Michael F. *The Fate of Their Country: Politicians, Slavery Extension, and the Coming of the Civil War.* New York: Hill and Wang, 2005.

Hooker, Richard J. "The American Revolution Seen through a Wine Glass." *William and Mary Quarterly* 11 (Jan. 1954): 52-77.

Hooper, Osman Castle. *History of the City of Columbus Ohio: From the Founding of Franklinton in 1797 Through the World War Period to the Year 1920.* Columbus: The Memorial Publishing Company, 1920.

Howells, W.D. "In an Old-Time State Capital, First Paper." *Harper's Monthly Magazine* 129 (Sept. 1914): 593-603.

Hunter, Ann Arnold. *A Century of Service: The Story of the DAR.* Washington, DC: National Society Daughters of the American Revolution, 1991.

Hurt, R. Douglas. *The Ohio Frontier: Crucible of the Old Northwest, 1720-1830.* Bloomington: Indiana University Press, 1996.

Ignatiev, Noel. *How the Irish Became White.* New York: Routledge, 1995.

Jacobson, Matthew Frye. *Whiteness of a Different Color: European Immigrants and the Alchemy of Race.* Cambridge: Harvard University Press, 1998.

James, Stephen Elliot. "The Other Fourth of July: The Meanings of Black Identity at American Celebrations of Independence, 1770–1863." PhD diss., Harvard University, 1997.

Jewell, Frank. "Looking Backward, Celebrating the Fourth of July." *Chicago History 7* (Summer 1978): 120–22.

Johnson, Paul E. *A Shopkeeper's Millennium: Society and Revivals in Rochester, New York, 1815–1837.* New York: Hill and Wang, 1978.

Jortner, Adam. "Cholera, Christ, and Jackson: The Epidemic of 1832 and the Origins of Christian Politics in Antebellum America." *Journal of the Early Republic* 27 (Summer 2007): 233–64.

Kachun, Mitch. *Festivals of Freedom: Memory and Meaning in African American Emancipation Celebrations, 1808–1915.* Amherst: University of Massachusetts Press, 2003.

Kammen, Michael. "Commemoration and Contestation in American Culture: Historical Perspectives." *Amerikastudien* 48 (2003): 185–205.

———. *Mystic Chords of Memory: The Transformation of Tradition in American Culture.* New York: Alfred A. Knopf, 1991.

Kamphoefner, Walter, Wolfgang Helbich, and Ulrike Sommer, eds. *News from the Land of Freedom: German Immigrants Write Home.* Translated by Susan Carter Vogel. Ithaca, NY: Cornell University Press, 1991.

Kazal, Russel. "Revisiting Assimilation: The Rise, Fall, and Reappraisal of a Concept in American Ethnic History." *The American Historical Review* 100 (April 1995): 437–71.

Kellogg, Susan, and Steven Mintz. *Domestic Revolutions: A Social History of American Family Life.* New York: The Free Press, 1988.

Kerber, Linda K. "The Republican Mother: Women and the Enlightenment—An American Perspective." In *Toward an Intellectual History of Women: Essays by Linda K. Kerber.* Chapel Hill: University of North Carolina Press, 1997.

Kirsch, George B. *Baseball in Blue and Gray: The National Pastime During the Civil War.* Princeton: Princeton University Press, 2003.

Klement, Frank L. *The Copperheads in the Middle West.* Chicago: University of Chicago Press, 1960.

Knobel, Dale T. *"America for the Americans": The Nativist Movement in the United States.* New York: Twayne Publishers, 1996.

———. *Paddy and the Republic: Ethnicity and Nationality in Antebellum America.* Middletown, CT: Wesleyan University Press, 1986.

Kornblith, Gary J. "Rethinking the Coming of the Civil War: A Counterfactual Exercise." *Journal of American History* 90 (June 2003): 76–105.

Lawson, Melinda. *Patriot Fires: Forging a New American Nationalism in the Civil War North.* Lawrence: University Press of Kansas, 2002.

Leary, Edward A. *Indianapolis: The Story of a City.* Indianapolis: The Bobbs-Merrill Company, Inc., 1971.

Lee, Gerald Stanley. *Crowds: A Moving-Picture of Democracy.* New York: Doubleday, Page, & Co., 1913.

Levine, Bruce. *Half Slave and Half Free: The Roots of Civil War.* New York: Hill and Wang, 2005.

Levine, Peter. *A.G. Spalding and the Rise of Baseball: The Promise of American Sport.* New York: Oxford University Press, 1985.

Levy, George. *To Die in Chicago: Confederate Prisoners at Camp Douglas, 1862–1865.* Gretna, LA: Pelican Publishing Company, 1999.

Litwicki, Ellen M. *America's Public Holidays, 1865–1920.* Washington: Smithsonian Institution Press, 2000.

———. "Visions of America: Public Holidays and American Cultures, 1776–1900." PhD diss., University of Virginia, 1992.

Lupold, Harry F., and Gladys Haddad, eds. *Ohio's Western Reserve: A Regional Reader.* Kent, OH Kent State University Press, 1988.

Manning, Chandra. *What this Cruel War was Over: Soldiers, Slavery, and the Civil War.* New York: Vintage Books, 2007.

Martin, Scott C. "The Fourth of July in Southwestern Pennsylvania, 1800–1850." *Pittsburgh History* 75 (1992): 58–71.

———. *Killing Time: Leisure and Culture in Southwestern Pennsylvania, 1800–1850.* Pittsburgh: University of Pittsburgh Press, 1995.

Maxwell, Fay. *Early German Village History, South Columbus, Ohio.* Columbus: Elic Press, 1971.

McConnell, Stuart. *Glorious Contentment: The Grand Army of the Republic, 1865–1900.* Chapel Hill: University of North Carolina Press, 1992.

McDaniel, Caleb W. "The Fourth and the First: Abolitionist Holidays, Respectability, and Radical Interracial Reform." *American Quarterly* 57 (2005): 129–51.

McGerr, Michael. *The Decline of Popular Politics: The American North, 1865–1928.* New York: Oxford University Press, 1986.

McIlvaine, Mabel. *Reminiscences of Chicago during the Forties and Fifties.* Chicago: Lakeside Press, 1913.

McPherson, James M. *For Cause and Comrades: Why Men Fought in the Civil War.* New York: Oxford University Press, 1997.

Mehegan, Sean. *Restaurant Business* 104 (September 15, 2005): 46–47.

Merriner, James. *Grafters and Goo Goos: Corruption and Reform in Chicago, 1833–2003.* Carbondale: Southern Illinois University Press, 2004.

Miller, Carol Poh, and Robert Wheeler. *Cleveland: A Concise History, 1796–1990.* Bloomington: Indiana University Press, 1990.

Miner, Curtis. "And They're Off! Pennsylvania's Horse Racing Tradition." *Pennsylvania Heritage* 31 (2005): 26–35.

Mintz, Steven. *Huck's Raft: A History of American Childhood.* Cambridge, MA: The Belknap Press of Harvard University Press, 2004.

Moorhead, James H. *American Apocalypse: Yankee Protestants and the Civil War, 1860–1869*. New Haven: Yale University Press, 1978.

Morrison, Michael A. *Slavery and the American West: The Eclipse of Manifest Destiny and the Coming of the Civil War*. Chapel Hill: University of North Carolina Press, 1997.

Neff, John R. *Honoring the Civil War Dead: Commemoration and the Problem of Reconciliation*. Lawrence: University Press of Kansas, 2005.

Newman, Simon P. *Parades and the Politics of the Street: Festive Culture in the Early American Republic*. Philadelphia: University of Pennsylvania Press, 1997.

Nolan, Alan T. *The Iron Brigade: A Military History*. New York: The Macmillan Company, 1961.

O'Leary, Cecilia Elizabeth. *To Die For: The Paradox of American Patriotism*. Princeton: Princeton University Press, 1999.

Oriard, Michael. *Sporting with the Gods: The Rhetoric of Play and Game in American Culture*. New York: Cambridge University Press, 1991.

Ownby, Ted. *Subduing Satan: Religion, Recreation, and Manhood in the Rural South, 1865–1920*. Chapel Hill: University of North Carolina Press, 1993.

Page, Brian D. "'Stand By the Flag': Nationalism and African-American Celebrations of the Fourth of July in Memphis, 1866–1887." *Tennessee Historical Quarterly* 58 (Winter 1999): 284–301.

Parish, Peter J. *The North and the Nation in the Era of the Civil War*. Edited by Adam I. P. Smith and Susan-Mary Grant. New York: Fordham University Press, 2003.

Parkinson, Robert Glenn. "Enemies of the People: War and Race in the New American Nation." PhD diss., University of Virginia, 2005.

Pasley, Jeffrey L. *"The Tyranny of Printers": Newspaper Politics in the Early American Republic*. Charlottesville: University of Virginia Press, 2003.

Pickenpaugh, Roger. *Camp Chase and the Evolution of Union Prison Policy*. Tuscaloosa: University of Alabama Press, 2007.

Pope, S. W. *Patriotic Games: Sporting Traditions in the American Imagination, 1876–1926*. New York: Oxford University Press, 1997.

Potter, David M. "The Historian's Use of Nationalism and Vice Versa." *The American Historical Review* 67 (July 1962): 924–50.

Quaife, Milo. *Checagou: From Indian Wigwam to Modern City, 1673–1835*. Chicago: University of Chicago Press, 1933.

Randel, William Pierce. *Centennial: American Life in 1876*. Philadelphia: Chilton Book Co., 1969.

Renner, R.W. "In a Perfect Ferment: Chicago, the Know-Nothings, and the Riot for Lager Beer." *Chicago History* 5 (1976): 161–70.

Rhodes, Greg, and John Snyder. *Redleg Journal: Year by Year and Day by Day with the Cincinnati Reds since 1866*. Cincinnati: Road West, 2000.

Richardson, Heather Cox. *The Greatest Nation of the Earth: Republican*

Economic Policies during the Civil War. Cambridge: Harvard University Press, 1997.

Rielly, Edward J., ed. *Baseball and American Culture: Across the Diamond.* New York: The Haworth Press, 2003.

Rippley, La Vern J. "The Columbus Germans." *Report—Society for the History of the Germans in Maryland* 33 (1968): 1–46.

———. *The German-Americans.* Boston: Twayne Publishers, 1976.

Roberts, Randy. *Papa Jack: Jack Johnson and the Era of White Hopes.* New York: Free Press, 1983.

Rorabaugh, W. J. *The Alcoholic Republic: An American Tradition.* New York: Oxford University Press, 1979.

Rosenzweig, Roy. *Eight Hours For What We Will: Workers and Leisure in an Industrial City, 1870–1920.* Cambridge: Cambridge University Press, 1983.

———, and David Thelen. *The Presence of the Past: Popular Uses of History in American Life.* New York: Columbia University Press, 1998.

Ross, Steven J. *Workers on the Edge: Work, Leisure, and Politics in Industrializing Cincinnati, 1788–1890.* New York: Columbia University Press, 1985.

Ryan, Mary. *Civic Wars: Democracy and Public Life in the American City During the Nineteenth Century.* Berkeley: University of California Press, 1997.

———. *Cradle of the Middle Class: The Family in Oneida County, New York, 1790–1865.* Cambridge: Cambridge University Press, 1981.

Scheiber, Harry N. *The Old Northwest: Studies in Regional History, 1787–1910.* Lincoln: University of Nebraska Press, 1969.

Schlesinger, Arthur M. *The Age of Jackson.* Boston: Little, Brown & Co., 1945.

Schultz, Duane. *The Most Glorious Fourth: Vicksburg and Gettysburg, July 4, 1863.* New York: W.W. Norton & Co., 2002.

Shalhope, Robert. "Toward a Republican Synthesis: The Emergence of an Understanding of Republicanism in American Historiography." *The William and Mary Quarterly* 29 (Jan. 1972): 49–80.

Sittler, Margaret. "The German Element in Columbus Before the Civil War." Master's thesis, The Ohio State University, 1932.

Smith, Henry Justin. *Chicago's Great Century: 1833–1933.* Chicago: Consolidated Publishers, Inc., 1933.

Sollors, Werner, ed. *The Invention of Ethnicity.* New York: Oxford University Press, 1989.

Speer, Michael Sheppard. "Urbanization and Reform: Columbus, Ohio, 1870–1900." PhD diss., The Ohio State University, 1972.

Spillman, Lyn. *Nation and Commemoration: Creating National Identities in the United States and Australia.* Cambridge: Cambridge University Press, 1997.

Stanley, Amy Dru. *From Bondage to Contract: Wage Labor, Marriage, and the Market in the Age of Slave Emancipation.* New York: Cambridge University Press, 1998.

Sullivan, Dean A., ed. *Early Innings: A Documentary History of Baseball, 1825–1908*. Lincoln: University of Nebraska Press, 1997.

Summers, Mark. *Party Games: Getting, Keeping, and Using Power in Gilded Age Politics*. Chapel Hill: University of North Carolina Press, 2004.

Sweet, Leonard I. "The Fourth of July and Black Americans in the Nineteenth Century: Northern Leadership Opinion Within the Context of the Black Experience." *The Journal of Negro History* 61 (July 1976): 256–75.

Teachout, Woden. *Capture the Flag: A Political History of American Patriotism*. New York: Basic Books, 2009.

Teaford, Jon. *Cities of the Heartland: The Rise and Fall of the Industrial Midwest*. Bloomington: Indiana University Press, 1993.

Thomas, John L. "Nationalizing the Republic, 1877–1920." In *The Great Republic: A History of the American People*, edited by Bernard Bailyn, et al. Lexington, MA: Heath and Company, 1977.

Thornbrough, Emma Lou. *Indiana in the Civil War Era, 1850–1880*. Indianapolis: Indiana Historical Bureau and Indiana Historical Society, 1965.

Tolzmann, Don Heinrich. *The German-American Experience*. Amherst, NY: Humanity Books, 2000.

Tootle, James. *Baseball in Columbus*. Chicago: Arcadia Publishing, 2003.

Trachtenberg, Alan. *The Incorporation of America: Culture and Society in the Gilded Age*. New York: Hill and Wang, 1982.

Travers, Len. *Celebrating the Fourth: Independence Day and the Rites of Nationalism in the Early Republic*. Amherst: University of Massachusetts Press, 1997.

Trommler, Frank, and Elliott Shore, eds. *The German-American Encounter: Conflict and Cooperation Between Two Cultures 1800–2000*. New York: Berghahn Books, 2001.

Tuveson, Ernest Lee. *Redeemer Nation: The Idea of America's Millennial Role*. Chicago: University of Chicago Press, 1980.

Tyrrell, Ian R. *Sobering Up: From Temperance to Prohibition in Antebellum America, 1800–1860*. Westport, CT: Greenwood Press, 1979.

Verter, Bradford. "Interracial Festivity and Power in Antebellum New York: The Case of Pinkster." *Journal of Urban History* 28 (2002): 398–427.

Waldrep, Christopher. *Vicksburg's Long Shadow: The Civil War Legacy of Race and Remembrance*. American Crisis Series. Lanham, MD: Rowman and Littlefield Publishers, Inc., 2005.

Waldstreicher, David. *In the Midst of Perpetual Fetes*. Chapel Hill: University of North Carolina Press, 1997.

Walters, Ronald G. *American Reformers, 1815–1860*. New York: Hill and Wang, 1997.

Warren, Charles. "Fourth of July Myths." *The William and Mary Quarterly* 2 (July 1945): 237–72.

Watson, Harry L. *Liberty and Power: The Politics of Jacksonian America*. New York: Hill and Wang, 1990.

Weaver, John B. "Ohio Republican Attitudes Towards Nativism, 1854–1855." *Old Northwest* 9 (1983–1984): 289–305.

Wendt, Lloyd. *Chicago Tribune: The Rise of a Great American Newspaper.* Chicago: Rand McNally & Company, 1931.

Wheeler, Robert A., ed. *Visions of the Western Reserve: Public and Private Documents of Northeastern Ohio, 1750–1860.* Columbus: Ohio State University Press, 2000.

Wilbert, Warren N. *Opening Pitch: Professional Baseball's Inaugural Season, 1871.* Lanham, MD: The Scarecrow Press, Inc., 2008.

Williams, Richard Brady. *Chicago's Battery Boys: The Chicago Mercantile Battery in the Civil War's Western Theater.* El Dorado Hills, CA: Savas Beatie, 2008.

Wittke, Carl. "Ohio's Germans, 1840–1875." *The Ohio Historical Quarterly* 66 (Oct. 1957): 339–54.

Wright, Marshall D. *The National Association of Base Ball Players, 1857–1870.* Jefferson, NC: McFarland & Co., 2000.

Zelizer, Viviana A. *Pricing the Priceless Child: The Changing Social Value of Children.* New York: Basic Books, Inc., 1981.

www.ingramcontent.com/pod-product-compliance
Ingram Content Group UK Ltd.
Pitfield, Milton Keynes, MK11 3LW, UK
UKHW031846110225
454967UK00004B/379